Passions of the Mind

Passions of the Mind

Unheard Melodies: A Third Principle of Mental Functioning

Harold N. Boris

New York University Press
New York and London

NEW YORK UNIVERSITY PRESS
New York and London

Library of Congress Cataloging-in-Publication Data
Boris, Harold N., 1932–
Passions of the Mind: unheard melodies :
the third principle of mental functioning / Harold N. Boris.
p.   cm.
Includes bibliographical references and index.
ISBN 0-8147-1204-5 (acid-free paper)
1. Psychoanalysis—Philosophy.   2. Sociobiology.   I. Title.
RC506.B64   1993
150.19′5—dc20   93-15084
                            CIP

New York University Press books are printed on acid-free paper,
and their binding materials are chosen for strength and durability.

Manufactured in the United States of America

10   9   8   7   6   5   4   3   2   1

Heard melodies are sweet, but those unheard
Are sweeter;
Therefore, ye soft pipes, play on;
Not to the sensual ear, but, more endear'd,
Pipe to the spirit ditties of no tone.

—JOHN KEATS
Ode on a Grecian Urn

Contents

Foreword

I once spent a wonderful summer with a jazz pianist who told me he spent much of his life just playing, and only later, when he needed to teach, did he try to figure out what he did when he played. I suspect Harold Boris spent much of his life figuring out what he did as he went along, but the playing is there first, and the thinking is part of the playing. What Boris plays is psychoanalytic music and his thinking creates a score for the notes that keep pouring out of him.

In his introduction, he fastens on *the kaleidoscope* as an organizing image. New configurations come into view with each turn. Boris has a lust for turning the kaleidoscope a hairbreadth at a time, and relishes the startling shifts each turn makes to the texture of our beings.

"A room looks very different to a small boy with a shiny new black and chrome hammer in his hand than it does later that night when he cannot fall asleep," Boris writes. The psychoanalyst shares the small boy's journey between form and formlessness, between assurance and uncertainty, between joy and dread. Configurations shift in perceptual, emotional, and intellectual ways. A wonderful thing about this book is that Boris is true to the *living experience* of psychoanalysis, the living experience that psychoanalysis is. In Boris's hands, not only does psychoanalysis come alive in new ways, but through his psychoanalytic kaleidoscope/prism/laser beam, life itself gains in intensity.

The tone of this book is both serious and puckish. It is tinged with black humor and irony. A profound appreciation for tragic-comic elements of life pervades it. It is filled with play of meanings, hint adding to hint, overtone to undertone. The snake of meaning never stops undulating, but is not merely clever or cute. Meaning grows out of affective contexts that are life and death matters. This book is a mind to mind, navel to navel affair. It tingles with automatic aliveness, lacerating intuitions, and searing questions that keep psychoanalytic living open.

The Great Twins or Counterparts

Boris's formal conceptual framework is in the tradition of "polarity theories," which emphasize interplay of dualities. One force or principle opposes, offsets, balances, contributes to its "opposite." Such a framework is inherently dramatic, since it charts shifting relationships between characters with different agendas or programs. Growth depends on tension interweaving between competing claims.

Boris's great twins or counterparts or *dramatis personae* are the selection and pleasure principles, especially as they work via the pair and couple. The selection (pair) and pleasure (couple) principles carry into the psychological realm something of tropism in biology. They function as predispositions to organize experience along specific relational lines. For example, the pleasure or *lust* principle is associated with appetite and gratification *now:* when gripped by lust one may be quite willing to compromise standards. The selection principle involves the tendency to hold out for ideal satisfaction.

> Hunger's wish to mate is inimical to the wish to mate perfectly; the wish for perfection must be appeased too. (137–38)

> We are not merely to live, but to live well; not merely to breed but breed well. When Mr. or Ms. Right Now is also Mr. or Ms. Right, hope and desire fuse, the *Pair* and *Couple* integrate, selection needs and needs to choose and be chosen are all met, and the baby and the future converge. (277)

How wonderful it is when selection needs and pleasure needs converge. So often they are antagonistic, conflictual, seemingly irreconcilable. We are lucky indeed when they work together in ways we can say yes to. Boris suggests many ways these tendencies counter each other, a sort of division of labor, and add to the richness (if difficulty and complexity) of living. For example, the interplay of hope and desire:

> The term *Couple* carries the valency of the pleasure-pain principle; it is based on appetitive desire and it seeks repletion. The term *Pair* . . . [is] rooted in hope and seek[s] closure and completion. In the states of mind *Couple* vs. *Pair*, one's presumptive or actual partner looks as different as the room did in the earlier example.
> These paradigmatic states of mind—*Couple* and *Pair*, pleasure and selection—live a paradoxical existence. They compete, and, in competing, offset, modify, and coalesce with one another. Hope (a leading element in the *Pair*), for example, keeps the desire in *Coupling* from being merely propinquitous. Hope's choosiness calls desire to "finer" possibilities. Desire coerces hope from forever studying (if not writing) the menu of possibility. It will be readily seen that time/space will be quite different relative to the convergence of the two. (8)

Coupling feeds on difference, often complementariness (for example, complements of elongations-openings, such as mouth-nipple, penis-vagina, baby-uterus, and the many imaginative variants). Pairing feeds on sameness (a motor of group togetherness). Boris's chapters are replete with ways sameness-difference informs clinical work, human relationships in general, and biosocial structures. Special treats for the clinician include discussions of anorexia, psychosis, and a variety of narcissistic and borderline problems. More generally, this book is filled with generous portrayals of sexual warfare and problems involving goodness or perfection of fit.

Of the many rich discussions of clinical issues, I would like to single out one of special importance to me. Boris suggests that a sense of ideal sameness in *Pairing* plays an important role in identity formation. He hearkens back to hints in Freud that some sort of primary identification precedes loss.

Identification is not simply a secondary defensive operation (although it may be), but a primary mode of being, a significant, originary state in its own right, a state of heightened affective cognition. We grow through identifications. We move from identi-

Identifications

fication to identification like stepping stones. Identification plays a primary and positive role in who we are and how we live.

At the same time we can be crippled by identifications and our identificatory capacity. What an amazing capacity this is, to experience others as ourselves, ourselves as others. We twist ourselves out of shape with our identifications, and twist ourselves out of shape fighting them. Boris suggests that early identity formation can go awry because of deleterious identifications, which misdirect psychic development. These are not merely substitute formations but mishaps at the core of the personality's ability to process experience.

Boris gives many examples of ways people sort experience via couple and pair paradigms. Coupling makes use of our capacity to compare and contrast. Pairing makes use of our capacity to level differences. When these two work well, life opens up. A wrong turn or warp in unconscious sorting processes can poison the "feel" of a life, without the person being able to finger what is off.

Boris offers his terms as counters for further discussion rather than as dogmas. He offers perspectives on how the psyche structures and reshuffles experience. He makes us understand and feel what it is like to live in the world of the couple, and the world of the pair, and the importance of moving between them.

> As with *Couple*, so with *Pair: each exists at the expense of the other, each exists as an alternative to the other, each functions to modify the other,* to provide freedom and choice and relational possibility within the shifting adaptational parameters of one another's constraints.

Add "between" to "within," so as to underline, in Boris's words, "the paradoxical dialectic between paradigms" (150).

The Right to Live

What happens when an infant does not feel selected by the pair, or chosen by the couple? An infant that does not fit into early pairing or coupling processes may feel off the map personally, socially, sexually, even outside the species. The problem a fetus may have as to whether it ought to be born or not is more than matched by the newborn's dilemma as to whether it ought to grow, or be at all.

Boris sharpens discussion of fit/lack of fit between parents and offspring, by bringing out unevenness and variability between pairing and coupling processes. The child and parent may fail each other's needs for sameness and/or difference in gross and subtle ways. The sense of being unwanted (or wanted-unwanted) can be broken down into ways pairing and coupling processes work or fail to work. One can feel oneself coming to life in one realm, and dying out in the other, now needing sameness to thrive, now needing difference.

The Right to Live and the Selection Principle

For Boris it is especially important whether or not the individual is selected in the *Pair* (Group) to flourish and propagate. To love and be loved in the *Couple* is not enough. One may be jealous in the couple, but envy arises in pair-group deficits and inequities.

Motivation in the couple is egoistic, sensuous, pleasure-oriented. Group motivation works vicariously via identifications ("social-istic"). The species puts its weight on the side of the group. Identifications one has and how they work are part of the essential mechanics of group (species) survival. The unit of survival is the group, and if one does not have the "right" identifications working in "right" ways, one is (or feels) lost.

More broadly, Boris feels he can predict when groups hold and split by discerning when internalizations are used for identity formation and when for object relations of a different kind. He argues that alternative hypotheses (e.g., "reality" and "death" principles) do not have the same economics. There is much to think through here.

A Note on Psychic Deadness

Many pages in this book portray psychoanalytic sessions dealing with psychic deadness. One gets a feel for patients battling for their right to live, flickers of aliveness rising and falling in dead seas. One gets a sense of what patient and analyst are up against when neither feels wanted by the other, when coupling and pairing processes fall flat or work against each other.

Boris portrays associative streams of patients in sessions, but he also portrays the analyst's associative streams. What emerges is a sense of both patient and analyst fighting for life against great odds. The analyst's struggle is not only with the patient and himself, but also with his group and profession. Boris trenchantly portrays ways that assumptions which make for professional unity can deaden analytic work. He shows how the analyst both nourishes and deadens himself (and his patients) by necessary ties to professional groups.

The group itself is torn apart and nourished by variable pairing-coupling needs and difficulties. For example, the psychoanalytic group as a whole struggles with society for recognition. It must deal with wanting and not being wanted in varying keys.

The baby called psychoanalysis struggles for survival in many ways, on many levels, within and outside itself: in individual sessions, and larger societal processes. Psychic aliveness cannot be taken for granted, but is a precious gift that must be carefully nourished.

Life at the Boundaries

The major influence on Boris was the psychoanalyst Wilfred Bion. Bion was concerned with the struggle for aliveness against deadening processes within and between personalities and groups. Bion treated groups as individuals and individuals as groups. He elucidated ways individuals/groups found aliveness dangerous and how dangerous feeling alive can be. He showed how psychic aliveness is evacuated, killed off or spoiled, or never comes to be. Bion's message is pertinent today, when evacuative products of civilization threaten to poison life.

Like one of his heros, Socrates, Bion valued ignorance. Whatever he "knew," he knew he didn't know more. He "knew" his knowings were structured by individual, biological, and group selection processes. Bion was not only keenly aware of the many hands on the elephant, but also that the elephant keeps changing. Something original keeps coming through openness, in spite of the odds against it.

Boris, like Bion, lives originary openness. He is true to the creative moment in psychoanalytic experience. Freud-Klein lines of association permeate his sessions. We feel the sexual intensity of primal scene and oedipal musings, and struggles around nourishment. At the same time erotic imagery interlaces with evolutionary ideas, especially depictions of how "selection" works in genetics and neurology (Mayr 1982; Edelman 1987). If Bion reached into religion, astronomy, and physics for intuitive models for psychoanalytic visions, Boris is drawn to evolutionary genetics, biology, and neurology. With a turn of the Borisian kaleidoscope, we see selection processes busy at every region of being. Selection problems run through life at all levels: erotics, aesthetics, politics, ethics, how and what one sees and experiences.

At times Boris's pages are like action paintings, so many impulses, voices, and attitudes having a say. He shares with us twists and turns of the human psyche as he knows it, as it speaks through him and his patients. Guiding structures crystallize out of the flux of experience. One thrills to inklings of hidden order in the flow of events. Boris refuses to compromise his dedication to the living moment, and to ordering processes he finds there.

MICHAEL EIGEN

Acknowledgments

For permission to quote entire passages, where I felt that the writer was the clearest source there is, I am indebted to Donald Meltzer for *The Kleinian Development, Part III,* Basic Books for Gerald Edelman's *Neural Darwinism,* Harvard University Press for Ernst Mayr's *The Growth of Biological Thought: Diversity, Evolution and Inheritance,* D. Marcus Beach for *Windows of Insanity,* and Francesca Bion for graciously giving me permission to quote from the entire W. R. Bion *oeuvre.* Francesca brought Wilfred's *Cogitations* for me to read when it was still unedited in typescript: I am happy now to quote from it in print. There is far more to Beach's manuscript than I have quoted; he is considering working it up for publication. My mental discussions with Bion, whose thinking has been of the first importance to me, have provided much of the material out of which I write this book.

For their parts in discussions of various of the ideas in this book, I wish to thank Gerry Adler, Kit Bollas, Neil and Evan Boris, Dan Buie, Michael Casendino, Mike Eigen, Edward Emery, Marjorie Carter La Rowe, Terry Maltsberger, Andy Morrison, Paul Myerson, Adam Phillips—and others. Edward Emery read portions of this book when in manuscript and he, Eigen, Feiner, Grotstein, and Leston Havens provided introductions to or discussions of my presentations to the various institutions or societies with which they are respectively affiliated.

I offer special thanks to Kitty Moore. Not only did she find a home for this book, but stayed with it as its editor.

To Carol Lounsberry Boris, who wrote so much of it with me, I am pleased as punch to dedicate this book.

Part One

Paradoxes and Paradigms

Introduction

The ideas put forward in this book started out as interpretations in the psychoanalytic consulting room. I illustrate their derivation and use in the second part of this book. Some readers may want to read that section first, returning to the first part, as they would to the discussion section of a clinical paper.

I do not begin there myself because so much happens in a session that making any sense of it at all requires selection— requires, metaphorically speaking, frameworks, receptors, or lenses. The purpose of interpretation is to provide the circumstances by which a patient can experience, indeed, *re*-experience, life through such alternative sets of realizations.

The purpose of writing theory is different. Writing theory and, as in this case, metapsychology, make *the system* of interpretive realizations itself discernible. Gradually some of what I found myself saying to patients and others over the years began to be visible to me as containing particular perspectives that traveled from patient to patient. As I began, in various papers, to write of these perspectives, they seemed to become paradigms and paradoxes that together refashioned some of our current psychoanalytical dialectics (Boris forthcoming a). On still further analysis, they seemed to me to prescribe a principle in the sense that Freud used that term in his essay "Formulations on the Two Principles of Mental Functioning" (1911).

These perspectives do not concern new facts, but current facts juxtaposed in slightly new configurations. New developments in science often follow from new instrumentation. My instrument of discovery might be said to be the kaleidoscope. Old and durable facts imply old and durable relationships between them. The turns of the kaleidoscope which reveal new relationships are, as Kuhn (1962) and others have demonstrated, potentially generative of new facts. A room looks very different to a small boy with a shiny new black and chrome hammer in his hand than it does later that night when he cannot fall asleep.

The behavior and experiences of people look rather different when viewed psychoanalytically from the way they seem from a different, say an economic or a biochemical, perspective. Within psychoanalysis, there are schools and traditions from which the "same" datum, if there is such a thing, also looks widely different. For example, an explanation that includes a death instinct makes a different construction, even within the object-relations point of view, from explanations simply dealing with aggression or hate. At one point I wrote of people I had seen (e.g., the anorectic or bulimic patient) thinking that it was they who carried the difference to which I wished to draw attention. Now I am writing as if the distinction lay not in the "cases," but in the perspectives I take on people. The kaleidoscopic shift I am introducing in the pages that follow features a third principle which I am calling a selection principle.

This can be thought of in three ways. One is that there *is* such a thing as a selection principle. Another is that it is only true that people *act as if* there were one. The third is that what we think or how we act is an approximation, good or poor, of something else entirely. I do not doubt that those who feel a theory or an amalgam of theories already explains human psychology will feel impatient with my proposal for rethinking motivations. But as I shall hope to make clear, founder as it might on explanations already serenely in place, the question once asked is not so simply wished away.

Suppose that people do act in accordance to this third, or selection, principle. Does that contribute some functional adaptability to the nature of things? How might one describe that adaptive function? One would, I think, have to say that those species which survive today have inherited a *choosiness* in respect to their activity—a choosiness in which those deemed most fit are favored not merely, passively, by an "asteroid"-nature in the ecological sense, but by having made a series of bioactive choices in the social milieu—particularly those influencing reproductive choice and the rearing of progeny. How would such a system of preferences make itself manifest? In many creatures by a kind of genetic programming that leads them in some sense to the better and the best. How do they know which choice is better? They don't. It is necessary merely to suppose they are "wired" to prefer one thing or event over another. Better, for example, might be (and often is) bigger or more vivid, in whatever way those traits might be made manifest. Suppose such a built-in tropism for whatever is bigger or more vital or some other kind of "er-ier" were not in place? Then reproduction would return, as it were, squarely to chance.

There are species whose reproduction quickly reflects "asteroid" changes in the ecology: guppies previously troubled by the chiclid alone, which consumes only large adult guppies, were placed in waters in which resident predators ate only the small, young guppies. In just eleven years, thirty to sixty generations later, the guppies evolved to have fewer and larger offspring (Kolata 1990). But creatures like ourselves may well have found our adaptation enhanced by a disposition toward slower genetic change (cf. Gould 1987). Moreover, making reproductive choice may seem to us better not left to chance, even if we cannot know which set of choices are the more viable. Consider the poor pea hen whose "ideal" is so freighted with magnificence that he can barely escape the fox; still whatever in her says, "Look no further, your Prince is here!" seems to find validation in the fact that, freighted as he is, her Prince has (so far) escaped not only the fox, but rivals and parasites and all manner of things more. If she dreams of a time when sleek and minimal will win the day, she may not even know how to put that dream to herself. But whatever the dimension—today's or tomorrow's—of the Peaonic ideal, she is honor bound to fulfill it.

Though an avid student, I am far from an expert on evolutionary biology. I rely on others, and quote extensively from, in particular, Mayr on biology and Edelman on neurobiology. Their theories are consonant with my own that *the* key factor in carrying out the system is that each individual *must offer selective choice* to others and that *each must be correspondingly choosy*. (I shall presently show the implication of this for what we think of as narcissism and for suicidal depression.)

But here I am already ahead of myself. For I imply, of course, that were there such a tropism in the nature of things it would be psychologically as well as biologically relevant. In saying that people act as if there were incumbencies in their selective processes, I am saying that biology informs psychology, that the biologic tropism is represented in psychological dispositions and functioning. I shall map this in some detail, particularly in the matter of the way we selectively attend to experience, and by this means create (edit and destroy) our experiential world. I shall also try to show a kind of universal occupation with the two key elements within such a predilection: an aesthetic, having to do with the celebration of the true and the beautiful; and a metaphysics having to do with the ideal. I will anticipate myself here by noting the possible relevance of the fact that there is no known culture without a religion or a kinship system (Boris 1976). One should also have to suppose that since the question of selective breeding is oriented to survival in the generations to come, these aesthetics and ideals would concern a generational life after this one. One would also suppose there would be scientific theories like the one I am here advancing. But for all intents and purposes, there are not. This would suggest either that I am talking through my hat or that much of what I am alleging we experience is not ordinarily apprehensible. The latter would make the case for writing a book.

A woman speaks of a man she met at a party. What she does *not* say is this: She walks into the party. What does she do? She checks her hair, dress and makeup at the first mirror she sees. She then looks not so much at who is there, but at what the other women are wearing. She hopes to be neither over- nor under-dressed. She hopes she is not wearing "someone else's" dress—more, even, perhaps, than she hopes no one else is wearing hers. In like way she qualifies the people she sees, and then heads or allows herself to be brought to those with whom she feels she has something in common. To further find or establish things in common will occupy some time. It will only be after this that she and her newfound friend will feel free to venture onto their differences. If she is interested in meeting a man, she follows much the same course, moving from commonly held factors, slowly onto differences, of which not the least, but usually the last, will be their respective sexes.

It is possible to reflect that the woman has said nothing of this because she is unaware of it—despite the anxieties and bits of embarrassment the occasion gave her to feel. She could describe it, as later she did, and she could understand it in her own life history, but she could not explain it. She "presented" but the analyst wasn't quite able to get hold of it. When he did "hear" it and when he looked beyond it further, he was able to see which of the psychoanalytical patterns or dynamics it fit. This, however, left out half of it. To hear the other half he would have to newly discover old ideas.

For experience is apprehensible only when attention is paid it. But attention itself is not in our freehold; we cannot pay it out at will. Rather attention is commandeered by deeper forces. These deeper forces—or principles—select how attention shall be paid and to what. The "same" elements in an experience will be experienced quite differently depending on which force or principle has taken attention into its service. We analysts are trained to attend to our patients' experiences. We encourage our patients not to worry about "going on and on" and repeating themselves because we are prepared to find in the "same" material how first certain relationships come into focus, then others, depending on the state of mind of the moment. Thus what for our patients seems at first blush to be more of the same is for us an ongoing revelation. Yet every analyst knows those times in which nothing seems fresh, new, or leading someplace. Sometimes this is a deliberate contribution of the patient. But sometimes it follows an occasion when we have felt that there has been something presented that we have not quite been able to get hold of. Accordingly we have given the patient the same old interpretation, little knowing that the (kaleidoscopic) relationships between the bits of experience had, however minutely, changed without our changing with them. When somewhat later we do take in the changes, we can look not only at them—but past them into the patterning of human nature.

Of the two principles Freud used, one propounded a "proto-mental" state of mind (and state of affairs); this one is, of course, the familiar pleasure/pain (*Lust/Unlust*) principle. The other has been the reality principle. This was derived from the pleasure principle and was not itself rooted directly in the bio-core of our being. I now propose a third, another proto-mental state of mind, having to do with a subservience to the imperatives of natural selection edicts in our biological and social lives.

These principles and their descriptions are, of course, abstractions, metaphors. They allude to motivations which themselves are felt in quite different sets of feelings and states of mind. The state of mind which I attempt to encompass within the term *Couple* carries the valency of the pleasure-pain principle; it is based on appetitive desire and it seeks repletion. The term *Pair* I use to encompass those motivations which are rooted in hope and seek closure and completion. In the states of mind *Couple* vs. *Pair*, one's presumptive or actual partner looks as different as the room did in the earlier example.

These paradigmatic states of mind—*Couple* and *Pair*, Pleasure and Selection—live a paradoxical existence. They compete, and, in competing, off-set, modify, and coalesce with one another. Hope (a leading element in the *Pair*), for example, keeps the desire in *Coupling* from being merely propinquitous. Hope's choosiness calls desire to "finer" possibilities. Desire coerces hope from forever studying (if not writing) the menu of possibility. It will be readily seen that time/space will be quite different relative to the convergence of the two.

Inner and outer also are paradigms in paradoxical tension. Looked at in a field theory (Lewin 1951) and especially in a general field theory, they can be seen to have spacings and edges that shift with the sands of moment-to-moment experience. If the urge to *Couple*, geared as it is to the discovery and use of differences, is being requited in relations in the world of affairs, inner-object relationships will grey out and dim. However, if the urge to find belonging and community with others, that is to *Pair*, is going well, then the urge to exploit differences may be, by way of postponement, redirected to internalized objects. Freud's little aphorism—"the man with a toothache cannot fall in love"—by way of going on to say that analysis is impossible for those in mourning or in love—expresses part of this.

Psychoanalysis has had a motivational basis: the polymorphously perverse, psychosexually libidinous id in conflict with ingrained forces of self-preservation. Later elaborations, like Klein's and Bion's, are rather more anxiety-based: in Klein the death instinct and its vicissitudes play a major role; in Bion the inability to suffer pain and anxiety are at the core. Interpersonal theories like those of Fairbairn and Sullivan are based on an innate need for object relations, and their focus is on the individual as a contemporary social creature, albeit landlocked in time, and the dynamics therein. More recently there have been Self theories in which the establishment, maintenance, and in Kohut's (1977) words, "restoration" of the self are the critical issues; Self theorists speak of integration and disintegration of the self (cf. Greenberg and Mitchell 1983; Mitchell 1991; Eigen 1991a, 1992). Winnicott tended to view the establishment of the self as sometimes assisted, sometimes interfered with, by the unruly passions.

The "existence" of motivational bases are reached by a process of inference along the following lines. People act (do, feel, think, sensate, etc.) as if X were the case. If indeed X is the case, then it follows that Y.... In such an inferential derivation the "if" is often lost, with the result that a logical fallacy takes place: to wit, people may act as if such and such were the case without its at all *being* the case. Interpretations in the consulting room follow this derivation, but sooner or later, as the analyst and patient progressively fill out the picture, they are self-correcting (though see Glover 1931). In theoretical formulations each proposition depends on others. In the data that led Freud to the death instinct, he simply could not find good connections either to the pleasure principle or to the reality principle. Others tried to help him out by supposing the compulsion to repeat was an attempt at belated mastery, but this added to what Freud probably felt was already a conceptually overburdened ego. Was it some longing for symmetry that took Freud away from the ego (and its reality principle), fuel-supplied with neutralized energies over to two biologically rooted principles? Or was he onto something for which the formulation required a bit more knowledge than he had at his disposal?

Like most motivational theories, the dialectic of the selection/ pleasure principles rests on an economy of shortage. If there were enough for all, selection would be unnecessary, and if selection were unnecessary, so too would be the range of qualities to choose from. Pleasure could be itself indiscriminate: there would be no need to make kinship systems and keep track of who bore what relation to whom. The disposition to do this might well have been bred out of our species long since. But, through the eye of my kaleidoscope, people act as if there were or had been an economy based on shortage, such that of the people available, some must be used for *Pair* and *Group* formation and some for exchanges suitable only to the *Couple*, whether that *Couple* be the "nursing couple," the warring *Couple*, or the reproductive *Couple*. As people move (or are moved) from one category to another, shifts in the entire individual and *Group* economy take place. An addition to the *Pair* or *Group* sphere means a loss in the repertoire of *Couple*, and vice versa.

This sorting, involving as it does comparison and contrast, works on a twin axis. One seems to sort for who is us and who is other. The second seems to sort for gender. The first scan operates from the *Pair* assumption, the second from the *Couple*. Together, it is as if the goal of these categorizations were to find an us who was also of the opposite sex and a twosome who wasn't. Neither of these motivations is sufficient; both are necessary. This twin-branched motivational base need not be conscious (if everyone *were* conscious of it there would be scant need for this book). It is enough that these root motivations bring about states of mind—or what Bion (1961) called "Basic Assumptions." These assumptions are proto-mental: they are what we experience from among all possible experiences. We hear music in octaves and in a 20 khz range; we see four colors, not a continuous stream of light, and we are essentially blind to infrareds and ultraviolets of the range; and so forth. According to Bion (1961), when people took themselves to be in a group situation, they all immediately made certain assumptions without knowing them to be assumptions:

> The basic assumption about the pair is that they meet together for purposes of sex. . . . The basic assumption is that people come together as a group for purposes of preserving the group. . . . My second point is that the groups seems to know only two techniques of self-preservation, flight or fight. . . . It is the basic assumption that the group has met together to obtain security from one individual on whom they depend. (Bion 1961: 63–66)

It was as if that were what groups were made for, and everyone knew that without need of discussion or agreement. It is in this sense that I use the concept "assumptions," although it will already be clear that while I agree with Bion on the nature of such assumptions, I see no reason to view them as emergent only in the face-to-face or reference group. Rather I regard them as inhering in the *Pair*, of which the *Group* is a natural extension, and beyond the *Group*, the Species. (Bion's interchangeability of "preserving the group" with "self-preservation" implies that Darwin's works [1859; 1872] on the preservation of the species and emotion were not far from his mind.)

As the observer alters *his* or *her* assumptions regarding people's assumptions, the facts seem slightly to rotate: *Pair* formation can be seen to be based on mutual identifications, identifications which are *not* secondary to loss but are as primary as primary can be. These require analytic study in their own right, the more so because there is an entire class of patients who are not crippled by guilt or the talion anxieties that forerun guilt, who nevertheless do not appear to live life simply for life's sake. For them survival seems to mean something more (really, other) than maximizing gain within the constraints of self-preservation and freedom from the anxieties that attend the various conditions of self-preservation. Moreover nothing seems to happen unless it is seen to happen, unless it is acknowledged, verified, validated. The idea that there is but this one lifetime (and this one analysis), though all believe it, does not seem to make much sense to them. Accordingly they are prone to wait, or await, as if *not maximizing* gain has at least as much value as living their lives to the fullest.

To these patients it is as if survival meant something different from self-preservation—and different, too, from trying once again to fulfill the unmourned wishes of childhood, *powerful as those desires are!* Rather survival is experienced as if it involved a great obligation to being choosy and providing choice to others. It is as if their survival went beyond a lifetime and beyond the immediate preoccupations of the self. It is as if they felt themselves put on this earth for some different or higher purpose—and to this obligation they must be obedient. But it is also as if they lacked a reason for feeling so. They offer memories of trauma, but shrink away in horror from any indication that the analyst might take their stories and memories to have historical truth to them. Often, as it turns out, they don't have truth to them; their memories are hopeful attempts at fitting into a psychoanalytic treatment organized for the study of the *Couple* and its vicissitudes, some bits of realization for the *Pair* issues that cause such pain yet (outside the existential) lack even a language.* It is easy enough to think of such patients as suffering from the "neurosis of success" or from "survivor guilt" (Freud 1916). And indeed, they find such interpretive constructions helpful; through them they are at least partly able to find the realizations they need. But another little twist of the kaleidoscope shows yet a different pattern: the entitlement such patients evince is at once provocative and furious. They are entitled because they have prepaid. However audaciously they act, they do not deem themselves to be among those who *do* feel that they have every right to live and flourish. Their offense in living is not against mother or father or the unborn and born siblings or even the proverbial starving children. It is against God or Fate or Destiny or whoever controls selection and says who will live, who will die, who may flourish and reproduce, who "must step aside and only stand and wait."

In being communicated, these differences have distinctive rings to them. And these same rings inform the patient whether the analyst is relating to him as a fellow member of a *Pair* or as a member of a *Couple:* In a supervision, for example, the analyst or therapist might tell his or her supervisor:

"Well as usual the patient came in late. . . ."

The supervisor, unbothered by my own or other systematized sets of formulations may nevertheless guess that, before long, the patient will have said, "I don't see the point of this; nothing is happening. I keep coming and coming. . . . Perhaps I am not cut out for this kind of therapy."

*In common usage, interestingly enough, it is Alfred Adler's language that is used: "subconscious mind," "inferiority complex," "compensatory over-reaction," "insecurity," etc. From Freud there are "projection" and character descriptions like "anal-compulsive or retentive," mostly used to describe others. Adler's language of reaction and power seems to give realization to what people feel describes themselves.

Read in a *Couple* context, the analyst or therapist is being given an anatomy lesson by the patient about other possible relationships ("coming and coming") between points and cut-out places.

Read in a *Pair* sense, the patient is feeling angry and wounded. The session for which he has hoped has yet again not arrived. It seems to the patient that there is precious little alliance on the analyst's part, and this threatens to turn nothing into a "no-thing," except . . .

Except that the analyst also despairs of the current session, believing in and hoping for a better one. In this analyst and patient are allied. Neither wants to give himself or herself over to too "cheap" a consummation. Both believe in perfectibility and a session-life hereafter, as indeed, the selection principle *would* have the *Pair* and *Group* bring about. Each member of the *Pair*, accordingly, has felt the session, as poorly as it started out, to have been a good one. Each member of the *Couple* has been staved off by the analyst's reading of the patient's opening line.

Were the analyst able, over next few sessions, to do so, there would in both matrices be opportunities for interpretation. One line would follow from the patient's feeling that his and the analyst's bodily parts are being misused and wasted. The other would follow from the patient's flight from opportunities for *Couple*-realizations out of his hope-bound devotion to better and more— the more so because the analyst is too.

Upon approaching the void left by the crises of this patient's past, the analyst is very glad to have his theories. These help him to stand the confusion and turbulence that ensue each time the patient yields over one of his paramnesias and gazes anew into the void. As they wait for the figures and events, obscured first by the amnesia, then by paramnesias, to belly forth and stand revealed, it is a comfort to both that the analyst has a theory. As a practicing analyst myself, I know this very well. (In my life this was called by some of us the Myerson phenomena. We could stand how thread-bare our theories were because we all knew Paul G. Myerson would know. When Paul then asked in some surprise how any of us thought he would know if we didn't, we all felt reassured. We knew he was kidding, though often, of course, he wasn't.) How rude then it is to have propounded a theory that causes a certain amount of jostle with one's own and others' well-worn theories! It can only be forgiven if it helps—otherwise away with the accursed thing!

Although I have tried as best I can to write this book in English, I have had to find recourse in those bits of jargon the reader has already met. While these look like nouns, they are actually verbs meant to describe the way the individual experiences or attempts to experience others and have them do likewise to him. Another bit is ahead. I use P as a shorthand for patient and Ψ to represent the psychoanalyst, therapist, psychiatric social worker, counsellor, and those others who also work in the psychoanalytical vineyards. And I use the expression, —*click!* to convey the eureka experience that takes place when preconception or premonition meets a realization.

1. The *Couple* and the *Pair*

Ψ [the analyst] has furnished a consulting room. It has a comfortable chair for himself, another for his patients, and generally it
will have a couch. It has been furnished with some care to unobtrusively reflect his tastes and personality. Treasured icons make
discrete links to his family, his profession, and his past. He will
not, for example, have color photographs of his wife and children
but he may have a vase that one of them bought him or a letter
opener that once belonged to his father. The references in the
furnishings to period and to color will also express his identity,
whether they are of glass and chrome or Early American. And he
will be there in the spareness, the choc-a-bloc-ness, the tidiness or
the mess. Depending on how much of a piece he is, he will be
saying either "This is how I want you to think of me," or "This is
who I am." (His patients will know which.)

   At or about the appointed time the analyst opens the door from
the waiting area to the consulting room. The session has now
officially begun. If the patient is present, he generally will enter.
The two are likely to offer one another a conventional greeting.
Both may want hubbub and hurly-burly to be contained until
patient reaches his chair or the couch, and both have learned to
count on their respective conventions and routines to restrain
such potential for turbulence. The development of these small
courtesies and their almost daily application rivets enough attention to make these transitions neither too revealing nor too exciting. The ceremonial repeated seems to say, "We both still know

that today again we're here for business. There are safeguards against the abyss." If the patient and analyst must pass one another, say at the door or as each composes himself at the juncture of couch and chair, these ceremonies help against touching or hitting, embracing or wrestling.

Insofar as the analyst can perform these rites mechanically and count on the patient to observe them as well, the analyst can busy himself with what he is here to do, and that is find out who has arrived. For no matter how pale and perfunctory the ritual, the patient inevitably brings in with him, like the scent of ozone after a summer storm, a burst of pure being.

Looks are sometimes deceptive. The analyst may think he has met this patient before, but of course he has not—not this patient. For today's patient is today's and can never have been here before any more than one can put a stick in the same river twice. The patient is brand new.

The patient may not know this, any more than the analyst may know that he also is brand new. The familiar rituals repeated would, indeed, seem to argue against it. But that is their little collusion.

The assumption that practice makes perfect is widely held. Both the analyst and patient may feel that being good comes out of an accretion of small achievements, one upon another and that progress means being better than before. For these, starting afresh and being each time new and different is a continual setback. On the other hand, they may take the vantage point of the *Couple* and seek out, not distinctions in degree in which the differences are more or less of the same, but differences in kind. The patient allows this difference from himself in order to play at *Coupling*.

So what are the facts today? Shall patient and therapist be meeting in fusion or fission? This question comes into being in the small plosion of the encounter. They may have quite different wishes. The analyst may want to draw the patient back into the frame of mind in which the patient can be looked at as deviant, immature, or ill, while the patient may want to draw the analyst's attention to differences less pejorative to his soul, more gratifying to his body. The analyst certainly does not want his 3:00 P.M. session to be given over to some stranger who, the moment the door is opened, marches in and lies down on his couch. (It may be bad enough that this happens in his 3:00 A.M. "session.") There are jokes about this—about lending to someone who has forgotten his dream one's own. But these are jokes. The analyst, if he has practiced for awhile, will have had the experience of seeing another one of his patients turning up at an unexpected hour, and the likelihood is that his heart will jump as he rapidly reflects on his schedule to see if it is he who has made the mistake. But at least he will recognize the other patient. Imagine someone altogether new, and worse: not even acting as if he were new, but lying down and starting to speak quite as if that were an everyday occurrence. It is the stuff of which dreams are made—or nightmares. Yet it would be quite as bad for the patient, who may have dreamt of seeing another analyst, someone nice or helpful for a change, but not surely to walk into that other analyst's room, lie down, and start talking.

To move away from the turmoil and fright of the new, both the patient and analyst will tend to contract their spheres of attention to the familiar: Oh, he is wearing that tie again; I see she has her hair up again today. Indeed, a book missing from the analyst's shelves or a new folding of the afghan may be startling enough for the patient, causing him to glance twice at the analyst just to make sure. And of course in the patient's dreams, the analyst is never a settled state of affairs. The patient often dreams that time and familiarity are out of joint: that there are others present in the waiting or consulting rooms when the patient arrives; or that the analyst is different from usual. The analyst is by no means immune from such dreams either. Both long for a breakthrough, or at least a breakout; both fear a breakdown. But even when merely dreaming their dreams, they have prudently stopped synaptic activity in those portions of the brain involved in motoric activity. During most dream-sleep, only the eyes move. They may imagine, but must lie still. They may look, but not touch.

The analyst has settled into a tradition whose tenets and culture define his task. Remarkably, as analysts, they tend to cleave to a medical model. Close analysis of this model may well reveal it to be a nineteenth-century, racist, classist, scientifically elitist, masculine structure, imitative of these same qualities when they operate in medicine, making scant difference as to which stranger performs this function on which other stranger, just as it makes no difference to the structurally male elements in the role whether that role is carried out by a woman or a man. Or a Freudian, object-relations, interpersonal, or Gestalt therapist. The object of this structure, the element without whom it could not function, on whom it utterly depends, namely, by that or any other name, the patient P—cannot but return to it the hatred it imposes. All the same in becoming a patient, P enacts his or her reciprocal to the analytic role, making it possible for Ψ to remain a viable entity. This then links them both to the P ↔ Ψ *Group* together across the generations. More often than not the precepts of that *Group* involve ideas of getting (being, becoming) better. Rivalry among members of every *Group* over the means and ends of improvement is resolved by appeals to the preeminence of tradition. On his part the patient, by even becoming a patient, shows he has been acculturated as to how to be a patient. He comes already imbued with the tradition of all patients everywhere: it is he who must take the inferior position. His understanding of that reveals he has taken the first step in joining what his analyst will call the therapeutic alliance. He has become a member of a *Pair* linked to the traditions of a *Group*. Though he will also develop what the analytic *Group* will call a transference, he will be asked not to enact that transference, for it arises out of the area having to do with *Coupling*. And psychoanalysis has been deemed a matter of the *Pair* studying the *Couple*.

In what follows I shall put forward the idea that people sometimes behave as if they were members of a *Couple*, sometimes of a *Pair*, and such behaviors take rather different perspectives on making relations with other human beings. In his classic work on groups, Bion referred to these different perspectives as basic assumptions. He argued that these assumptions were of the nature of tropisms—casts of mind that alternated with one another depending on the group's objective. However, although Bion referred to human beings as political animals in the Aristotelian sense of that term, he did not quite decipher if and how the basic assumptions that he observed when people took themselves to be members of groups played themselves out in the individual psychology of any member; that is, where and what are Bion's basic assumptions when there is no group to be observed? As will become increasingly clear, I view these basic assumptions as residing in individual psychology while also maintaining that there is no such thing as an individual psychology except in reference to others, including the *Group* and species.

Nevertheless, were Bion writing this, he might speak of the two states of mind I believe I have observed as vertices not unlike his own and refer to them as Basic Assumption–*Couple* and Basic Assumption–*Pair*. And indeed what I mean by *Pair* encompasses a good deal of what Bion meant when he spoke not only of the pairing group but much of what he meant by "basic assumptions" in a "proto-mental" state as well (Bion 1961: 62–65).

*I refer to people under Basic Assumption–*Pair *as being of a state of mind in which only the thought that one or more people are and should be bound by* identifications *makes any sense at all. This state of mind begins the self and ends with the self's relations with the self.*

*When people are under Basic Assumption–*Couple, *the vertex of the* Couple, *their interest in the one and the several is* not *in identity and identifications but in the* discovery and exploitation of the differences between objects—*for instance, of species and of gender. All differences that obtain or can be invented among people (such as the relation of mouth to breast and breast to mouth) become in this state of mind a basis for the feeling "Vive la différence!"*

Regarding (for example) a mother and her baby, they may be seen in two lights: as the Nursing Couple, to borrow a phrase used by Winnicott, and the mother-infant *Pair*. In the first state of mind the two are interested in exploring and exploiting the differences that are there for them to use. The baby, its sensual and sensuous pleasures in being fed, held, and cuddled, the mother in the precise reciprocals of feeding, holding, cuddling. At times the two of them are at work narrowing their differences and becoming as if one, replicating each other in sound, movement, and facial expression (the intersubjectivity dance). In these respects they are preoccupied and occupied with becoming a *Pair*. It has long been understood that the mother or other will have in mind the socialization and acculturation of her baby through these *Pair* activities. It has been less well recognized that the baby i
a niche for himself in the ecological hι
equally stimulated by preoccupations having to do with the *Pair* in the same sense that both are stimulated by the opportunities inherent in the Nursing Couple. The two parties do not, however,

always "agree" on which posture to take toward each other; conflict and compromise are ongoing between the two states of mind and the two states of affairs.

The *Pair* and the *Couple* are motivational systems, each with a life and logic of its own. Each expresses itself in two ways—as experience experienced or realized and also as precursors of conditions of mind and affairs. Biologically rooted motivations do not necessarily declare them*selves* as subjective states. Their effect is more subtle, sometimes so subtle as to be nearly undetectable. For example, a central function of these motive forces is to orient the experiential apparatus toward certain data and certain constructions of that data. We are by no means necessarily conscious of either orientation being operative and so do not ordinarily allow for its bias when contemplating the data it brings into experience. When I look at you, do I see you as a lover or friend, as rival or sex object?

P speaks of a dreadful experience. She has been asked by other members of the staff not to attend a particular daily meeting. Is this the exclusion from the mother/father *Couple* of the primal scene and the oedipal configuration—or is this a shunning, a sending to Coventry, by the *Group*? P is feeling so horrible at the moment that she guides her associations along lines particular to the *Couple*. As P appears to be attempting to make, not a *Couple* but a *Pair* with the analyst by being more Catholic than the pope, the strain wears on P. She slows to silence. Suddenly she feels gripped by anxiety. The room tilts, the couch wobbles —her knuckles are white; she feels spun into outer darkness. The analyst's associations refer her to the time, as a two-year-old, she fell down the toilet. Wouldn't take "No" and "Go Back to Sleep" for an answer. Unwelcome in the parental *Couple*, she formed a *Group* of her own. In her *Group* the motto was, "I Can Do It Myself." Unrescued from her cot, she made her way through the dark and hoisted herself onto the toilet. But there was no one to pull the seat down. Slipping into the chilly bowl, hubris was, as usual, repaid by fate: the rim of the seat came down around her, imprisoning her until she was forced into cries and finally "They came" (and Oh, what a funny sight—youshouldhaveseenher—she was!) to her rescue. Now she had to reform in order to re-form with the *Pair*. The triangle excluded her; she had to form a *Pair/Group* by giving up her independence, her alternative *Pair/Group* of me, myself, and I. The function of the copulating *Couple*, rather than reproducing, was to gain an audience and her role in this division of labor was to make sure that they had an audience for every one of the 110 variations (this number took account of the fact that the parents were at times of the same gender: see Phillips [1992]).

When *Pairing* is the dominant consideration, a second person will be examined in terms of his or her likeness to the self and a third person for his or her likeness to the first two. He will also be compared, as is each self by itself, to an ideal. Specific qualities of that ideal will be learned and formed out of identifications, but the idea of *Pairing* is very much to lay down such elements, as one might lay down wine, for later use as ideals. Thus, from the beginning, a nascent aesthetic impulse is at work. When *Coupling* is regnant, the third person is likely to be seen as superfluous or as a rival. The *Group* is an extension of the *Pair*, the Oedipus complex, of the *Couple*. Depending on the state of mind, which is to say depending on the motivation, the same triad can constitute now a triangle, now a *Group* in the mind of any one of them. The behavior of these three people, that is the state of affairs, will not only vary but be variously interpreted, depending on their states of mind. In the state of mind in which *Couple* is ascendent, there is a great likelihood for two or more of the three to feel jealous and to act accordingly. When *Couple* perspectives recede, the events in the state of affairs will involve prospects of envy and/or admiration. Because so much is open to interpretation, one function of the *Pair* or *Group* is to lend support for certain interpretations, particularly those which for various reasons (such as being untrue) are open to doubt or vulnerable to disputation. Among those interpretations most vulnerable to dispute are matters of taste. There is no denying whether a good meal is a good meal; the sense of being comfortably replete informs as to that. But whether that meal consisted of good food is another question answerable not in *Couple* terms as nicely full, but in *Pair* terms.

Following Bion, I am inclined to think that what is so "basic" about these assumptions is that they are preconceptions. The mind appears to be so organized as to focus sometimes on differences, sometimes on likenesses. I view mentation as organized around comparison and contrast. When the state of mind *Pair* is regnant, similarities are found. By "found" I mean that both "similarities" and "differences" are embedded in the potentia of experience, much like the profiles and the vase are both embedded in the well-known figure/ground plate. When the state of mind *Couple* is lively, differences are prized out of what is embedded. This distinction is not, of course, absolute; and what is or isn't "there" has a good deal to say about how it is or isn't experienced. Nevertheless the sleights of mind are such as to contrive experience when pushed to it.

Taking the idea of differences: those of interest in the *Couple* originate in the domain of differences in *kind*. Differences of *degree* work in the domain of relative likeness. But under certain conditions (the sway of envy, for one [see Boris 1992a]) more and less of the same can be treated as if it appertained to differences in kind: homosexuality is one outgrowth of this. In a similar way differences in kind can be transformed into differences rather of degree. Fetishism is a stage property for one such variant of this.

Whether two people fashion an experience contrived out of identifications or one exploiting the reciprocal (or unreciprocal) use of their differences is a matter negotiated by the two of them. The agreement to negotiate expresses a membership in the *Pair*. It is a cusp that surrounds and contains a mutuality of engagements in even such seemingly antagonistic activities as warfare. Thus wars show a degree of *Pair*-formation that is absent when the Other is deemed to be of a species different from Us or Ours. Predation of one species by another shows the absence of even that cusp. The line is a wavering one, however. Many people will not eat certain animals, or any, because of a sentimental tie, a feeling of identity. Starvation may make the line move. Some people cannot marry in the faith; only someone clearly Other makes *Coupling* possible—or, as in the use of prostitutes, certain sorts of *Coupling* possible. It may be recalled that Lewin's work during the Second World War showed the degree to which distastes for certain cuts of meat shifted only when the shift took place in a group connection (Lewin 1951).

Thus there are two states of mind, the *Pair* and the *Couple*, each with its speciality; each comes into its own to make and map the world. They are "meant"* to function in harmony but until they do they are bound to function at the expense of one another, and the lines they draw in the matters of kind and degree waver. At the point where the wish for direct (particularly sensual) experiences is too far or too long displaced, the line will move to exclude more people—out of Us and into Other. At the juncture where there are satisfactions aplenty for the body, more discriminating tastes and discernments will come into play. But the need for affiliation in the *Pair* dimension means that there is a limit on the solipsism of the mind: we are bound to see (or believe we see) matters as our *Group* does.

Differences of all sorts are used by the *Pair* to form *Group*s with a common purpose, such as the division of labor or a specialization of function. The only defense afforded to the *Pair* when it comes to discovered differences is to incorporate those differences as differences of degree rather than of kind and to use them by way of divisions of labor and specializations of function. Nevertheless in drawing fusion-fission lines those differences as organized for purposes of the *Pair* or *Group* remain fault lines. When the crystal splinters, it will be at those points of differences. This is so because the *Couple* will want to grab those differences for its own uses. Sally may be playing second base on an otherwise all-male team; so long as the team is successful, Sally will remain one of the boys. Should the team's fortunes sag and its differences from other teams become painful, it is Sally who is likely to become the first choice for purposes of *Coupling*.

From the point of view of the *Couple* it is easy to see specialized members of the *Group* as ready-made objects suitable for coupling. Recalling the figure/ground metaphor, a man may become a girl in the boarding school or prison and a man once more in the presence of women, depending on which state of mind is in force. ("In force" is defined by urgency of whichever motivation, *Couple* or *Pair*, is being frustrated, but also by "Newton's First Law," which in sociopsychological life also means that relationships in motion tend to stay in motion; this latter "law" may turn out to

---

*This is tautological, of course; I will try to make my meaning clear in chapter 4.

have come into play as a block against imprinting and being imprinted—a lag-phase to preserve species-specific postnatal development. For in order to select the "better" or "best," there must be a wide but not endless assortment of possibilities.) Objects whose morphology or function has become partially efficient and differentiated from the me, myself, and I-self object, or "we-go," stand upon or indeed provide the borderline between *Pair* and *Couple*. This object will seemingly shift the self into the *Coupling* mode unless it can be retained as an object of specialization or tool for the division of labor. The number of degrees away from selfness and out toward otherness makes it like a loose ion, something volatile which more than anything else could create the shift from *Pair* to *Couple* status; that is, it could become different in degree or in kind depending on the point of view of its contemplator.

The *Couple* exists for purposes of copulation, for the taking of pleasure whose ultimate reach is mating. Infantile psychosexuality, driven by the pleasure-pain principle, is a way of describing this *Coupling* providing that the co-determinous motivations to *Pair* are given their proper weight. As a state of affairs, *Coupling* is lively when the appetites are in need of refurbishing. At this point, at least one person is interested only in discovering or even inventing differences of the sort that increase sensual pleasures. Sensual appetites can be satisfied providing the kind of differences required are discovered. The Other whom the first might wish to employ as his object in that endeavor may have reciprocal needs, adjunctive needs, or needs that might initially require various degrees of *Pairing*—which is to say make the encounter into, or take out of it, a partnership. ("Say 'please' first!" might be the simplest example of the latter.) Despite the Other's disposition, the first may feel free to rape, plunder, or pillage. The needs of the sensual cornucopia cannot be only partially satisfied satisfactorily; there must come a point of repletion, short of which nothing less will do.

Shades of grey come into the picture with the advent of the capacity for vicarious feelings. Vicariousness is the medium of the *Pair*. Through one's identifications, one can feel that "there but for the grace of God go I," which is the source of empathy, sympathetic imagination, and the capacity for pity and fear that Aristotle identified as requisite for the cleansing catharsis of tragedy.

In its beginning the newborn experiences an ecstasy of hope and despair in the wilderness of sense impressions and dark, inchoate messages arising from within, insofar as there is a within. The hope is that matters will make sense, that preconceptions will be met; the despair is that he will be unable to wrest from the welter anything that he can recognize based on those preconceptions and predilections. At some point infants do begin to expect something. That expectation is more than simple anticipation based on extrapolation from previous experiences. Attached to certain anticipations is an emotional investment in having the anticipation be as it is supposed to be; there is a wish to find a world that is seemly and fit, a world that makes sense to infants and they to it. The feeling of the infant is to be linked to Something. What is the something? Of what does it consist? Is it infantfeelingmothersensationworld? The theory is that such an outsized experience is overwhelming and that the infant can't manage it any more than the reader could manage that all-at-once word. The infant, like the reader, might break the experience/word segmentally in order to attend to the various elements one by one. He can, for example, distinguish his mother from all the other people going in and out of the infant nursery at the hospital in which he was born; he can track her as she comes and goes. As his experience expands, the infant's attention becomes more mobile; soon the infant can separate figure from background, one from another, and can create Two where One was. Psychoanalysis has it that among the first of these divisions is mother from breast. In a paper called "The 'Other' Breast" (Boris 1986), I have argued a different distinction. I have suggested that when the baby discovers or invents the two "breasts," he now must choose: and this leaves him with the sorry, sometimes unbearably painful task of preferring one to the other.

The infant wishes the breast were as much a part of him as thumb, foot, or even bellyache. The breast, or at least the "good breast," is the source of all good things, and the infant wants it for himself—not so much to adorn that emerging outline of "myself" as to have it as much at his disposal as he has his fingers, eyes, or mouth. The idea that the breast travels with mother is not a pleasant one to entertain.

The infant exists in just such a state of greed. Choices between one thing and another are barely endurable, so vivid are his elaborations of (in Frost's words) "the road not taken." In desperation he limits his array of choices so that desire faces only a binary choice. He, of course, so hates the potential choices, different in kind and not just degree, that he occasionally discovers; they tease and tantalize him and excite in him a retaliatory wish to persecute them with disdain.

Our young draftsman, accordingly, draws up a rough plan with the deployment of his attention in which the good breast is his and the bad breast—the breast that frustrates by its independence and absences—belongs to mother. But of course, he need not even put mother in the worldview he is crafting. He needs something there to which to ascribe the badness and destructiveness, but a simple construct of the bad breast will do. All goodness will flow from the one and all evil from the other. Thus by the division— "splitting"—he has effected, he can separate the good from the bad and the one breast from the other, link the goodness with the one and the badness with the other, and thereby organize his life.

Bion asked Klein how the baby knew the good breast was good (Bion 1979). Kleinian theory rests heavily on good and bad personifications of experience. But is this deprivation based on repletion v. frustration in the libidinous sense? Or is there more to it? Kleinians know there is more to it, but theirs being an anxiety theory, it plainly features the degree and even kind of anxiety in an experience as co-determining its goodness and badness along with the libidinal contribution of the experience. I do not doubt this formulation, but I think it might be expedient to trace back the anxieties—the badness—to frustrations in the experiences of *Pairing* and the sense of the goodness to approximations of the preferences that lie prefigured in the roots of the *Pair*.

The development of vicariousness is what makes possible the titration of ruthlessness with concern and with repentance for hurtful actions.

As the infant develops he discovers two objects, himself and others, and as Freud (1921) remarked, "Love of self knows only one boundary, love of others." But an object is barely an entity until it is defined; one might say an object is an entity awaiting definition. The infant's hand and the infant's mother are objects, as is his hunger or his bladder. As is the mobile someone thoughtfully placed above his crib. But these have no meaning until they acquire a relationship. The *Couple* and the *Pair* are such relationships. They await, in their turn, objects with which to link. A succinct way of putting such matters is that the mind is a set of relationships waiting for objects to employ. No object exists except tangentially—as a part of a potentia—until its place in a relationship is accomplished, as often as not by analogy.* Freud's remark concerned the relative power of narcissism as against object love, of auto- v. other-eroticism. His implication, of course, was that the erotic impulse would finally link up, in whatever polymorphous way, to another body and perhaps person. It would *Couple.* But before that it would enjoy a state of primary narcissism, an ocean of bliss, a fabulous melt, in which relationships, even to the self as an object, did not yet sprout links waiting to happen. I prefer to regard this state as a prefiguration of union.

Earlier I noted that the states of mind did not have to make themselves felt as explicit motivations except as mental orientations, ways of paying attention, toward giving preference to certain sorts of experience. There are states of feeling that serve as intermediate motivations. In the *Coupling* mode these motivations are hungers, frustrations, excitements, and satisfactions on the one side and the reliefs, gratifications, and sensual and affectionate well-being on the other. It is possible that a hormone like oxytocin or another endorphin marks the achievement of repletion. In the *Pairing* mode the reach is between isolation, emptiness, and despair to affinity and affiliation, fullness and hope. The sense of bliss that comes from an experience of absolute unity—of fusion and union—is to the impulse to *Pair* what ecstasy and purring contentment is to the *Couple.* One can say that the *Couple*'s stock in trade is repletion, the *Pair*'s is completion.

Identification, the medium of the *Pair*, was variously described by Freud as a defense and as something proactive in its own right. Its most famous function was the resolution of the Oedipus com-

* I will return to this in chapter 3.

plex. The child abandons its interests in *Coupling* (and *Decoupling*), that is to say, its sexual interest in one parent and rivalry with the other, and adopts an object other than its parent's lover as the new recipient of its wishes to *Couple*. In making its further identification, the child permits the family to become a *Group*. Identification in this sense was the fallback alternative; the child adopted it out of love for its contestant and out of fear of sexual retaliation. But it can equally be said that in leaving the *Pair* for the *Couple*, the child loses its precious sense of identity with the family *Group* and particularly its *Pair*-partner. Even as the child aspires to conquest and triumph, it longs for the old identities that it is losing. The child's solution is to create new and other objects for *Coupling* purposes—the boy or girl next door—and thus retain its primary investments in the *Group*.

By analogy to states of affairs, elements can be incorporated in states of mind such that goods can be bought and stored. But these goods may be used as supplies to feed the self or can be used by the self to supply to others. To incorporate something speaks only of one part of a fantasied act. The other part concerns where what is incorporated is deposited. Freud wrote that identification grew out of fantasies of incorporation. Such identifications and their close cousins, introjection and internalization, are rooted in the domain of the *Couple;* that is to say, they are deposited for use in object relations in which the relationships are based on differences. For example, a cannibalistic relationship may occur between superego objects and the "I." Or the two objects, the internalized self and the representation of the other, may continue relationships based on the physical body's relationship to its fecal masses (see also Boris 1984a, 1984b, 1988). On the other hand, in his work on group psychology, Freud wrote of what I regard as identification in the domain of the *Pair* in which each object becomes the other's subject or combines to form an "us" object. In this sense identification as a fantasy or an act is bound together by its mimetic goals. It is key to any discussion of identification to consider how the now–internally represented object is used in relation to the ego or self. Just as one's relationship with people will shift from those based on *Coupling* to those on *Pairing* and back, so one's relationship to internally represented people or bits of people will vary. Indeed, as I hope to show later, both the world of interpersonal relationships and the world of internalized object relationships are but two aspects of a larger field in which successes in one realm affect the motivational status of the other. Freud had this in mind when he noted that losses of persons occupying an individual's state of affairs will be taken up and laid down for use in his internal relationships and thereby replace the loss of the actual object and its anticipated power in regard to the self (Freud 1917). In short, the relationship's the thing.

For the infant, the alimentary experience is a rich source for framing mental activity of incorporation; the body model is eating. Disincorporation is to be found in burping, vomiting, urinating, defecating, or crying pain or badness out of one's system. If the infant wishes, he can imagine that he can translocate the undesirable attribute by one or another of these means: if the purported discovery of unwanted or other traits in the Other disfigured or deformed the it, so much the better; at least, no matter. Or the Other might be filled with good stuff, its shape is not to be disturbed. Now the badness will be evacuated into the Self, leaving a space, and goodness will flow from the Self into the space in the Other. The Other is idealized and the Self deprecated.

Clearly, before this can happen, the Self must be differentiated from the Other, so that the either/or-ness of selectivity can ply its trade. Where for babies less in need of effecting this sort of transmigration, the Self-Other boundaries can remain a matter of indifference, the infant who needs to transport qualities across the boundaries between Self and Other needs to be cartographically exact about where one ends and the other begins.

There are procedures by which the Self can engage the Other in acting consonantly with the idea that something has been emptied from the Self and taken in or on by the Other. If the Other does not comply with the idea that what is being "discovered" in him is the result of a projective transfusion, the behavior of the Other cannot be attended to, or at least not unselectively. People who depend on this notion of the evacuation of Self qualities into Others, so that these qualities are not associated by the Self with the Self, but rather with the Other—people generally called paranoics—often feel it prudent not to get too close a view of the Other into whom they have deposited their unwanted attributes. This is due in part to the fear that proximity may invite a rapid redisposal. But another motivation lies in the fear of discovering that the transfusion did not "take." (One such practitioner could tell the "presence of the enemy" by the pattern in which the city lights came on at night, but sly dogs that they were, each night they changed the pattern!)

By regarding identification as *the* means by which people are members of a *Pair* and then, by extension, of *Group*s, I am supposing that identification is a fundamental alternative to *Coupling* and like any alternative can be used for defensive purposes. The same holds true of forming a *Couple*. It can be what one or both people come to when their identification with one another in the *Pair* falters. Where earlier they saw much in common and could experience events vicariously, now their differences become obtrusive (at least to one of them) and they are drawn either to abandon the relationship or to *Couple*. So-called masochistic submission of one party to another is an example of this (Ghent 1990). As the choice of domains (internal/external) exists, so the choice of the kind of relationship *(Couple/Pair)* exists as preconceived alternatives for use as circumstance dictates. Now it is true that there is a certain play of will as to which state (mind or affairs) and which motive *(Pair* or *Couple)* an individual will employ, and this element of will can be displayed to a patient in the consulting room. P, for example, dreams over a weekend two dreams involving the analyst. P jokes, "Now I need come only three times a week." This is reminiscent of Freud's explanation of dreams as a hallucination in the face of the unavailability of the breast—in this case the two breasts. But we must ask: how volitional is this re-representation? Is not the dreamer as much prone to what the dream is as to the deprivation that his dream attempts to deal with (Grotstein 1983)?

Perhaps the clearest way of taking note of the shifting quality in states of affairs is by considering that both sets of needs must be accommodated. Since it would be inconceivable for all people to form a *Group* (in that posture what would become of their need to *Couple?*) and a waste to have a world full of differentiated objects (for what would supply the need to affiliate and harness differences?), the ongoing question appears to be how to put particular Others to best use. Other may make a good opposite number in a *Couple,* but who then will play second base? The Analyst may make an excellent analyst, but who then will play Papa? Take away the Cold War, and a dozen other wars spring up because an antagonist is needed. Bring East and West together, and someone will be needed for them to unite against.

2. The *Couple,* the *Pair,* and the *Group*

In infancy the mother or mothering person is partly disposed to be a member each of *Couple* and *Pair,* as is the infant—but since they only have each other they have to agree on (or contest) who is what when. Though excellent work has come from Stern (1985) and others (e.g., Beebe and Lachman 1988; Anders 1989), confirming and detailing the infant's activity in shaping this "intersubjective agreement," no answers as to what motivations are in play have been given. But there can be general agreement that the mother bears more than the provisioning function ascribed to her in the more primitive version of psychosexual theories: she must be receptive also to the baby's communications and indeed to his efforts to lead and orchestrate. That is, in his effort to gain his mother as a partner in a *Pair,* he must stimulate in her an inclination and ability to move toward him and identify with what he is like.

By saying that infants act as if they were sometimes a member of a *Couple* or *Pair,* I mean to emphasize that the two are states of mind which coexist, as figure and ground coexist in the picture of the profiles that are also the vase. Sometimes one comes to the fore, sometimes the other. That is, sometimes one person looks at another in such a way as to look for differences and sometimes in such a way as to look past or over differences and find aspects in common.

Two people may agree on how to regard one another or they may not. But one person may not agree with himself as to how he regards another since the way he pays attention, and so what he experiences, may not be settled. I think a person takes note of both sorts of qualities in a brief and rapidly oscillating way. Each makes a claim on his attention. Each way also offers a sort of refuge from the claim of the other (see in this respect Feiner 1982).

For the infant, a mother, whole and indivisible, particularly when making her claim about one of the states of mind *(Couple* or *Pair)*, would so rivet his attention as to veritably mesmerize him. In the Darwinian sense, she would select him, for with her presence she fills the horizon as the only experience to apprehend, as all the cells with which he apprehends experience would comport themselves to the shapes, smells, and sounds of her. He could not see the trees for the forest of her.* The young, however bent they are to have their pleasures, are not altogether immune from the dangers attendant on the pursuit of pleasure or the evasion of pain. They have a sense of survival, of self-preservation. Pleasure and pain, self-preservation and the survival of the species—these are the preoccupations of the young and so the constraints on attention. They *select* attention. As Freud (1917) put it, "The man with a toothache cannot fall in love."

If the draw to the *Pairing* mode were somehow excessive, he would become her. But if he is able to switch off this representation of her, and this is only possible if he can move to the *Coupling* mode, he could escape being a clone of her and discover again the differences he could enjoy.

P has had two dreams. In the first she is in the presence of an attractive man—possibly Peter O'Toole as Lawrence of Arabia. She fashions her mouth to receive a kiss, and is so alluring that he is compelled to kiss her in a lingering fashion. Then their bodies seem to cleave together in a perfect embrace, capped off for her by the evident stirring of an erection. P gestures to her mouth, her torso, her pubic region. She remarks, "That's funny, in the dream I was in a fetal position."

In the next dream, P dreams of herself sleeping and awaken-

---

*I shall return to this condition later; for now I wish only to note that the capacity to "split the object"—that is, to divide by two, is a predilection born of the *Couple* principle and enabling the self, accordingly to be taken as *its* own object.

ing in surprise to find her finger is in her vagina. She examines it, and it looks dew-moist and flecked with a pearly substance. In her dream she goes back to sleep, but not before putting her finger back in.

In her associations to the first dream, to Lawrence of Arabia, she associates his full close-up handsomeness and his great blue eyes, the hood of his cloak swept around his mouth, and his status of being in a desert. To the pursing of her mouth she associates a mouth opened circularly, as in Christmas cards of children singing carols. To the second dream she associates her pleasure in masturbation and the unselfconsciousness she can only feel in dreams— which Ψ then gets off on listening to, making it shameful. To desert, P associates a recurring image of something newly born, still in only a membrane, unable to crawl away, doomed to burn to a crisp. Relative to the second dream she contrasts the unselfconsciousness she feels in the dream with the experience she is having telling the dream.

To look at these dreams along *Couple* and *Pair* lines, we must for the moment "blind ourselves" to the person who dreamt them and take note only of the precipitates.

In *Couple* terms, the following may be among the obtrusive elements: the face as one might remember it from nursing at the breast; the desert as an experience of dryness and thirst and of feeling deserted; a successful infusion of desire from mouth to breast; the erection of the nipple; the conversion of an infantile nursing scene into a grown-up sexual scene; the hiatus that stops the consummation; the need, then, to dream a second realization in which the consummation is fulfilled in an autoerotic fashion; the conversion of frustration at the hands of the nipple and penis into the ability to self-fulfill with even the provision of semen by the hand-thumb-penis no longer even requiring a man to substitute for the mother—something that appeases both sensual wishes and those driven by envy, the discovery of which will exact envy and anger from Ψ.

From the *Pair* point of view, here is a creature who is doomed to die, even before she is fully born. What will it take to be allowed to live on? To and with what has she to reconfigure herself? One image is of the little carolers, singing for their suppers, perfect mouths perfectly open—O. This formation is at once neutral and polymorphous. It is O for orifice. She is not yet specialized; nothing is yet vestigial. This brings forward the good object. His mouth is cloaked; he will not make a meal of her. His great eyes look at her. They see that she is good. He pours himself into her, step by step, in stages. But those eyes see that she is desirable. . . . At this P stops the dream. In the second dream self-sufficiency replaces excitement and desire. Nevertheless the responsibility to provide progeny for the race is intact: P has what it takes. The dreamer goes back to sleep. There is time yet before she has to differentiate in order to *Couple*; time yet before she has to die. For now One is one and only one, and it is OK.

Just so the baby: shall it be in a position of coming around to a like mind with mother on the subject or fighting the question out? That like-mindedness is an expression of Basic Assumption—*Pair*. Without a shared assumption, either party to the transaction could only be felt to exist at the expense of the other—a predatory or, worse, parasitic relationship. For this not to happen (or long endure), the states of mind, *Couple* and *Pair*, need to be negotiated. I would like to say that the cusp of Basic Assumption at once expresses and defines the shared view that the people involved are of the same species; such ideas of negotiation are not extended to those viewed as being of a different species—or those sub-speciated by the *Group* of which (in this case) the mother and baby are members.

To keep him from taking a wholly predatory view of her, and particularly a parasitic one, the mother may want to enlist the infant into membership with her in a *Pair*, in order to find some new object for the infant (and perhaps the mother) to take as a sensual possibility for *Coupling* with. This last is not alone a connivance of the mother. If it is to work it requires agreement from the baby. He must agree to switch his intentions (in state-of-mind language, his attentions) and see his former *Couple*-object as his new *Pair*-friend.

This precise situation also occurs in aggregates of people. They too have choices as to how to regard one another: as objects for *Coupling* and perhaps mutual or unmutual predation, or as that large *Pair* we call a *Group*. On a dark and deserted street, one is always relieved if the other who shows up is wearing the uniform of our *Group*. A *Group* forms out of common concerns; the aggregate forming the *Group* puts aside its differences—and does so as if with one mind. Since at least some possibilities for *Coupling* within the aggregate are going to be sacrificed to the identifications that are the glue of the *Group*, the members of the *Group* will need to find opportunities for *Coupling* elsewhere. Ordinarily, therefore, aggregates come together to form *Groups* when it seems to them that by relinquishing one another as objects for *Coupling* they will *Couple* better en masse with yet others.

In pondering this state of affairs regarding tribes keeping track of kin and kinship ties, Freud felt that the incest taboo was being observed: when each person knew who was family, one knew also who was available for sexual concourse. Lévi-Strauss (1973; see also Boris 1976 in forthcoming b) saw family and tribe rather as a means for bride trading, which he thought to be *the* basic commodity exchange. Perhaps inherent in both of these uses (or hypotheses) is that one *Group* requires at least one other person with which to have *Coupling* commerce—one other object from which it can both feel itself to be different and do the things that exploit that difference. In seeing itself as people in common, the aggregate must overlook or subordinate all that is different among them. It is easier to do this when the someone whom one is going to call Other or Them is quite different. Commonly *Groups* heighten their differences from other *Groups* by wearing clothes or developing languages or traits that are unique to them. *Pygmalion* and *My Fair Lady* tell one side of this story, the yellow star and "Jüden" quite another.

The Other is founding member of the *Group* of which the Self may be invited, while very young, to take a part. The rules of such *Groups*, as of any and all *Groups*, are very simple: all members must pay attention to certain things in certain ways and not pay attention to the fact that they are paying attention to certain things in a certain way.

Indeed, the very conception of who is part and who not part of the *Group* rests on the idea that those who are part have more in common with the other than they do with those who are not part of the *Group*. Often this can only be a result of how attention is paid to the issue of commonality. Does one take note of size? shape? color? gender? Plainly one has to select—and to feel that selection to be more vital than selections based on some other characteristic or set of characteristics.

Since this is no different from any one person's methods for attending selectively, it is easy to become a member of any *Group,* including the first one. The difficulty arises, if it does, when Self and Other disagree on what to pay attention to and how. If one is prepared to join in the formation of a reciprocally collaborating set of opposites, one can remain part of the *Group* of non-Us people. For "we" and "they" are *Group*s in which what is in common is that "they are not we" and "we are not they."

Still, it is easier and more reliable to know who is "in" when one knows who is "out"; this is a simple variation on the Either and Or of all selective procedures involving attention. Thus the old adage: common enemies make common friends. The selections that are held in common are not threatened by the Other, for there is a quid pro quo involved. One of the tasks that lies before the infant is to establish ways of experiencing his own experience that also bear out the ways the Others in his life select out from their own range of experiential possibilities. The infant might wish to notice things in such a way that his mother will have none of. He might, for example, wish to believe that it is a matter of "won't" for his mother rather than "can't." Such a belief may inspire him with hope but might infuse her with guilt. His implication that she is refusing him what in her view she simply cannot give him —a view often enough expressed in the sort of crying an infant does—may seem to her far from a vote of confidence, hence reproach. She may take it as an accusation as unfair as it is worrisome. If he wants to join *her Group,* he had better be of like mind. A nice cry of sadness and then some sleep-that-will-do-wonders is the ticket she has written for him. This enraged, accusatory crying had better stop and soon. But the infant feels, "Why won't she, since she can? What else can I do to make her do so? For if she does so, not only will I enjoy what she does, but my belief that she can and could all along do so will be restored—and, in the same stroke, I shall be hauled back from the bright edge of disillusionment." The infant is infuriated. At the moment, needless to say, they are not of a mind—not in a *Group.*

At the *Group*'s edges, of course, is where the tensions lie: here people are specialized—are different enough from the *Group* mean to be a hair's breadth away from being used for *Coupling*. *Couples* who are very much alike are in danger of becoming instead a *Pair*. Fighting (as opposed to athletic contests) is an activity whose lust places it in the domain of the *Couple*. Fighting is sometimes what keeps the *Coupling* alive for sex (though it may sometimes be so successful that the twosome may instead make its meal of it). There is a kind of fighting that arises in the *Pair* and expresses the outrage of one party with the other.

The source of this outrage is envy. The envy is based on the issue of influence—who influences whom in service to the *Group*. The stronger of the two parties will be the one who most feels he or she has the right to live, flourish, and survive. To the person less in doubt of that right, the other must give way—or abandon or be abandoned in the *Pair*. Such deference confirms for both parties who has the superior quality upon which the rights depend. The other can only envy the winner. For if he were to stay in the *Pair* he is at risk of feeling so unequal and so controlled by the superiority of the mother that he can only attempt to rectify the imbalance by the despoliation of the other. When things are in better balance, the *Pair* can feel that any power granted in the *Pair* by one to the other is used on behalf of both.This fighting has as its goal the despoliation of one by the other, as an expression of the quality in the state of mind of the *Pair* that any power granted by one to the other should be used on behalf of both. By the mutual agreements that create the *Pair*, the junior member has ceded to the superior member the right to bestow grades of membership and quality: "I dub thee . . ." An identification projected by any one party must be accepted by the other. "I am!" cries the one. "No you are not!" replies the other. "However, by virtue of the authority vested in me, I now dub thee . . ." Such are the power and the pleasures invested in the *Pair* and the *Group* on behalf of the species.

The divisions the mother and infant shape are heir to all of these tensions. In Kleinian terms the breast is a triangulated object spun out for purposes of *Coupling*, while mother and baby form a *Pair* regarding it. The breast is by no means absolutely discovered as a part of mother, but rather is given the status of a Part-object that mother and infant and often others share. The discovery that the breast is indeed a part of mother is a depressing one (the anaclitic depression, in the Freudian vocabulary—cf. A. Freud 1965). But the trouble is worse than that. Not only is the breast not one's own, which is a narcissistic blow, it belongs to one's partner in the *Pair* who has now turned out not to be one's partner but one's rival for the breast—a member of a *Group* hostile to oneself. I suggest it is in these terms Erikson's attribution of trust and mistrust to this stage of infancy might be further understood. The infant has a mouth, a hunger to suck and take nourishment, to be held and cuddled and burped; these characteristics are suited, as the infant desires them to be, to the mother's nipple and breast and milk and body. When these attributes work reciprocally, all is well, but when that reciprocity is not evident, another sort of to-and-from comes into the picture. The infant may not only have to idealize his mother but veritably to inspire her. He must bring his caretaker around to joining him in the point of view that the breast or its substitute should not be regarded merely as an object delivering nutriment and pleasure. The infant must stimulate her to the conviction that the *Coupling* exchange can also be used as a conduit to the infant's efforts to get its ideas across, the first of these being the one just mentioned: that the breast has a giving and a *receiving* function. The infant's hope that he has a mother who is a "can" or "cannot" depends on engendering a mother who shows signs that she shares his idea. If so, the other "flow" can go from the infant into the mother. But he needs a signal that his transmissions have been received—feeding and feedback, a two-way flow.

In considering the basic assumptions of people in *Group* situations, Bion made essentially three points. The first was that what is true of *Group*s arises only when those involved somehow consider themselves members of a *Group*. The second point was that when people do consider themselves to be members of a *Group*, the assumptions are presented as inevitable by-products of that condition, which is to say the members might dispute whether or not one or another of the assumptions should prevail, but they would agree that only one or another should and did prevail. The third point was that when these basic assumptions were the foundation for all subsequent interactions, they replaced the dynamics endemic to what he referred to as the primal scene:

> The impulse to pair may now be seen to possess a component derived from psychotic anxiety associated with primitive oedipal conflicts working on a foundation of part-object relationships. This anxiety compels individuals to seek allies. This derivation of the impulse to pair is cloaked by the apparently rational explanation in the pairing group that the motive is sexual and the object reproduction. (Bion 1961: 163)

Bion's basic assumptions were Dependency, Pairing, and Fight/Flight. These assumptions arose in respect to an object that was of, but not in the group—for example, some other group or the leader of the group. How this other was perceived by the group was in part a function of that Other's behavior and in part a function of what particular assumption the *Group* was making at the time.

Bion also referred to the "work group," by which he meant a group in which the three basic assumptions (Dependency, Fight/Flight, and Pairing) were tolerant of the primal scene and therefore not merely traded off one for another.

Though he observed that society at large contained subgroups devoted to one or another of the assumptions—the Armed Services for fight/flight, for example, the Church and the Aristocracy for certain aspects of pairing, the Leadership for dependency—Bion's interest was and continued to be in the mentality these configurations implied. What made them basic assumptions lay in their unthought nature: they existed as preconceptions of what observed experience was or might be.

Other systems theorists—such as Minuchin, Rosman, and Gailer (1978), Birdwhistell (1970), Saussure (1959)—also see the means as more basic than the meanings. That is, people do without knowing what or why. Under such circumstances study of the meanings and motives is as wildly inapplicable as the attempt to explain the behavior of subatomic particles by ascription of reason and purpose. "Thoughts," Bion was to write, "require a thinker." The mentality that created the basic assumptions he had earlier described as outgrowths of groups was also a mentality that created objects and events whose experiential status was akin, not to ideas and percepts, but to things and doing—things-in-themselves. It required a further sort of process—alpha—to transform events and things from a status of being real and so (being "beta elements"), into ideas of things that could be thought with.

In general outline this explication extended Kleinian thought about symbol formation into more general purpose conceptualizations. Roughly analogous to the work group there were degrees of freedom by which the mind freed itself of its innate assumptions under the terms of which things and events had only one condition—actual. At the same time, analogous to the emergence of the work group from the basic assumptions, there were degrees of freedom by which the mind's view of relationships between things escaped metonymy and homology. One such relationship was the primal scene; other assumptions such as dependency, fight, and pairing could be made. In time analogues could be formed. One of the examples Bion liked to use concerned a patient of Hanna Segal's who would not go to a concert given by a famous violinist because he disliked the idea of people displaying their masturbation in public. The patient's construction of the concert left out the idea of music, but what if he thought that the performance was only one of playing the violin? The analogy would have been lost now in the other direction.

Freud also thought that people unconsciously hold constructions—fantasies—of objects doing something to other objects. For various reasons Freud wished to emphasize the dynamic unconscious—the unconscious of the repressed. One can speculate that he emphasized this to maintain Freudian psychoanalysis's distance from what Jung was writing of the racial unconscious on the one side and what Klein, from her work with very young children, was saying was basic to the child's nature on the other. But from the days of the *System for a Scientific Psychology* through chapter 7 of *The Interpretation of Dreams* and onward, Freud established a vocabulary and grammar (condensation, displacement) that was exclusively that of the primary unconscious and thus the fashioner of experiences and dreams. His universal was the Oedipus complex: that was the relationship sine qua non. Sooner or later it would out as the basic idea people had on what was what, and as the erotic nature of the phases of infantile sexuality changed, the version of the complex, not the complex, would change. The Oedipus complex was for Freud a state of mind, more even than a state of affairs. It was an associational web that wove observation and impression into basic configurations of intent and meaning.

In classical theory it is the ego, of course, that has the syntactic and grammatical repertoire with which to figure and transfigure the data that are experienced. There are not only the mechanisms of defense by which potential experience is given form and meaning, but there is that most powerful of all means—consciousness, at the ego's disposal. Early on in his formulations Freud used the concept of attention to explain how the ego took up experience, or did not, or did so partially in order to transform it in the process. As time went on, Freud wanted a term to express attention that endows the object with love and lust, which cathects it rather than merely noting it, and he coupled attention to cathexis in the word "Beseztung." The result was, as it had to be, that the different varieties cf paying partial attention were reified into mechanisms of defense. Attention itself was no longer to be found in Freud's vocabulary.

In his work Bion started out securing the ground. The language of psychoanalysis had taken on such a "penumbra" of meanings, he often wrote, that he wished to begin again with the fundamentals—with, indeed, the Alpha and Beta! He thought that using the previous jargon would bring in with it all the old senses and contexts that the words were embedded in or coming from. Accordingly, Bion tried to see what he could do with the concept of "attention," which Freud had abandoned in favor of attention *cathexis* and with such basic feelings as love and hate. For this simplification Bion chose Love and Hate. He used the concept of attention as I do, to describe the means by which knowledge was created, recreated, and destroyed. He went further than I can in parsing out the various ways in which attention was used. These became categories in his famous or infamous Grid. In its simplest terms knowledge was a plus or minus affair; not knowing that the violinist was playing music and not knowing he was sublimating a masturbation were indices of minus K.

From this standpoint basic assumptions were claims on attention that resulted in particular forms of K (knowing) and of -K (not knowing). To K of *Pairing* was to -K of *Coupling* and K-ing only about *Pairing* in order to -K about the primal scene was a kind of supra-unselfconsciousness. From this K and -K it can be

seen that one of the attributes of *Group* assumptions is sharing K
and -K among the members. Little boys who knew about the
emperor's new clothes were uncivilized so far as basic assumptions went—if, that is, the emperor happened to be a member of
their *Group.*

For Bion, knowledge and its management turned out to be the
commodity and task of the group but also, plainly, of the mind:
what does the individual do with knowledge that he has which is
not deemed to be either respectable or true or even to exist by the
group? In the psychology of the individual this is a sidelight, left
for social psychology and sociology to contend with. But Bion's
experiences persuaded him (if he needed persuading) that man
was, in Aristotle's sense, a political animal.

The difficulty was that even as Bion said man was a political
animal and that knowledge was politic, his studies took him to
the mental life of man as an individual being. At the end he was
writing of the caesura of birth; quoting Freud, he wondered if too
much was being made of birth as the start of mental life. He did
not live to know of studies that show responses of infants to stories
read aloud when they were in utero compared to stories they are
hearing postnatally for the first time. Had he known of this he
would have noted the surprise of others at the novelty of this
notion.

3. Paying Attention

By supposing a *Couple* and a *Pair* to be orientations of mind—basic assumptions in Bion's sense, unconscious fantasies in Freud's and Klein's—I am drawing the human as a political animal into one being with the creature whose preoccupations reflect an individual life lived for a utilitarian mix involving the minimization of pain consistent with the maximization of pleasure. I shall presently go into what such a concatenation implies, but for now I will confine myself to what I think to be the two basic points of view. From early Freud and late Bion, I take the concept of attention as the means by which these orientations of mind are made possible.

Attention, I shall suppose, is for all intents and purposes an either-or affair; there is no on-and-off about it. It is something in motion, as life is in motion, and though it can be steered, it is also susceptible to capture. Experience has irresistible claims on our attention; there are expectations, predictions involved. We are geared not only to respond to certain experiential data, but to do so in preordained ways. Certainly some of these constraints are inherent; they come in the general cornucopia of species-specific genes. Some also come with the genes, but are specific to the individual. Some are learned and come with the culture. Some are self-learned; they are the result of autonomous, often self-conscious effort. Ascertaining which is which is no easy matter.

As I write, thoughts come to mind. One competes with another. Meanwhile a summer storm abounds with the sweet full rush of rain and the throaty rumble of thunder. When the writing goes well, when the *mot juste* comes readily to mind, I barely heed the storm; neither do I attend to the memories and associations that such storms rekindle. But when I feel uncertain as to what to say or when in the order of things to say it, the storm intrudes. So while I think and say I steer through the conflicting claims on my attention, it may be quite as accurate to say that thought and fantasy and perception steer me.

Were I more afraid of such storms than I am, I would seek refuge in the port of this writing, and feel vexed if I could not lose myself in that safe harbor. I would feel afflicted by the sounds, smells, and sights of the storm, but no less, perhaps more, by the insistence of their demand quality, as the term goes. I might suspect myself to have been selected—selected out for the occasion, as if I had been "gifted" with receptors especially attuned for the experience. I might suspect that it is precisely such gifts as artists and nature lovers covet I find a curse; I might feel awkward about complaining about how I could not shut out the storm. Privately I might feel somehow carved as if the storm's sounds, smells, and sights had special runnels in me: as if I had been previously selected (ruined and accursed) to be hapless when it came to being able to ignore the experience.

Perhaps, given the pain and sense of persecution I would be feeling, I might draw upon my analysis where I may very well find that such a tumult of natural sound was a version of the primal scene: a representation and misrepresentation of it. The thrall of the current storm might keep me from recalling the primal scene and the feelings it evoked in me. The storm commands my attention because I have asked it (as previously I asked its predecessors) to shield me from the perceptions and then the memories for which it is a screen. As for most apprentice sorcerers, it is easier for me to do than undo a screen. My attention is likely to feel riveted (as they promise in book reviews): I will not be able to put it down.

The constraints on the range and ease of selectivity in the paying of attention has then, paradoxically, to do with choosiness. Predilections limit choices. Accordingly, the situation is as follows: there is a range of matters—potential experiential events— among which to choose. Some claim our attention; we have little choice in regard to these. We must attend to them. Others lie outside our ken. They do not belong to us as a species, at least yet. Still others impose themselves upon us, not because of their nature, but our own. We gravitate to them out of our own predilections. We select but such selectivity would be pointless without anything to choose among. But choices are no less pointless without a disposition to make choices.

As it happens the demand quality of stimulus has been the object of study by psychologists for some time. What it has ordinarily meant is that the sound of the gunshot is irresistible no matter how intense one's absorption in other mental activity. It has also meant that the Zeigernicht effect, under which unfinished tasks exert a hold on one's intentions more than other tasks, comes from Gestalt theories and implies the motivational effect of closure. Perhaps Chekov had both of these ideas in mind when he counseled younger playwrights not to put a gun into a scene or onto a set unless it was going to be used. The stimulus exerts a compelling effect.

In some stimulus deprivation tests, the compelling effect was removed because much of the normal sensory input was blocked off—sight, sound, touch, etc. The effect was that subjects reported hallucinatory or dream states of great intensity. In the absence of exterior stimulation, it seemed, interior stimulation either increased per se or attention had nowhere else to go. Analogies were made to sleep and dreaming. In sleep, when attention is withdrawn from sensory titillation and motoric discharge, REM sleep begins. All of this evoked Proust's cork-lined room and seemed very satisfactory. But its premise was that attention shuttled across an established (generally, a learned) sensorium, fetching now this, now that. Internal motivation and the availability of stimuli combined to make one stimulus-bound or stimulus-free.

In some respects this was the model available to Freud. His concept of complex invoked not only the organization of the tendrils of association, memory, and perception into patterns, but he held that such complexes were the basis of compulsions, obsessions, and fixations, including idée fixe. New stimuli did not enter to free associate with whatever they chose of other contents of mind by the primary process, but were often caught in the web, becoming thereby yet another road that led to Rome (or Rome's opposite or otherwise surrogated number). This was, in short, a state of response-boundedness in which quite improbable stimuli were intertwined with the kernel of the complex.

Freud insisted that captured attention would only give its cryptically contrived nexus up to the free associations of the analyst. For the analysts to have free associations rather than complexes of their own, they had to have their own analysis. Even then they were ever wary of being captivated. The patient's complexes were secure only in so far as they could bind their analysts to them and by doing so clip the wings of the analyst's associative freedom. In the interactive sphere as well as the intrapsychic one, attention was subject to being put in compromising positions.

It was to take the work of two others to fathom what Freud knew he could not himself work out if he was also to do psychology. One was Chomsky (1972) and the other Edelman (1987). Chomsky's contribution was terse: the program for learning language was encoded in the brain; languages had to be learned, but the syntactic templates and formats were intrinsic. Children could utter sentences they had not been taught.

Edelman came to neuroscience from immunology, a field in which he had won a Nobel Prize for demonstrating that the white cells which give the body immunity to infectious diseases are "selected" by the infecting bacterium or virus—given, in acts of contact, the precise antishape required to stifle and ultimately nullify the infection. The invading cells find and instruct the defending ones; the defending ones, equipped now with the characteristics necessary specifically to attack the intruders, freely circulate, leading the life of specialists, ready to do battle with the very *bête noirs* that were their creators and mentors. The text creates the antitext.

In Darwin's thinking concerning natural selection, species exist to further exist. All members of a given species unwittingly collaborate to forward the best of their genes unto the next generation. The poorest specimens not only die on the vine and become easy prey for predators—thus being helpfully taken out of the running —but they also fail in the competitions within the species for advantage. The runts of the litter get the poorest nourishment and fall further behind; and the weaker or less endowed of those of mating age get shunted aside by the stronger, richer, or better endowed.

If nature were parsimonious, a shaver with Occam's razor, then, Edelman reasoned, this selection of the respondent by the stimulus should be found in other systems of the body—indeed in the formation of the morphology of the body itself. His analogy was to natural selection in Darwin's sense of the term. Cells could be thought of as naturally occurring organisms: broadly constructed as to types, but needing either to specialize further to find an ecological niche or to be found unadaptive or redundant and sloughed off. The response-cell's fate was thus curiously in the gift of the stimulus. Many might be called, but fewer chosen. Thus like the antigenic T-cell the N- (neuro) cell would reach a point of evolution determined by its particular DNA. It would then be open for use by one or another part of the brain; that is, it would be open to recruitment by clumps of cells that were forming to cope with the signals the neurosystem was being peppered with. When language was being learned, for example, huge clumps might form to attend to everything from Swahili to Classical Greek to English. When it turned out that only English was being learned and "Mama" was sufficient, a sort of compaction took place as the result of this natural selection by the family from among the potential brain colony of polyglots. The çlump or colony, having specialized further, could now be analogized even further to a species. These cells had interactions among themselves that were bounded, feedback systems that informed them of their specialized nature in a whole of which they were functionally a part, but a distinctive part. Once chosen in the way of specialization they moved from being a N-cell to being a N-sub-lingua cell with primary links to their own sub-kind and few or none to other N-cells.

Edelman's work, to which I have not done justice (but see chapter 4), also accounts for the rerouting that takes place as, for example, the stimulus changes its nature. Blindness where there was sight occasions a drop-off of cells devoted to transmission from the optic nerve; bounded self-referential linkups of these now unnecessary cells or clumps might, in their atrophy, blur their specialty and be open to offers from, for example, hearing bundles that may need to amplify.

Edelman's thinking opens a further perspective on attention. Attention is the conduit by which signal information cultivates the brain. But one can see the inevitable problems of any specialization, the loss of range and scope and flexibility. To the extent that the rudimentary ability to volitionally deploy our attention gains in scope, by dint of practice and the development of the brainpower, our mind gains proportionate freedom from what was previously thrust upon it. We can turn away, though only—forever—by turning elsewhere. Now we cannot know. To our two eyes and ears we have added a third—the blind eye and the deaf ear. We have gained obliviousness by learning also how not to notice one event by altogether noticing another. Newly minted psychoanalysts frequently suffer from hearing all utterances in their newly developed way. Happily most regress and can hear things in several ways, with the obtrusiveness only secondarily assigned. Is this akin to a "basic assumption" mentality becoming a "work" mentality?

For Edelman's schema to work as for Darwin's, there has to be a built-in limitation in resource. Without it there would be no need for selection, for any morphology or functional attribute would flourish. Variation would occur in the random way of mutation and only Lady Luck or the fin de siècle depravity of the reproductive partner would take it further or leave it to its brief splendid eccentricity. "Heard once and then no more," as Keats might have said. These models have therefore implicit in them something that doubtless made sense to their originators on subjective experiential grounds, limitations of resources on the one side and of energy on the other. Since I am considering attention and not whole-person selection (which I shall do presently), I point out that attention in all models is limited.

Delimited attention means that any use of attention is at the expense of any other use of it. Only the most extraordinary mind and robust constitution allows one to be a Renaissance man *and* a specialist. Most people cannot be both. Soon enough they discover that their greedy wishes to absorb more than they can in more ways than they can are almost as frustrating as their wishes to compel all that they can in as many ways as they wish. The experience of a mind limited in its attention (and attention span) is one of hatred and grievance in the same degree as a rewarding mind is a joy and a pleasure.

The compensation for limitations of attention comes when the mind is in danger of informing its owner of things he would rather not know. Defenses require a rather specialized view of things. Reaction formations require a deep and fervent knowledge of sadism and harm, but an equally great knowledge of one's own distaste and, just to be sure, an equally vivid knowledge of the pleasure others take in the slaughter of the innocents, and just to be surer still, a deep and constant knowledge of one's repugnance for those others and their barbaric spirit. All of this taking of rather partial views is in danger from a robustly vagrant attention, which like an unwatched child might get into anything and come home with strange and dangerous ideas.

Among the paradoxes, then, is the value of the amount of attention—and of its freedom. It takes a good deal of attention and vigilance to maintain the set pieces of attention necessary to maintain a reaction formation: one has to remember what to remember and what to forget, what to ascribe to self and what to project into others. When such reaction formations enlarge, as they are likely to, the depletion of the stores of energy shows up in the decrease in *élan vital,* one of the hallmarks of a depression. But the depression is not merely a result of keeping so much sadism unconscious and feeling bad and sad about it as well. The diminution of free energy keeps the reaction formations safe from re-realization—the return of the repressed. In this sense people who have their mind firmly made up on every conceivable subject and do not talk politics, religion, or matters of taste have tied up attention so securely that they have some free energy to spend.

The scanning we do, making the *tour d'horizon* of which the French speak, goes on. But in time we become canny. We remember where to pause and where to look quickly. We steer our attention arriving at our destination via a series of tiny corrective moves, but we know and remember where that which we wish to steer around is located. Still, we are in the position of that character of Kipling's who was told that, after following a number of steps and directions, he would own a treasure, providing that at the moment of discovery he did not think of the words "White Rhinoceros." Plainly there is no repression possible here. What might be possible is to prepare a surrogate thought so well that one can instantaneously turn one's attention to it: "Purple Elephant," perhaps?

Certainly it would take some doing to keep the surrogate thought (image, percept, sensation) fixed in place. (Men who struggle not to ejaculate before their partner reaches her orgasm sometimes have quaint tales to tell of what they fix upon to think about to keep the arcing sensation from being noticed not wisely, but, as it were, too well.) Experience has an undeniable impress; unconsciousness is difficult to achieve. Not infrequently lives are given much of their shape in an effort to keep the unnoticed staying unnoticed and unknown while White Rhinoceri have a way of recurring even to the wary.

If we wish to forget something, we don't want any reminders. Yet all around us, inside and out, are reminders. If we do not want to live lives of absolute isolation, we must surround ourselves with people of like mind, people who also want to forget, people who also want to know only of elephants, only of purple. Being relatively immobile the young cannot choose their circles, but must adapt. But circles would not be circles, I have argued, if they did not give some help with the problem of fixating surrogate knowledge in the gunsights of attention. In return, quid pro quo, one does as one has been done by. One conforms one's mind, which is to say, one tailors one's attention to the mode. That way the collectivity assures that certain matters will be regarded as so, certain matters as not so, and certain others as nonstarters. (Orwell's *1984* was surely a poignant illustration of this very point.)

This perspective has attention as two-tiered. There is noticing and there is noticing what one notices. The first Freud called preconscious; the second, conscious; add a third, and we have an unconscious that, in his view, consisted of what we resolutely do not take notice of (and will, if we can, resolutely not take notice of) and what we try not to notice we are not taking notice of. According to his theory, we are not likely to recover this material in a replay of the last several minutes. It will appear as an absence —like the infamous eighteen-minute gap in the Nixon tapes—or more likely as a memory cleverly counterfeited to look as if it were the real article, a "screen" memory designed to obscure the fact that censorship had been at work. The manifest content of the dream consisted for the most part of such screens. This is what makes the interpretation of dreams at once possible and necessary. To each element or fragment of the remembered dream, there is an associational complex. (Erik Erikson somewhere recounts a patient's dream that consisted of a single word; that, so to speak, is what at first blush she recalled of her last five minutes. Together, however, they reconstructed something approximating the core of her life story.) Thus even were we to replay our last several minutes, we would find only what had been preconscious; and some of that would be counterfeit. If we were to go further and push against the counterfeit (assuming we could know what was and what wasn't), we would come to what was replaced almost in the very act of noticing. This will be our old friend, the White Rhinoceros, which was adroitly hidden behind the screen of the Purple Elephant.

In the two states of mind, *Couple* and *Pair*, courtship proceeds by careful mutual "interviews" directing attention to what the two have in common—what interests which person. This is done in part to deflect the possibilities for aggression that follow from mismating and in part to deflect the vis-à-vis that might too soon lead to *Coupling*. Mainly it is done to build up a basis of *Pairing* that could stand or withstand later differentiation. With a good base of *Pairing*, *Coupling* can be introduced—contest or conquest. The mutual feeling by both that they have a good deal in common of the right stuff acts as a releaser. Of course, part of what they will or won't have in common is the idea of what the "right stuff" is. Once two or more people begin to establish their bona fides— frequently this is about their relation to the host or Host or the other inspiritor of the occasion—the ardor to establish their ties (or lack of them) does not always maintain a faithful relationship to the truth. The need to have or find attitudes and interests in common, indeed enemies in common, is so powerful that people often lie without quite knowing it.

Psychoanalysis is about representations: about images, signs, and signals. Thus the dream and the transference are central to all schools of psychoanalytic inquiry. In saying this, psychoanalysts, perforce, must say there is a world in which things and events are as they are: they are actual; the mind can be trained and disciplined to perceive these accurately, to remember them clearly, and to recall them faithfully. One can learn to think dispassionately and in a cordial relationship to consensual or empirical traditions.

There is a Real out there; a historical real and a current real, consisting of actual time and space, of actual people and doings and of defined ways and procedures for apprehending them—for example, the methods of logic and experimentation.

Psychoanalysis also says that there is a primary mind or process at work whose relationship to the real and the actual is imaginative. It doesn't record, it represents; it doesn't discover, it invents; it doesn't recollect, it re-presents its duplicitous images shaped by longing, tailored by fear. Wishful thinking, wishful dreaming, wishful perceiving, and wishful remembering.

Psychoanalysis speaks of the tension between the secondary and the primary process and the forces that drive them—between the self-preservative and self-actualizing forces that edge us toward things as they are and the self-protective, pleasure-seeking forces that take us toward matters as we would wish them to be. This tension consists of a dialectic; at the same time what is, what we wish were, and what we feel ought to be coexist in uneasy proportion and in temporary compromise. At any given moment truth exists only approximately.

Suppose the world of facts was no more real than that of representations of those facts. To put it another way, suppose that the Real as a category was filled merely by representations of the real and that these representations were as tangential to what they represented (or claimed to represent!) as are the imagoes and phantasms of the unconscious and its dreamlife.

If we suppose that, then we have a world represented by the canonical letter X of which we are of two (or more) minds. The superiority of the one mind to the other doesn't come into question any more than the superiority of French to English or of Latin to Russian comes into question as a way of communicating between people about experience. What does come into prominence as mentocentrism recedes are the nature and characteristics of the various ways of apprehending X that cannot be known.

We are dealing with two mental constructs, which are functionally reciprocal. Together they constitute a duality, each portion of which serves as an alternative for one another—as one might say sleep and wakefulness do. The construction of each of these worlds provides definition for the other; they tell each other apart by providing comparison and contrast. A fact helps us to know what is fictional about a fiction as a fiction helps us to know what is factual about a fact. At the same time, however, both fact and fiction require protection from one another.

It is only partially useful to know our fictions are fictional; we need illusion, dream, make-believe, hope, play, metaphor—all the as-ifs, and we don't want to have them exploded by facts. The same holds true of our facts; facts also need to be protected. Between fact and fiction there exists an equipoise, an equilibrium in individual and cultural homeostasis. Each depends on the other's particular weight of means or force, to complement it and to distinguish it, an ecosystem in which a delicate balance must be maintained. In this allegory, facts and fictions prey upon one another, competing for conviction; yet each requires the other to survive. Neither can grow so large, fierce, or predatory as to destroy the other.

For functional purposes fictions should not be too fictional and facts not too factual; where one moves in one direction so must the other. If fact and fiction function so as to provide alternatives for one another, and fictions are created by wishful or fearful thinking, what impels the creation—the discovery or invention— of facts? Is there a different motive force, or do facts also fulfill (or seem to fulfill) wishes and allay fears?

The traditional argument is that facts do have such functions. They serve wishes for self-preservation, for which a respectful knowledge of the real is necessary. The reality principle needs its reality. Facts concerning reality must be thought to be real and true even if they are not.

Each individual arrives at the amount of reality he can bear. At the same time, the status of the fact is organized and mediated consensually—the truth of a fact is a matter of agreement. When Self and Other cannot agree on the trueness of a fact—one man's fact being the other's fiction—a crisis is bound to emerge. The two may take refuge from one another (as my interlocutor did from the enemy who was patterning the city lights), or they may hope to change one another's mind by force of argument or, failing that, simpler force. Or they may agree to disagree. Disagreement safely preserves both facts, the true one and the false; neither is lost; each can be found alive and well in the Other. This "conservation" functions like a mutual projection: both parties agree not to have the fact, but to hold it safe for the other. Thus each can contemplate what he does not own, as one might go to a museum. If attention wanders, there is a place it can go to. Most important is that the facts and fictions one wishes to maintain within the container of Self can more precisely be discovered there when one knows where else to look for facts and fictions from which one disassociates one's Self. Attention always requires an Or for its Either, if its selective processes are to function with security and ease. In this regard it is easy to see that there are such things as good enemies. These are Others who so plainly and indisputably contain the attributes—the intentions, qualities, and characteristics—that we do not wish to notice as our own. They are the ones who disbelieve our beliefs and believe our disbeliefs. They can always be spotted and often they can be so ludicrous, so extreme, so singleminded, so unopen to argument, that it is plainly stupid to take them and what they think seriously.

Attention is subject to summonses from the demand quality of experience, including the power of portions of experience to stimulate other portions with which the former were once associated. This associative binding was Freud's initial meaning of the word "complex." He had hoped to suggest that experiential units were indissolubly bound to one another, in a kind of neuronal web. There is a way in which the raw stuff of experience has a webbing: sight with sound, sensation with feeling, emotion with thought, memory with anticipation, perception with remembrance: and a way, therefore that when these are severed by selective uses of attention, there remains a tendency for each portion to drift toward the others (consider in this regard Proust's madeleine.)

Since the construction of an experience by selective attention is a fabrication, both in its factual and fictive aspects, this tendency toward reunification has to be countered by continuing affirmations that the fabricated experience is the truth, the whole truth, and nothing but the truth. There must be no gaps, no holes; the fabricated experience must appear seamless and seemless.

Every subsequent mental fabrication, every ascription of particular matters to the domain of fact, others to the realm of fiction, needs, accordingly, to be looked at not alone for what it contains by way of fact or fiction, but for the use to which the thinker puts it. Every mental product could be looked at not only for its meaning, but for its function in respect to filling the place it does. For, paradoxically, facts hide truths as well as fictions do, and sometimes better, even as fictions reveal and illuminate truths as well as or better than facts. If we know more of merely the psychic truth, we increase the light, but also the density of the obscuring shadow. The void is held at bay by the cheerful light of the campfire, but so too is what else might be out there.

Both fact and fiction are equal in their potential for conveying pain and hence fright—and for protecting from it. When one piece of either feels too menacing, it can be replaced and the experience reconfigured. Fact or fiction can replace whatever bit is being excised or needing transfiguration. The only requirement is that it fit so seamlessly into the fabric that its counterfeiting presence is unnoticed. Once again, it is the use of the idea that must engage us. Fact or fiction, one no less than the other, can transform an unbearable experience. Each can be used truthfully—or otherwise.

The dialectic—we can't stand to know and we can't stand not to know—is the crucible in which what we discover and tolerate as facts and what we invent and preserve as fictions is fashioned. When a bit of either sort of knowledge has to be omitted something must fill the gap it leaves. The filling must block out the gap, but it must not call attention to itself. What remains must look as if it always were.

Fact can be useful to generate the illusion that the truth is known. Answers to questions can be indefinitely postponed in service to the quest for further knowledge. Facts can be accumulated by painstaking research in order to establish that the quest is productive. Looked at with a less cordial eye, this same accumulation of facts can be seen to rationalize a quest that is itself quite possibly false. The quest to know may be in service of the wish to doubt or to postpone or to fill out a gap that is meant to conceal or obfuscate what is known. The quest may be less in search of the real than of the irreal, the heard than of the unheard melody; a quest more designed to fortify versions preferred by that *Group* which has fortified one's own versions of the truth than of the truths that fall where they may. The fate of these irreals and instead-ofs, these seeminglies that are being taken as so, is often at the mercy of others. The fox who proclaimed the grapes sour could have found a number of alibis. He could have said there were no grapes there, or that he was not a fox, or that foxes don't eat grapes. Each of these might have served his need to rationalize his failure to seize the grapes hanging out of his reach. But what if he were observed by other foxes?

The usefulness of the *Group* to both support what is fact and what is fiction and to help obscure that these determinations are wrought artifactually by selectivity of attention cannot be overestimated. The threat to the *Group* to maintain innocence of this fact equally cannot be overestimated. The *Group* is a mighty bulwark against the tendency of attention to gravitate back to what once was so and thereby to undo all that selectivity has wrought.

Many experiments in the area of social psychology show how memory and perception are both influenced by the need of an individual to *Pair* with the "stooges" who, for example, falsely claim that one line on the blackboard is longer than another; similarly, the individual, despite the signs on the "shockometer" warning of lethal danger to the recipient, will dial the electricity right up there to comply with the suggestion of the expert or authority figure (see Milgram 1974). Dissonance, cognitive or otherwise, with the consonance required to be at one with the other member of the *Pair* (members of the *Group*), is unwelcome in the extreme: attention must be paid to what the *Group* believes. This rush toward agreement is sometimes thought to be a measure of the need of the less secure individual to ingratiate himself with those who were seemingly more confident: and there is little question that if the distance to a point of agreement from either side of a disagreement were measured, the insecure might travel the greater distance. Yet were he to show signs of fight or flight, the duty of saving the *Pair* would shift because the *Pair* is often so necessary to the *Couple*.

P arrives for her Monday session in despair. She has "done it again." Instead of being content with a calm, open weekend in which to garden and otherwise enjoy the outdoors, she "had" to call C . . . and one thing led to another. During the act she was entered from the rear and this powerful way of being taken was very exciting indeed. After this, he said nothing more, left soon, and didn't so much as call. Fucker! she said to herself of him.

Fucker! she had said to herself of Ψ as she left Friday's session, all the way home. In fact, on arrival home, she had called C. On Friday Ψ had called P's attention to the fact that her worry and concern for Ψ when he had been late for their session represented a choice of sorts. Others might—she might—have had other thoughts as to what detained Ψ.

Two possibilities might suggest themselves at this juncture: P might have conjoined Ψ with someone (equalling Fucker!) and then got herself a Fucker of her own. This is what P thought. But she had a dream that did not go with this hypothesis.

She dreamt of a ten-inch or foot-long brownie made of dense fudge. It seemed enormous to her, much too large. So she cut a piece off it. And then she got another dish for it, a banana-split dish, which she then showed to R., a woman friend of hers.

P thought that in the dream the brownie represented a wish for her own penis, one which she would make anally and then slot into her vulva. From this perspective, the liaison on the weekend served to make her more of a Fucker! herself, a member of a *Couple* for the purpose of thereupon being a member of a *Pair*. But she was not yet entirely conscious of her wish to avert jealousy as a woman via identifications with man-as-fucker: a plague on both C and Ψ—I'll do it with R.

There is of course a great deal more to be made of the experience (the "rear-entry" position as one that hints of sodomy and suggests a homophilic act, for example; and the banana reference, as a breast that is a penis). But it is a dream par excellence that displays the tension between portraying things and events as belonging now to the *Couple*, now to the *Pair*. What for P is incomplete in the *Couple* she regains vicariously in the *Pair*.

The two states of mind being to a degree interchangeable enables us to use each to snuff the other.

P is thirteen and after pretending to look for something—anything—to talk of, he talks of something awful, a regular nightmare, that happened that summer: P's parents and L's mother suggest P and L see a movie together. "Have yourselves a date."

But what was so goddamned awful was the idea, "date." Was he supposed to make out with someone with whom he grew up (summers)? He and L were the next thing to best friends, and if someone ever asked whether they ever tried something together, P would sneer that that would be like kissing your sister. P was going to say no, but now, worse and worse, L said, sure, why not?—which made P feel deserted and lonely. OK, he said, if that's how it is. . . . He had formed the idea of being a Neanderthal and grabbing some tit in the movie and then kind of forcing himself all over her afterward. Yet when they were in the movies he felt more lonely than ever and wished only for her friendship. What he wanted, come to think of it now, was to leave the goddamned movie and talk things over, like in the olden days. But just then she put her head on his shoulder, like every other—'scuse the French—cunt in the theatre. And, well, he just wished the whole thing was a dream so that he could wake up.

As a member of a *Pair*, what the *Group* thinks imposes great weight. P feels pressured into becoming a *Couple* with L, especially when L seems to agree. But paradoxically that very pressure is calling on him to be a good member of the *Group*. For P this means fidelity, honor, loyalty, and nonlibidinous feelings and other such codes: can they really be calling on him to dishonor all that? If so, he will do it, but with a vengeance (Boris 1990a). But L's lifelong relationship with him has been as member of a *Pair*—what he calls a sister. Should all this mother/sister/L stuff be junked? Are these now, all of a sudden, to become people unencumbered by the incest rule? Ah God, if she only didn't have a cunt. . . .

The next summer P and L do begin sex. L feels she is giving P the best gift a woman can bestow. P is bitter: he feels he has sold his innocence for sexual pleasure. He showers and scrubs after each event, but not all the perfumes of Arabia. . . . He then gets a funny idea: he and L should sex around with someone else.

4. A Selection Principle

It will not have escaped the reader that the subtext to what I have so far written is a dualistic model: *Pair—Couple,* Preconception—Conception, which has biological roots. One, that governing the *Couple* as a state of mind, is scarcely distinguishable from Freud's pleasure principle. (I do and shall take my differences from it, specifically to it as Primary Process, in chapter 7, Realization.) But for the present, I turn to the function of that other root, that root out of which the impulses to *Pair* evolve.

As I do so, however, I must ask a degree or two of self-consciousness in the psychoanalytic reader. To some extent or another we are members of "the Viennese delegation"—words courtesy of Nabokov—and though we have formed several schools, we have taken on the attributes of every *Group:* we have established, as *Group*s must, a hierarchy. We have one for ourselves, we have one for our patients—and we have one in and at the base of our theories. Most of us have an eye on developmental considerations: we organize our facts, indeed obtain our facts, not so much along the lines of changing repertoires, but along lines of development, maturation, and the like. We tend to think bigger is better. Neurotic is better than borderline and borderline better than psychotic. Primitive is somehow worse than post-oedipal as genital or really post-genital is better than oral or anal or narcissistic. Healthy is better than pathological. In some sense this means that two-year-olds are better, more mature, than ones and less so than threes. For a very long time these assumptions went counter to

Melanie Klein's observations, for how could tiny infants have so much mental ability? Klein's inferences may be correct or incorrect, but by what standard? The scientific standard is an outgrowth of that other Viennese school, logical positivism, so it is a fair question to ask why positivism's entire hierarchy is superior to another standard. And so on.

In this exposition I have expressed a point of view that objects are potentia awaiting relationships to select them and give them realization: empty but configured categories await filling out. *Pair* and *Couple* are two of these, Present and No-thing Present are two more. These at once drive attention and awareness to, and are filled by, its selectivity. How, as the analytic *Group*, should we be aware of this process operating in us, and how, being incognizant of the process, should we know of the biases in the data it provides to us? The red and blue we see are . . . well, are. How should we know that according to physicists the light stream is continuous, but that we by nature see it discontinuously in four primary colors? And, in any case, what are we supposed to do with that bit of information? For the moment we might let us take our facts as selective items discovered or invented out of deference to the *Pairing* system.

For example, it has so often been said that man is a monogamous animal who mates for life that we may have forgotten to take a grain of salt with not only this assertion but also with the other qualities ascribed to man: that we are the only tool-using animal; that we are the only animal capable of language and speech; that we are a social animal, and as social animals we contest for individual dominance in our ascending and descending social orders, and because dominance means authority and control, these mean the right to choose turf or mates.

Equally it has been said that we simply are, are as perhaps a harp is, strummed by the ineffable winds of fate or chance. No matter then who or what we are or are capable of being or becoming, activities far beyond our reach (global warming? ultraviolet increase? chaos?) are determinative.

Is anatomy determinative? Is character destiny? Or do, as Adler said, the *protests* against feelings of inferiorities set the strings? There are neither answers to these questions nor any reason to believe these are the right questions.

But they are inevitable questions. The *Pair* and the *Group* cannot do without them. If selection is the name of the game, there must be choices to choose from, and one choice must be in some way better than the next. Indeed such is the robustness of the system that choice, like energy and matter, must be conserved. Though our *Pair* and our *Group*, having made up its mind to it, cannot use certain portions of the palate, we are only too pleased to help construct a *Pair* or *Group* who can.

One of the ideas behind assigning man a social and monogamous nature was to distinguish Us from Them, the beasts from the heathens. As our knowledge of Them grew wider through travel and deeper than the simple observations of the partly domesticated countryside, distinctions between Us and Them became, if anything, more attenuated. Even Alfred Russel Wallace broke with Darwin over the latter's steadfast determination to see in man a continuity with all the other creatures of God's domain. Wallace saw a quantum leap—so *much* brain, that increments no longer mattered (this did not appear to help with the matter that women have smaller brains than men!). Later this same debate recurred, as these debates often must.

The entities of the wilderness and jungle appeared to be in a continual oedipal struggle for rights to the female of their kind. Not only was the law of the jungle the struggle for existence, for prey, and for grazing, but it was fang and claw, antler and brawn, for the rights to the female. It was as if Sophocles wrote his female role as: "Have a safe trip, Laius honey." "And, Oh, Hello! Don't I know you from somewhere? You look somehow so . . . well, familiar."

While the Oedipus complex is a preoccupation of man, it hardly serves to sever us from other animals. Indeed the female's choice is coming to be recognized as a potent force in the descent of the species: the bravado that shook the woods and scorched the turf to establish dominance in a male hierarchy is now seen as also constituting an Olympiad designed to win the favor of the ladies. They are ready to take anyone: for them the number of disparate copulations is their dice role with chance. The Bower bird builds impressive bowers for such ladies as may be out for a stroll; if the ladies enter and pause with their Baedekers or Michelin Green Guides, they will be mounted within seconds by their hasty hosts.

But they may pause outside and say, "Not here; this is glitz and glimmer but nothing solid for the children" and so look for other choices.

This problem of who or what selects, who or what is selected, burns through current Darwinian thought, and it may be worth a moment to look into the issues involved. At first blush Darwin seemed to be saying that there is a jungle out there and the race is to the swift and the strong—the fittest. This meant that nature—the ecosystem—would quite mindlessly weed out some species and some strains in species, "rewarding" others, and the surviving species and strains would with their particular characteristics and traits have the bold hand in shaping the generations they sired. The species would propose, nature dispose. A species that bred in variety would mathematically have a better chance to weather the winter.

However, on further inspection, it was to appear that among the traits which may be favored are those that help nature along by taking a hand in the destiny of their species. This meant that reproduction could be a blind spasm of parthenogenesis or mating, or that the creatures involved could show predilections in making their reproductory choices. As with the Greyling butterfly, which distinctly prefers the color of jet black in their mates—a color that has not yet appeared in nature—these propensities or choices could be entirely unknowing, but they would not be random. Neither need they be conscious, because the value of consciousness, as I am trying to demonstrate, is primarily in its offer of the opportunity for choices not based on "egotistical" attraction or aversion—contra choices. If individuals of a species mated selectively or reared their young selectively, that might help or hinder—and the more "informed" the choice or basis for choice, the better. Which basis for choice would prove to be the more "informed" would come out in the wash; all one could suppose is that like other, more obvious (because morphological) traits, propensities existed along a varium, and were accordingly selected.

Even from this enlarged point of view, traditional theory used the individual creature as the unit. It was his or her reproductive advantage that was in the calculus. Mayr (1982) writes that studies have proved that females, both vertebrates and invertebrates, are very careful in their choice of males with whom to breed.

Indeed, the selection of the male which finally is admitted for copulation is often a very protracted process. Female choice in these cases is an established fact, even where the criteria are not yet known on the basis of which the females make their choice.

This strongly contrasts with males, who usually are ready to mate with any female and quite often do not even discriminate among females of their own and of other species. The reasons for this drastic difference between males and females were pointed out ... on the basis of the principle of investment. A male has sufficient sperm to inseminate numerous females, and his investment in a single copulation is therefore very small. A female, by contrast, produces relatively few eggs, at least in species with female choice, and may furthermore invest much time and resources in brooding the eggs or developing the embryos and in taking care of the brood after hatching. She may lose her entire reproductive potential by making a mistake in the selection of her mate (for instance, by producing inferior or sterile hybrids). The principle of female choice explains also a number of other phenomena that were previously puzzling, for instance, why polymorphism in species of butterflies with Batesian mimicry is usually limited to females. Females would discriminate against males that deviate too far from the species-specific image of the mating partner (releasing mechanism). (Mayr 1982: 597)

The thesis that the individual is the principal unit of selection has been challenged by some evolutionists who postulate a process of *group selection*. Those who support this kind of selection claim that there are phenomena that could not possibly be the result of individual selection. They refer in particular to characteristics of entire populations, such as aberrant sex ratios, rates of mutation, distance of dispersal and various other mechanisms favoring either in-breeding or outbreeding in natural populations, and degrees of sexual dimorphism. Such differences among populations, say the proponents of group selection, can be established only when an entire population (deme) is favored over other demes because it differs in its genetic constitution for the stated factor. Whether, and to what extent, such group selection actually occurs is still actively discussed in the current literature, but the general consensus is that most of such cases can be interpreted in terms of individual selection, except perhaps in social animals. (Ibid., 595)

And indeed the human female is not active only on the outside, but her ovum signals the sperm the path to true consummation. Whether there is a further act of selection, on the cellular level, is not yet known.

But are the body's cells social animals? Such an idea is put forward by Edelman (1987):

> The answer is that the selection theory, unlike information processing models, does not require the arbitrary positing of labels in either the brain or the world. Because this population theory of brain function requires variance in neural structures, it relies only minimally upon codes and thereby circumvents many ... difficulties. Above all, the selection theory avoids the problem of the homunculus, inasmuch as it assumes that the motor behavior of the organism yielding signals from the environment acts dynamically by selection upon the potential orderings already represented by variant neural structures, rather than by requiring these structures to be determined by "information" already present in that environment. (Ibid., 44–45)

> Selection is a competitive process in which a group may actually capture cells from other neighboring groups by differentially altering the efficacy of synapses. This process, in which groups that are more frequently stimulated are more likely to be selected again, leads to the formulation of a secondary repertoire of selected neuronal groups which is dynamically maintained by synaptic alterations. (Ibid., 45–46)

> Structural variability in the primary repertoire must be constituted in such a fashion that significant functional variability can occur within the secondary repertoires—a functional variability ultimately manifested in the perception and behavior of the animal. Since the dynamic formation of neuronal groups is considered to be necessary for learning as well as memory and since both of these are evolutionarily adaptive for the individual organism, there is survival value in the maintenance of repertoires of groups whose function leads to increased capacity for adaptive behavior. (Ibid., 46)

> We may define a primary repertoire as a diverse collection of neuronal groups whose extrinsic connectivities and potential functions in a given brain region are prespecified to some extent during ontogeny and development. (Ibid., 47)

> In order to develop the notion of selection from a repertoire of neuronal groups, it is essential to consider the general requirements placed upon such a repertoire, particularly those concerning its size and the nature of its diversity. A main requirement is that this repertoire be sufficiently large; that is, it must contain enough diverse elements to assure that, given a wide range of different input signals and a response threshold, a finite probability exists that for each signal at least one matching element in the repertoire can be found. Furthermore, for at

least some elements of the repertoire, the match with input must be sufficiently specific to allow distinctions among different input signals (i.e., to "recognize" them) with relatively low error. It is essential to understand that in a selective system such "recognition" can in general never be perfect—it can be only more or less good above some necessary threshold for recognition. The opposite assumption would either require a reversal of cause and effect in independent domains (world and brain) or necessitate the presence of an instructive mechanism. (Ibid., 47)

As we have seen, the abstract general requirements on any selection theory are (1) a source of diversification leading to variants, (2) a means for effective encounter with or sampling of an independent environment that is not initially categorized in any absolute or predetermined fashion, and (3) a means of differential amplification over some period of time of those variants in a population that have greater adaptive value. Such amplification may occur in a stochastic manner but must nonetheless eventually increase the ratio in the population of the more adapted. Effective differential amplification implies the existence of some form of heredity or memory, which assures that at least some adaptations are preserved and that they are not completely disrupted by the processes of variation that must also occur. (Ibid., 16)

These requirements obviously are met by evolution, in which mutation, recombination, and gene flow provide major sources of diversity, phenotypic function provides sampling of the environment, and heredity assures that some of the results of natural selection will yield differential reproduction of adapted phenotypes (Mayr). Each of these requirements is also met in the workings of a somatic selective system —the immune system—in which somatic recombination and mutation of antibody variable region gene segments lead to the emergence of a repertoire of different antibody binding sites. (Ibid., 17)

Such a theory emphasizes that the nature of the stimulus is dynamic and polymorphous, that there are two initially independent domains of variation (the world of potential stimuli and collections of neuronal Groups), and that the fundamental and prior basis upon which learning rests is perceptual categorization. (Ibid., 18)

The theory of neuronal Group selection insists upon the importance of variance in neural populations and upon the developmental origin of diversity within single nervous systems. The emphasis is upon two levels of selection, developmental and experiential. Ipso facto, this implies that one cannot construct an adequate theory of brain function without first understanding the developmental processes and constraints that give rise to neuro-anatomy and synaptic diversity. During adult experience, selection among populations of synapses becomes a key process; in most cases of postnatal experience, the rules for altering such synaptic populations supersede those for setting up new neuroanatomy. Reentry and mapping, each continually modified by behavioral processes, become the means by which such a hierarchical system can maintain internal consistency. In realizing the importance of generalization to problem solving and learning, and therefore the need to provide a neural substrate for generalization, the theory emphasizes the fundamental role of degeneracy of neuronal Groups in repertoires and of reentrant anatomy and function among the parallel systems and maps constituted by these repertoires. (Ibid., 18–19)

Neuronal Group selection comprises a series of somatic events that are historical and unique in each organism. With the exception of certain epigenetic events in development, individual selective events cannot have been directly influenced by evolution, in as much as they are all based on somatic generation of diversity. Such diversity arises evolutionarily because of the necessity in somatic time for categorization by degenerate networks under environmentally fluctuating conditions. This focuses attention on the question of the adaptive value of the mechanisms of Group selection. (Ibid., 67)

That "life" starts with conception, with the viability of the fetus, and that something else—another phase, perhaps—starts at birth, and that conception is in some way related to birth, are familiar ideas. We might add that birth or, if one prefers, conception, of an individual life is at once a culmination and a beginning. That beginning will then reculminate by means of a further conception twelve or twenty or forty years down the road. There must also be a dying point of life, beginning with the cell; otherwise reproduction would continue indefinitely in a geometric progression. And indeed there is—a cell can reproduce itself in a petri dish twenty-four times and no more. This ending point enables the cells to shift from one form and function to another, as needed by the body whole. From the DNA on, there is a communal organization that permits and regulates the population of the parts.

The model of homeostasis on which so many of us were brought up is not a good one. It assumes a stasis or balance to which the organism, when out of kilter, is motivated to *return*. Yet the open system by which each element of that system depends on the other to get reproduced means that within the tissue, within the very cell itself, must be a capacity to specialize in the direction of new homeostasises. Mutations are far more frequent events than has long been thought, and opportunism and adventitiousness must be considered engines of survival.

What I want to do, in speaking of the habits of the cell, is lay groundwork for the suggestion that at each dimension of complexity—cell, cell bundle, tissue, organ and system—there is an independent, yet parallel trope for reproductive survival. Freud commented that Copernicus, Darwin, and he himself had in turn dislodged man from being at the center of the universe: perhaps it is meet to reconsider our tendency to overweight the free-standing "Individual." Perhaps our views of him should include a person who, far from being the captain of his soul and master of his fate, is a man lumbered with the freight of his genes, a mere vehicle (though doubtless a limousine) of their destiny.

The question of the relation of the whole to its parts reiterates itself when we consider man in regard to his species. Man is a social animal, an element in the fabric of family, group, community, nation, and world. In this sense, is it Jack and Jill who have to flourish—or the species of which they are members? Freud's own ideas here were unsettled: he saw the gathering of the brothers as the means by which they could break the governance of the father, including his right to a harem of females, but, in his meditations on civilization and illusion, he also saw the brother or peer group as a moral force that strangled individuality. "Love of self," he wrote in his work on groups, "knows only one obstacle, love of others." In its context this seemed to mean that egotism and narcissism gave way to the sway of Other-love. In my terminology, *Pair*-love gives way to *Couple*-love. To take this distinction further, I attach to the *Pair* the accumulation of the urges or tropisms for reproductive success and to the *Couple* the means of seeing it carried out. Thus I would rephrase Freud to say, "Fidelity to the species or *Group* knows only one boundary, the love of pleasure and novelty gained in the exploitation of difference." This opposes self-, homo-, and hetero-love to each other, the latter being slightly more *Couple*-based than the others.

Sociobiologists have noted what they think to be yet another sort of "love," one they have called "altruism." They too regard the unit of reproductive survival as the individual creature, but they note that nature has bred nonreproductive insects whose function in the colony is not to reproduce themselves, but rather to improve the chances of survival of the offspring of others—the queen, for example. Biologists have also noted that among mammals there are *vicarious* breeding situations in which, for example, sister lionesses collaborate in rearing the cubs of one sister with her "agreement." Since the genes involved in sisterhood are more closely shared than those between mother and daughter, this observation is generally considered to represent the cubless sister's effort to achieve the next best thing to bearing her own. Such proxy activity goes toward a rethinking of the question of how far the individual is the unit of competition for reproduction and how far it is the species. Plainly the widespread observation that infertility develops in response to anticipated starvation or needs to travel long distances also suggests a trope of deference by the individual to the *Group*.

Ethologists bring back information from the field that those fang and claw fights for the right to dominance and thereby to females individually or in harems—the law of the jungle—are not so damaging to either party as once imagined. As soon as it becomes somehow clear who the winner is likely to be, the contender makes propitiatory and conceding gestures—and leaves to fight another day. While the strongest and the best is thus enabled to spread his seed far and wide, the contender is not without mates: in his challenge he supersedes other males, and by his deference to his conqueror he spares both himself and the top male such damage as would prevent both from breeding. The species is thus twice benefitted, genetically speaking, and there is a continuation of the social order.

In some species moreover there adheres to the female her mate's social rank. (It is not yet clear whether the female's rank gifts the males—other than her sons). Rank confers any number of privileges, among them first rights to food. From the point of view of the survival of the species, the generational reseeding, the eugenic, is carefully improved. Those best fit mate, those most fit enjoy privileges as to food and shelter, and their offspring lead a privileged life—a winnowing process is ever at work. But it is to be noted that this can only be the case if the system works—if the less privileged *allow* it to work.

As one might expect in an evolutionary system, with time the complexity of operation of such systems increased: selection against complexity was undoubtedly considerable, but selection against simplicity was even greater. Out of the increase in complexity of evolutionary systems, more sophisticated somatic selection systems emerged. (Edelman 1987: 299–300)

What I wish finally to suggest is that the system as principle be regarded as dialectic: a back and forth of "argument" between various forces—between cells, between cell bundles, between bundles and individuals as we know them (e.g., the whole person or our pet, the dog), and between individual as cellular entity in a colony or *Group*; the *Group* as an entity among subspecies. In this dialectic, forces on all sides—programs—come into and go out of being according to inchoate feedback messages, only a few of which, even on the macro level, have words. I think there are proactive forces toward individual and genetic success, and also counterforces to give way and die for the good of the species. As I shall show in the next chapter, I think neither of these are learned: that is, they preexist learning and are rather categories into which learned experiences are fitted.*

To speak of what the world is like is to speak of what the mind is like, and to speak of what the mind is like is to speak on a moment-to-moment basis. The mind defines itself by the categories it uses for interpretation, and those categories are created and recreated by the selecting environment. Once created, those categories define "new" experience in terms of previously constructed categories, yet the sheer force of the new entices the mind into creating categories it didn't use before. The *Couple* and the *Pair* are categories into which some of the same proto-data arrive, only to be differently construed. X appears. In what terms shall X be considered: as Mr. or Ms. Right or—Mr. or Ms. Right Now?

Experience is accordingly a function of a dialectic, and the monitoring of one person's experience by another, as takes place regularly and systematically in the therapy of psychoanalysis, is likewise the fruit of a dialectic. The unit or totality of experience can also be spoken of as an event, because it happens in time or a

---

*For an investigative model relating neurological and cognitive systems, see Posner (1988) and Posner and Presti (1987).

semblance of what we know of by the word "time." Bion maintained that the only thing the mind could properly be said to do was mentate; therefore, regarding the creation and destruction of experience, the mind could only modify what it knew or knew it knew of what it wished to experience or not. In the strict sense the mind couldn't modify—i.e., repress, project, displace—drives or feelings or memories, only its knowledge of these. This is the sense in which I use the concept: I understand the formation of experience as a function of the deployment of attention, but that deployment of attention cannot be regarded as an individual's freehold. Rather attention itself is severely curtailed and enlarged by forces more basic than it. Thus the dialectic of attention: while it shapes what is experienced, it is itself a subject of experiences more basic or primary than it is itself. And because of this, the adduction of the sources or agencies of the dualism plainly have had some jitter. They are in many ways reminiscent of the body-mind problem, the mind-brain problem and the particle-wave problem—to name a few. What is the relationship involved? Is it basic, emergent, or purely heuristic?

Principles are of course metapsychological terms and as such are abstractions and not clinical motivations. Hence Freud's use of terms like the pleasure ego. When speaking of a "selection principle," I do not consider it as a manifest thing—a phenomenon itself realized, but rather as something immanent that gives rise to manifestations in the domain of feelings and thoughts, memories and anticipations, perceptions and recollections. It "exists" as a category into which experience flows (I follow Kant [1781] here) and to which experience gives shape and definition. When I say it "exists" I am supposing that other categories do not exist; that they are somehow preempted by the "existence" of categories like the pleasure principle and the selection principle. I attach two kinds of significance to such a supposition. The first is that other creatures may have more or less of any principle than we, or more or less of the proportion of drive from either principle. The second is that the power and presence of such principles is a function of the accidents and chaos of natural selection. That is, we have it because it was somehow to our ancestors' "advantage" —evolutionarily speaking—to have it. Or, rather, to have its immanences and their manifestations.

I have noted that the state of mind we call "hope" is a manifestation of this selection principle. If, as I think, "desire" is a state of mind issuing from the pleasure principle, then hope and desire will be in dialectic tension, with hope motivating one toward Mr., Ms., or Mrs. Right, and desire, propinquitously, toward whomever, polymorphously or perversely, right now. If indeed such a state of affairs can be supposed to "exist," it is not difficult to imagine its advantage in natural selection as Darwin described selection. One would suppose that propagating with just any other creature including, onanistically, one's self, might well serve the immediate needs for pleasure. But this same "strategy" can hardly be imagined to benefit the survival of the species. Yet waiting a lifetime for the right other to come along before one is nudged into desire would scarcely do the species any more good than the former strategy. Hope and desire must conflict, yet yield. Of course this ignores the question of what must come to be before "hope" and its anticipations can be sufficiently satisfied to permit desire to ignite—and, equally, when "desire" is sufficiently enflamed to kindle hope.*

For on that dialectic selection—and in phenomenal life, *choosing*—depends. The pleasure principle depends of course on discovery; without knowing what's what, it cannot maximize pleasure and minimize frustration, deprivation, and other such pains endemic to its nature. But the selection principle has its own set of pains, principally the dread of not being among the survivors. And it requires the use of the capacity to pay attention (or not) to find its likenesses, its kind, its species, or if it cannot do that, to reinvent the world or the nature of its perceived self so that it can.

A species is defined by those creatures who can reproduce with one another. To propagate, like must find like. But if like absolutely finds like, the propagation will founder on narcissism or homosexuality. This means of course yet another aspect to the dialectic: different but not too, like but not too. (Goldilocks was also looking for "just right.") But by what standards and measures? The pleasure principle revels in difference. Attention, when driven by it, goes to the search for differences, especially those

---

*Love I suggest is the simultaneous fulfillment of both of those categories, the unification of Hope and Desire in one person, and even better, reciprocally in two people.

having to do with gender. When it encounters likenesses, its fund or pool of potential sources of pleasure is commensurately diminished. On the other hand, the selection principle relishes likenesses and identities, for with them its potential relationships are increased. Depending, therefore, on which principle is motivationally dominant at a given moment, the same object may be the bearer of good news or bad news.

Our perceptions, however, can be altered by the same sleights already described: differences can be ignored in favor of similarities, or vice versa, and the received experience of the encountered world accordingly revised. However, with two discongruent claims on attention from within, attention is, if not paralyzed, caught up. This makes our attention far more vulnerable to a deciding vote, and that vote will consist in the demand qualities of the world. Thus far from selecting our world, we are selected by it—another sort of dialectic.

For present purposes, however, such questions need not be accounted except to say that the old assumptions regarding the units involved, as well as fitness and selection, are undergoing continuing examination, leaving the psychological routes toward surmise quite wide open. One is rather free, therefore, to suppose that selection may have "rewarded" selectivity: that selectivity requires choices: that the necessity for choosing and being chosen constitute basic preoccupations or occupations for creatures so endowed: such that egoistic activity may at times and in places be counterproductive and would have to be modified by a principle every bit its strength and influence.

Breeding requires the preservation of others with whom to breed— this at a minimum. It also requires variety and mutation in order that breeding be successful—which is to say that breeding in the next generation passes on the DNA. From this viewpoint, the generationally surviving genes would be those in a good position to offer variety to the genes that in their turn may select them. One of the features breeding seems to reward is durability or survival. This may be false, because it can only be inferred from creatures that have survived and, in relation to the entirety of all creatures realized, those who survive, even in fossil form, can only be a fraction. To reason from them that survival is a value is like reasoning about populations from what may only turn out to be the first ten or twenty pages of their discarded telephone books. All the same, evolutionary biologists by and large feel that creatures act as if survival were a raison d'être; they hypothesize this all the while knowing the potential for teleological error and the pathetic fallacy. And if survival of the species were somehow a principle, then it would not (as it is not) be a jungle out there. As noted, individuals would take care, for example, neither to overgraze nor overpredate their food supply nor ruin their environs. Lest that happen, they would slow their rate of reproduction, turning to quality rather than quantity as the main means of assuring survival for their offspring. Such alterations of "strategy" do, of course, take place: "personal" or egoistic strategies seem modifiable in the direction of vicarious reproduction, of which the prime examples have been presented by Wilson in his treatise on sociobiology.

Wilson's work has been criticized on a number of grounds. I myself question the concept of "altruism" because it presumes individual creatures are each a unit of reproductive survival irrespective of one another, selfishly wanting, as it were, the propagation of only its own DNA. Were that the case selection would have had to be pulled away from parthenogenesis by failure after failure. More to the point, however, is the question of what the unit or entity of reproduction is: Is it the molecule, the cell, the organ, the man or woman, the group, the nation-state or the species? I regard this matter as unsettled. As I am attempting to show, the social unit—the *Pair* and *Group*—is in some respects superogatory to the individual human being. Is the individual human being in the same way superogatory to his individual cells by way of cell groups, as Edelman (1987) would have it, being selective of cells? It seems so.

Is it insect Y or animal X that wants sending along—or their DNA? DNA after all is what combines with DNA to inform the progeny. Is it possible to think that DNA uses the individual as a vehicle for its reproductory transmittal of genetic instructions? Is it possible to imagine that as the soma drives the psyche through the span of the id—to copulation, the soma also drives the psyche to get about the business of reproductory transmission—to breeding? If it were genes that freight the individual with their insensate urge to reproduce themselves "advantageously"—and not merely adventitiously—the egoistic drives of the pleasure ego would have to have play in several directions. There would be no use talking about sexual reproduction in the absence of other members of the species, for without them, while pleasure may be possible, breeding is not. Love, it is sometimes said, is a matter of chemistry. Gene calling to gene may be precisely that.

5. The Present, the Absent, and the Presence of the Absence

In one of the more notable scenes in *The Catcher in the Rye*, Salinger has Holden Caufield in troubled wonder. Holden sees the ducks in New York City's Central Park and wonders—where do they go when the ice is frozen? This question is aligned to the Zen inquiry about the sound of one hand clapping, which Salinger uses for his epigraph to *Nine Stories* and could apply to the later scenes in *The Catcher in the Rye* in which Holden and his sister, Phoebe, play at being the villain of the movie *The Thirty-Nine Steps*, whose little finger is missing its top. The implication seems to be that experiences exist even in their absence—perhaps especially in their absence. As Bion reflected, "You may not remember it, but that doesn't mean it forgets you." This was to lead to his remark on psychoanalytic listening:

> To the analytic observer, the material must appear as a number of discrete particles, unrelated and incoherent. The coherence that these facts have in the patient's mind is not relevant to the analyst's problem. His problem—I describe it in stages—is to ignore that coherence so that he is confronted by the incoherence and experiences incomprehension of what is presented to him. . . . This state must endure until a new comprehension emerges. (Bion 1970: 15)

That is to say that the patient's realizations at once conceal and reveal the elements of which they are made up, and to hear the presence of the absence, one must allow it to occur. From the patient's point of view it means that he or she will be thrown into a state of meaninglessness and chaos so unbearable that he will be driven to make moonbeams and auguries out of anything that stirs:

> P : I am so excited by my new car that I can hardly stand it. Not just the car, even the new plates. The plates read O69IYF. Which means "no more 69." I like to drive it up and down the highways. "In Your Face, guys!"

"In your face"—not "for your information." P is hearing the sound swell of anonymous voices to which she needs and wants to reply, also anonymously. It is one of the earmarks of the species that it offer anonymity to its individual members: individuals get "lost" in flocks, troops, schools, and herds. Within these *Group*s, signals flash quick as a flash. Although the alerting one momentarily puts his identity at risk, he is quickly able to meld into the anonymity of the *Group*, leaving the predator none the wiser.

In the *Group* of automobiles, P can flash the message, "In Your Face!"—and if faced with that, say, "How can you be sure it was me?"

The schoolteacher says to his class, "Who did that?" The class is silent. The teacher says, "Unless the person who did that comes forward and confesses, you all will be punished." The *Group* now evaluates the value of what the perpetrator did for it. X, who is not the perpetrator, confesses. How does he know it is his job to confess? That is his role in the *Group*, and at last he has his opportunity to play it. How did he and the rest know? It was his job in the repertory company, with a small stable of ingenues, heavies, and what have you—each playing his role like a dolphin surfacing from the sea: prominent one moment, invisible the next; distinctive one moment, indistinguishable the next. The species *Group* does a certain kind of business within its Self and quite another with Others. The former are extensions of the *Pair*, the latter extensions of the *Couple*.

For a system so complex as this, to be governed by an off/on switching system would be a tremendous burden. This position, except in linear forking strings, leaves too few options—which might be why computers can only approximate mentation. Still there must be switches or everything would be permanently either on or off, like living or dead, and surely a living system needs more options than that. I am proposing a model based on either/ or, with no real off-switch except coma and death. Freud had this issue very much in mind when he wrote his paper on negation (1925), in which he argued that the unconscious had no No's, that every feeling, impulse, and idea emanating from the unconscious was object-seeking and affirmative. It was the superego and ego to which he assigned censorious and censoring force.

Of course, the difficulty with that structure was with the problem of energies: did the ego and superego have forces of their own, or did they operate with energies borrowed from the id? Freud's initial solution was the latter. The ego neutralized, or, one could say, sublimated the direct energies of the id and used these to moderate the very unchained tiger from which it drew its force. This is still the classical or structural view of psychoanalysis.

But Freud I think was discontent with this theory. If the id working through the unconscious was so powerfully rooted in man's biology, shouldn't there be another principle equally rooted to match with it? In this vein Freud supposed a death instinct, Thanatos, and saw it in a dark struggle with Eros, the life or pleasure principle. The death instinct has not been taken up by many except for the Kleinians, who see in it the existential source of anxiety and dread. Most others see the dynamic as between the adaptive self-preservative inclinations of the ego, its ideals, and conscience and the devil-take-the-hindmost-pleasure and blood lusts of our atavistic nature.

As I have tried to illustrate, the anthropological, ethological, and biological backdrops with which Freud did his work have changed a good deal. Based on what I have discussed in previous chapters, I think it is possible to think of a kind of species or natural selection principle as counterpoint to the egoistic drive functions of the id. It is such a theorem on which I base this treatise.

If one were to start all over and describe and assign the dualities in human nature, the central dialectic would be between the individual entity of life and the collective systems of which it is a part. If one sets aside the rich cargo of death instinct—of self-preservation, the repetition compulsion and the drive to follow out the parabola that leads organic life back again into organicity —where is one left? I suggest that there is some difficulty about the last. Though it is true that living cells can reproduce only so many times, that is, repeat themselves only so often, this can just as easily be theoretically explained by supposing a stopping point at which the parent cell must give way to new growth. The compulsion to repeat even painful or especially painful experiences has by many been reattributed to the ego as a need for mastery. The dynamics to which Freud referred in the recurrent dreams of bad wartime experiences (what is now called Post-Traumatic Stress Syndrome) and which seemed to violate the wish-fulfilling nature of the dream can be reattributed to what I think is the dread of not being selected, that original anxiety that one is not destined to be among the elect—among those endowed with the right to life and reproductive life. To this I shall now turn.

Because the selection principle requires that we be prepared to make way for the Select, I think it is by no means clear to every infant, perhaps even to every fetus, that it may count itself among those destined to live and in time contribute to the gene pool of successive generations. I think such infants have to be convinced that their job is not to wither and die.

Implied in Freud's aforementioned work on negation and later in Bion's work on the "no-thing" (Bion 1963; see also Eigen 1991 and Grotstein 1990–1991), there is no such thing as nothing in people's mental calculus. In what might ordinarily be considered nothing there is instead an absence, an emptiness and a depression that is a function of preconceptions not met. Where there should be a mate for preconception, there is not a simple "not there" or "not yet." In the absence of what was supposed to be present, there is instead the presence of an absence. This presence, this no-thing, exudes menace. It is experienced as a some-thing which is aggressively preventing preconceptions from finding their realization (as Bion describes it, from forming conceptions). The no-thing is the stepmother at the Christening. It is antilife. This baby is not among those selected. It does not have the right to life.

People, of course, make additional attempts to achieve realizations of this no-thing. A common one involves people taking up the no-thing's inimical and hostile relation with themselves, such that it becomes the self that is hated and persecuted by the self. This is based upon the self's envy of its own audacity in continuing nevertheless to live (M. Klein 1952). If the no-thing is not too terribly envious it will abjure its darkest plans for a full hostile takeover, providing the self continuously feels itself to be an imposter, an outsider: teetering on the edges of social confidence, it must be ever ready to self-destruct its self-esteem. Under such conditions the self can be allowed its living death. But even a deep breath may become the hubris that restarts the no-thing's lapse.

One of the inborn preconceptions, perhaps more strongly in some than in others, derives from the selection principle that says that some must, for the good of the species, remain unselected. I imagine this principle to be found in life at various levels. As cells must give way and die unless they are selected by the environment as usable, so too must some people die, or as nearly die as makes no difference. (The resourceful cell has some give to it; its DNA pushes it only so far; for the rest, it adapts to selective pressures. But there are many more potential brain cells than are needed. Some must die.) The expression "Social Darwinism" has been used to describe this. There are ghettos everywhere in which supplies are so short as to cripple infants at birth and continue as life goes on.

In reviewing Jewell Taylor Gibbs's book *Native Sons*, Arthur Kempton (1991: 57) writes:

> In 1986, the last year for which the National Center for Health Service has collated information, there were about twice as many black women as black men in this country, and so many young men died that it depressed the average life expectancy of the African-American population as a whole. Lately, homicide has become the leading cause of death for black males between the ages of fifteen and twenty-four, who are dying at a rate that has increased by 67 percent in four years and is now six times greater than for other Americans the same age. Ninety-five percent of all the killings which accumulated into this statistic were attributable to guns.

In her 1988 book, Gibbs, a black sociologist, asserted, according to Kempton, that young black males

> are truly endangered—not only indirectly from society's neglect and abuse, but quite directly by their own actions and activities. . . . [They]

are continuing to kill, maim, or narcotize themselves faster than they could be annihilated through wars or natural diseases. They not only destroy themselves, but also jeopardize family formation for young black women [and] . . . the stability of the black community and endanger the entire society. (Kempton 1991: 57)

Kempton goes on to say:

There is a suggestion, both in her tone and in what she says, of something most of the young men she refers to have probably never had, the rebuke of a mother or grandmother which could both invoke and convey the used-to-be-unbroken tradition represented in the mind's image by the face of Mary McLeod Bethune but embodied in so many others. These women would have chastised their young by reminding them of the indignities their grandfathers endured in silence and the acres of white folks' dirty laundry their grandmothers labored over so that they could stand now at the threshold of opportunities that forebears worthier than they could only have imagined. Thus to behave like this was, for them, to betray that history of sacrifice as well as some essential part of who they were meant to be. (Ibid.)

"These women [who] would have chastised their young" fill the time and space otherwise filled by the presence of the absence of the no-thing. In chastising, they establish *Pair* and *Group* links to tradition. And with those links they supply a blockade to the nothing and those of its realizations that are filled by abject surrender to bad treatment by bad people. Freud's view was that "identification with the aggressor" is a way of coping with the loss and pain inflicted by the aggressor. Unable to beat him, one joins him; unable to *Couple* with him, one becomes him. But a question left over from that formulation is why those who are so treated accepted this situation. Have they indeed been "unselected"? True, the condition is imposed, and all too true, the odds against succeeding in pressing back are immense, because actual power is involved—not least the barrel of the gun. But against this there are the breathtaking events of the current era, in which millions of people in Eastern Europe broke out of a system that had kept them subordinate, some for over sixty years.

The explanation for such events has long been linked to the emergence of leadership, an explanation congenial to the "er-ierism" of the *Pair* viewpoint. And it is doubtless true that charismatic figures in the out- or subspeciated *Group*s can (and do) hurry forward to intercept such identifications before they link onto the persecutors, who otherwise would become the role models and figures for—the realizations of—identification. Here is a realization from Robert Browning's "Lost Leader" (1895).

> We that had loved him so, followed him, honored him,
> Lived in his mild and magnificent eye,
> Learned his great language, caught his clear accents,
> Made him our pattern to live and to die!

The "him" in this poem took thirty-two pieces of silver and left. But for the while he was the ego-ideal leader of whom Freud wrote in his essay on "group psychology and the analysis of the ego" (Freud 1921). The no-thing leader conveys the menace of frustration and despair. He or she seems to "care enough to do his very worst." This is a leader who extends from the *Couple*. The *Couple Pairs* and enters into a *Pairing Group*—but temporarily. Its objective, while deferred, is ultimately to enhance the individual's capacity to find objects agreeable or able to submit to a *Couple* relationship. Such leadership is, in prototype, modeled more on Moses than on Jesus. Though Jesus was to lead his disciples unto God-the-Father by giving his own mortal life as a sacrifice that purchased amnesty from Adam's Original Sin, he for the most part was not an instrumental leader in the sense Moses was. Moses led his people to the Promised Land, but did not go there himself. He brought down the sacraments and tablets, but these were not his. After his tantrum about the Golden Calf, an iconic realization of the Lord who had expressly forbidden such incarnate idols, he saw that he lacked the je ne sais quoi, as perhaps later Churchill did, to endure beyond the confines of his mission. Jesus was betrayed and denied as a Mosaic leader; the people wished instead for a Eucharistic leader with whom, by dint of wine and bread, blood and body, they could *Couple*. Matzohs are not in this way symbolic of Moses, but only a souvenir of the escape from Egypt.

Individuals convert frustrations on the *Couple* side of things into efforts to do business instead on the *Pair* side of things, not as a second best, but as an either/or. Mean and hurtful treatment—

doing one's "worst"—as a kind of selection can be understood in two ways: "Get lost and die, for all I care," or "You are bad, but there is hope for you if you reform." Obviously the second reading is less deadly than the first. Biologists speculate that bonding occurs as a result of mammals licking their young after birth; some speculate that the licking constitutes the signal to the young, a green light to go ahead toward further survival. Licking in the sense of "I'll give you a licking if you don't shape up" is, in its "if" clause, a conditional permission to go ahead and live, for it inspires hope and implies future time. Many children invite such lickings and lashings as a way of renewing their hope against the dread that they are simply unwanted. Baby rats, separated from their mother, do not survive if their mother's licking is replaced by smooth and rhythmical strokes from a paintbrush. They need strokes far more rough and tumble if they are to spell "M-o-t-h-e-r."

Infanticide is by no means a historical curiosity, and selective infanticide, such as the predilection against baby girls is another current practice (there is some indication that in the United States female children are put up for adoption at a rate twice that of boys). I cannot but suppose that akin to the chemical process that prevents pregnancy in times of starvation or uncertainty (lower estrogen in body fat preventing ovulation) there are counterpart processes affecting the carriage of the embryo to term and also affecting the degree to which the fetus feels superfluous or welcome. Babies who survive in utero assaults of the sort I am imagining may need more postnatal reassurances than those spared these attacks. Life is likely to be more a matter of life and death to them than for children not so chemically baptized. One may wonder if some portion of the fever in the so-called pro-life position on abortion is not an unremembered memory of how this unsure state—of being alive and not alive—must feel.

Just as at some point the infant can bring his hand to his mouth or grasp his foot, if and when he wants to, so he can deploy his attention. The phrase "if and when he wants to" contains the supposition of volition and intention—a Self. If the infant wants to believe that his mother "won't" rather than "can't," he has several alternatives. The infant is trying not to pay attention to something that may very well be so, namely that there is not much breast there for him; indeed, that the breast is a no-thing which will harm, perhaps annihilate him. He is also sorely afraid that if the breast keeps up its no-thingness much longer it will stimulate that latent but energetic thing in him that may already once or twice begin to whisper in tones of deadly menace: "You are not among the selected; you have not been chosen. Give over and prepare to succumb; your fate is to die so that your betters may live." These represent a double attack on him, the one coming from the hostile, even sadistic breast, which, since it treats him hatefully, he thinks must hate him; the other coming from within, announcing in almost religious terms his destiny. This latter appraisal is also so implacable that in the face of it he can only feel that there is nothing he can do. It will be obvious that as soon as he can he will want to develop a sense of sin, for that will give him the possibility of repentance and thus something to do to alter his fate and reduce his sense of helplessness. Or he might find groups in which there is the sense of being among the chosen people, among the selected, the elite and the elect: groups that have worked out an understanding with God or the Leadership concerning these fearful and inarticulate matters. But for the meanwhile, he has neither a sense of sin to save him nor any strong conviction that he is among the chosen. These may not seem like much in the way of choices, but a moment's reflection will reveal that the second position, because it provides hope, decreases the infant's helplessness.

At birth and afterward these infants feel premonitions about the no-thing springing forth from the chinks. They are more likely to see the man who "wasn't there again today/ [they, more fervently than others] wish to God he'd go away." I suppose every mother must have to balance what she needs for her own survival and well-being with what she can spare her children, and in this sense, to one degree or another, at some time or other, every child is going to be "rejected." How rejected will depend on how tenuous that child's lease on life is.

Freud nicely observed that "the superego skips a generation." That is a notation of the degree children are, in genetic terms, a means to an end. The fussing between parent and child can be distributed accordingly. The child is in large measure evaluated by the parent as to whether he or she will do in the matter of passing on the desired traits.

This supposition about desired traits leads, of course, to questions of what traits and who knows what traits these might be. Winnicott was always very insistent on the point that the future is extrapolated from the past: we anticipate what has already been. Jung took this one step further, arguing for a racial unconscious that brings ever forward the paradigms of the racial or species (speci-al, as it were) past, a past beyond the individual's experience of his personal past—a species-specific genetic past. This argument undermined Freud's wish to display the specificity of each individual's personal and specific experience as determinative of his present condition. But Freud held that there were universals—the unconscious, infantile sexuality, mechanisms of defense, the Oedipus complex, among them—which structured experience in a way Lévi-Strauss, Chomsky, Saussure, Klein, and Lacan were to take even further. But I think there is a simpler devolution. It is "more of the same." I think there is an openness about what the Same might be, but not about the More.

In English, more is a comparative, an "-er" domain. Whether Less is More or simpler is better or rococo is more lovely is each culture's and generation's construction of what is the true "-er" or the better "-er." The root experience is that more of the whatever it is, is better. This preconception drives the *Pair*, which wants bigger and better and more of whatever it is that the *Group* values, which is bigger and better and more of what the Non-G*roup* or the Other *Group* values.

This is how we know one another and how we can become serried into ranks (rank orders). "More" and "less" prescribe a hierarchy. I believe that in the *Pair* perspective this is the structure of experience and these the extant categories. The species survives by being and having more of the Same—whatever "same" turns out to be.

"Same" is important here: at its roots it defines the species. In the biological sense, a species is defined by those who can reproduce with one another in an ongoing way. "Ongoing" refers to those aberrations like sphinxes and centaurs and werewolves who are particularly greedy because reproductively they have no incarnation other than their present one: they cannot "sublimate" their desire for perpetuation by giving egotistic way to their sons and daughters because there are not to be any.* They are regarded at once as exotic and an error of nature. It is surmised that such anomalous creations are the fruits of incest, fruit that did not fall far enough from the tree. To stop the proliferation of these horrors, sterility is bred into the monster: either it bears no egg or seed or what it bears is a currency valid only beyond the species and therefore can find no redemption within it.

Bion writes of the mystic and the genius as being psychological counterparts of the one-of-a-kind monstrosities. In his chapter "The Mystic and the Group" (Bion 1970), he describes this peculiarly ambivalent relationship. The *Group* having established its status quo, and then only after some struggle and some loss of beloved wishes to compromise, now has an equilibrium going; in its efforts to maintain this hard-won consensus, the *Group* passes it off as *the* equilibrium: the God-given one-and-only ordained by the Founder and immanent in his works, e.g., the Constitution, the gospels, the Bhagavad Gita. This is the use of the breast by the *Pair:* The breast is font, not for food or succor, but as the source of all identifications. This attitude imposes a certain inflexibility in the face of change. Other *Groups*, growing up and established on the basis of other identifications with alternative fonts, may be showing greater initiative in regard to the ecosystem, which of course includes the materiality and ideology of each *Group* (and others) for both of them. Gould (1987) has demonstrated how resistant any *Group* (for example a hunter-gatherer *Group*) may be to change (into going over to food cultivation, for example). Once a realization for certain preconceptions and premonitions is found, only realizations that are more of the same seem to have any real currency. This tends to put a premium on moves toward extremism, conservatism, and autocracy. However, the counterfoil is the mystic. The question concerning the mystic is whether or not he is

---

*In Sophocles' *Oedipus Rex*, the encounter of the breeder with the nonbreeder is fateful. The nonbreeder asks a question in which "generation" is limited to a lifetime. It/she expects this ferocious breeder-to-be not to be able to conceive of a single lifetime. What a curious question—to ask about legs of one who knows legs in his very name!? He has the scars. He answers the hybrid, half-woman, half-beast, and then goes forth in the opposite direction—more and more of the same —and produces a plague: children who are in-bred: *too* much of the same.

the anti-"Christ"—or whether he presents a vision derived from the old god newly found. Acid tests that determine this appear to involve the rediscovery of this new reading or strain of enlightenment in the past (at or around the font): the idea that the mystic will suffer for (or surely not benefit from) his sin of being unique and that in accepting the mystic's analysis of what needs to be done and how, one is simply going back to primary sources and not abjectly taking a leaf or two from the book of one's competitors.

Under these circumstances, the Presence of an Absence is refuted by the *Group*. Its assimilation of the teachings and visions of the mystic has made the mystic, after all, no more than one of the *Group*—it is in such contexts that Bion uses the phrase, "Loaded with honors, he sunk without a trace!" This factor points nicely to the function of the *Pair*-cum-*Group* as the antidote to the Presences of Absences and their intrusions into experience as no-things.

Once we can get settled about nothing, the no-things tend to become ectoplasmic in the manner of the Cheshire cat. To be sure there will be a certain amount of turbulence as authentic absence gradually replaces no-thingness, but despair and hopelessness can and do go over into sorrow and relief, which in their turn, being grieved, open a way to new realizations, including the possibility of retaining the object for uses in the *Coupling* way. The child going to sleep at night has a terrain to get over until the some-things of dreams come and take him up. During the time of traveling over that terrain the child may feel unselected, hence chosen and made ripe for death. The immanence of the no-things is all around; he can hardly breathe—he can hardly dare breathe. What realization will serve him in this, the eternity of his need? Children differ, of course. Some, if they must endure any of this experience at all, will try to attend more to one part of it to escape the brunt of another part. If they are the sort of children who can tame by naming, they will find names, like those of the states in the United States: if their dreads are numberless at least they are not nameless. Other children, indeed, use numbers; they count innumerably to a hundred. Others turn the night into a light show: they are alive so long as the luminescence of their pressure-knuckled eyeball flows in its infinity of patterns. Others do not want to know anything beyond what they feel. If idea and feeling drift toward conjunction, alarm bells go off. These bursts of anxiety stop the drift toward conception and will soon be akin to having stopped the primal scene and especially the conception that may materialize from it.

In these maneuvers we recognize "neurotic styles" as Shapiro (1965) has named them: the obsessive-compulsive or idea-knower has selectively paid attention to that aspect of the no-thing experience and has established countermeasures that will organize and master the surplus of ideas that fill out the partial vacuum left by the child's disinclination to know of the feelings that are— or would otherwise be—part of the experience. The hysteric or feeling-knower takes up his sensorium with feelings, the surplus of which exaggerate the few ideas that remain. And so with the light painters and time counters, the space builders and the storytellers. Any port in a storm, but known ports make for lesser storms.

In these examples, the tensions and conflicts attendant on the *Couple* are not prominently in play. But they have launched the problem. The heartache inherent in separation, frustration, and jealousy are so painful to the child that to diminish the pain he must lessen his investment in the *Couple* and look instead to the Other in the garb of a member of the *Pair*. What counsel does the Other give the infant? First and foremost, it seems, something about the Other "Getting some rest" or "Having a life" or "Needing to work" or "Needing to be with another so to have another baby." Can these be taken seriously as conditions of absence, as no-things for much more than a moment? And what do these Others counsel? Give way, bug off, let go, drop dead. The preconception in the selection mandate coalesces with what the *Pair* is representing and puts the individual directly in the path of the no-things.

This might seem enough to drive the infant back into *Couple* modalities, and indeed sometimes it does. But before it is taken to the parental bed, light is brought in, the child is bounced and cuddled vigorously enough to shake loose the willies, ritual prayers are sung and the nighttime or naptime spells are spoken once again. The Good-*Pair* has been called upon to assert itself against the no-things, and in arriving and doing what needed to be done, it has proved its presence. This time the absences are filled with good presences (the good-*Group* conception) and the child drifts off with the feeling of being part of something bigger and better than its miserable craven self.

"Initially," Phillips (1986) writes, quoting Bollas (1979),

> the mother is "an object that is experientially identified by the infant with the process of the alteration of self experience." This earliest relationship becomes the precursor of, and paradigm for, "the person's search for an object (a person, place, event, ideology) that promises to transform the self." At this first stage, "the mother is not yet identified as an object but is experienced as a process of transformation, and this feature remains in the trace of this object-seeking in adult life, where I believe the object is sought for its function as signifier of the process of transformation of being. Thus, in adult life, the quest is not to possess the object; it is sought in order to surrender to it as a process that alters the self."

If, as I think, this is indeed the case, the wishes to *Couple* are under these circumstances not only supernumerary, but a nuisance. Such a finding very well fits with Winnicott's position that, in the construction of the self, the ongoing fractious irruptions of the drives and lusts are debilitating. Unless the pleasure ego can be insinuated into the *Pairing* motivation, they conflict. But many people do find a way of doing just this. The sexual acts are used as transformational acts. The wish for anal penetration on the boy's part is often as much a wish for incorporating the father's phallic strength as a sensual wish to be desirable and loved in and of himself or in an oedipal rivalry with the mother. Beating fantasies, like-wise. Since children are usually beaten in an effort to transform them, the fantasy and the reality are not so far afield. The proud, stubborn father, stiff-necked with authority, is going to knock some sense into his wayward child. The child, having already *paired* with that father precisely on the register of stubbornness, submits with a mixture of outrage and hope. The outrage is salved if the child can turn the beating or shaking into a sensual event: it says, "You may think you are hurting me, but I take from you pleasure, not pain. So you see, you can't hurt me after all." The hope resides in the idea, "So you think I can be transformed, after all!" The reiterated formula "after all" is the bastion within which hope abides. So many children who are perceived as looking for attention or testing the limits are in fact doing just that and more. Every scolding is a re-realization of "I can be better, I can be more. See, they haven't lost hope in me, even if I have."

The dread allayed by these acts is that "I have no potential and so there is something altogether lacking in me." This feeling, of course, produces the state of mind of depression; the depressions are felt to be quite literal; they are not absences, but rather the discovery of no-things, warts and all. The voluptuous surrender, the abject enaction involving such no-things—if they cannot be directed to the *Group*, in the Hindu sense of Darshan, or in being content, nay eager, to be but a cog in a wheel, or less even than that—will organize the *Coupling* in order that sensual gratification is taken (Bollas 1987; Phillips 1986; Ghent 1990).

When the *Coupling* urges cannot be insinuated into *Pair* purposes, they detract from them. Harmonies are established when preconceptions become fused with the cultural ideals (represented by Freud as the ego-ideal). Anna Freud in particular has noted the asceticism of adolescence (in many cultures) and the use of reaction formations to achieve that state of grace. But I would myself rather put it as the temporary triumph of the *Pair* over the *Couple* or the subset *Group* over the main *Group*. For example, there is certain gluttony among people accounted as the Beautiful and the Good, which is matched only by the gluttony of those achieving anorexia nervosa. Both of these *Group*s require of their members the sacrifice of individual laissez-faire. The members of each of these *Group*s are driven to extremes in order to keep the no-things in their places. The ability of the *Group* to define the experiential universe and to make virtues of necessities makes it also the necessary counterfoil for the experience of absence.

Hidden, however, in this commonplace is the too little asked question, by what means is the *Group* fashioned or founded? Let us say that two people are a *Couple* or a *Pair*. Three can also have that either/or nature. Three can be a triangle or a *Group*, depending whether three is regarded from the standpoint of the *Couple*, where it is an Oedipus complex, or the *Pair*, where it is the keystone for the construction of a *Group*. Three or more people can be seen as having both possibilities and in like way the forerunner of either. As with two-person dyads, there are preconceptions for one set of possibilities or the other—or both. What there seems to be almost no preconception for is the realization that numbers of people real or imagined don't imply either *Couple* or *Pair*. Stars appear to be in constellations; so do people. Are stars in constellations, or are these artistic illusions of the beholder? Are people in *Pairs, Groups,* states, nations? The "are" makes sense, or might, in other realms of discourse; in dialectical discourse, there is no question that experience so shapes the experiencer(s) that the answer has to be "Yes." Yet as we see all over the geopolitical map, what looked like nation-states of perduring viability dissolve as quickly as the turn of the kaleidoscope. As with the Cheshire cat, all that remains is the smile: but the smile is obdurate. It will shape new *Group*ings and *Pair*ings that will soon seem as inevitable and enduring as the cat once did. People who only see eye to eye see too little. In the therapeutic domain, I have described this in the following:

> When I speak of the problem of treatment, then, I have also in mind that the more carefully the elements in the anorexia are analysed, the more the analyst is in danger of missing what the anorexia hides. Unlike certain other symptoms or characterologic malformations, anorexia *contains* in the compromise formation less of what bedevils the patient than it *obscures* it. When the anorectic finally does give way and talks of her inexhaustible occupation with food, weight, and body image, the analyst will have a Scheherazade of a patient. The occupation will conceal the preoccupation, which is oedipal-genital in nature.
>
> The dynamics of the oedipal situation, however, are the same—profound desire competing with envious covetousness; projection as a primary defensive orientation; hypersusceptibility to stimulation and an urgent need for the release of excitement through orgasm or "displaced" orgasm.
>
> While her heroics about dieting or, at any rate, weight control are designed to stimulate admiration or, failing that, envy, the body is designed to look asexual and/or sufficiently androgynous as to evoke the most muddled sexual response in both men and women. Others, and, of course the analyst, are supposed to try to feed or fail at feeding and to coerce or fail at coercing. It is supposed to be as difficult to think about sex as it might in conjunction with a concentration camp victim or a saint.
>
> That there is a degree of vindictive spite in this will emerge later; as some patients for periods try to excite unrequitable longing in the analyst as a means of imposing retaliatory pain, so the anorectic denies the analyst the sensuous gratification he ordinarily gets from contem-

plating loveliness. But this is secondary to her effort not to "let sex come into it," as it is frequently put. (Boris 1984b)

Relative to realization—*click!* and to re-realization—*click!** The anorectic is attempting to understand everything in certain terms. There are women, for example, who upon the breakup of a relationship—a marriage, perhaps—lose weight. At first this may be due to stress, depression, worry of an essentially reactive sort. But then the weight loss becomes progressive and begins to express an "understanding" of the separation from the husband in terms of loss of mother or breast: I have been too greedy, so this is what happened. This understanding is at once "true" and "untrue." That is why it makes a good screen or cover story. So with the more extreme anorectic. Not only is she "understanding" what happened in oral and anal terms, *so must others.*
But:

P : It's so funny, when my folks were here, how much I masturbated, as if I was almost daring them to walk in and discover me at it.

The vast fascination with sexual matters needs to be systematically noted along such lines as this:

P : It's terrible on these days, like when I was walking here, wherever I look there is food—people eating, shops selling food. That's all I see.
Ψ: Instead of . . .
P : (Pause) Now that you mention it, I have been taking a new route over here. They have these beautiful women, soft mysterious, come hither. But it's all false. Even if you went in —I mean, what kind of women undress for people in places like that. [Note the attributions: "Now that you mention it," the "over *here*," the "if you went in," and how P spunkily attempts to make Ψ the author of the experience.]

---

*As indicated, this expression, —*click!*, is a metaphor for realization's expressing an act of recognition that makes one want to snap one's fingers and say, "Of course, that's it!" See chapter 7.

In meditating on the Wolfman, Freud wrote that one can think of the child putting interpretations on events at the time they occurred, at a later time in the light of subsequent information or fantasy, or at the time of narration or dreaming (Freud 1918). In terms of construction, anorectic patients pose just this problem more so than many others. It is often difficult to tell whether they mistook genital and oedipal matters as having to do with feeding and elimination, confusing breast and penis, pregnancy and puberty, because they always thought only in oral terms or because they reinterpreted everything to rid themselves of later discoveries too painful to be allowed to endure. To put it still another way, it is not easy to know when one is dealing with the adult's memories *from* childhood or memories *of* childhood. I would like to suggest that this difficulty is expressive of a particular function in anorectic patients.

Just as the location of contents crosses, as it were, *spatially*, back and forth between self and internal object, between self and transitional space, between body and food, and projectively between self and other, so too has the anorectic shuttled the contents of her experiences back and forth through time with the same frenetic and carelessly careful ease. The result is, I suggest, a *mélange* of experiences or rather of interpretation of experience. Prospective views, retrospective views, vision and revision, once served the same functions as the spatial ones do in the present. They protect against certainty—particularly the certainties of separation and loss and of ownership and disillusionment. And since uncertainty is itself so painful (for example, the haunting uncertainty attaching to what the body looks like or weighs after eating or purging), there has had to be created a quantity of understandings to compensate for the quality that is lost. Experience is always being attacked and lost to attack, interpreted and reinterpreted: confusion and fusion.

Re-construction is made inherently difficult and the difficulty is compounded by the anorectic patient who wants more interpretations to go with her own and has no intention of giving one up for another. The analyst's interpretations are valued since the anorectic projects into him the good material she craves. But they are feared, as food is, because the interpretations will add so much and have such weight that she will be lost in the confusion. She attacks interpretations with scorn and doubt and feels lost and uncertain. Then she takes an additive approach in order that no interpretation can be entirely true (or false). When this procedure causes its own difficulties, she perforce must look for certainty outside herself again. (It is characteristic of these patients to look to their parents to remember childhood for them.)

The anorectic's relationship to the analyst's interpretation has therefore to be a concern for him, not alone in terms of how they are symbolized and with what his giving of them is analogized (food: feeding, impregnation, etc.) but in terms also of the problems posed for the patient by certainty and uncertainty, his and hers. This is the more necessary because for periods of time the anorectic takes up a paranoid stance and proceeds with deception and stealth. Where others might complain of bad, useless, or "how's that supposed to help" interpretations, she may simply fight fire with fire, much as she returns silence for silence. For the anorectic patient the undoing of the "remembered" life history with the usual eye to historical accuracy engenders not only the usual resistances, but one rooted in a profound intolerance of ambiguity, uncertainty—of anything approaching Keats's "negative capability." Cooperation in the interest of discovery is an infrequent state of affairs: competition in access to what is so is the more pervasive atmosphere. More than with other patients, letting matters evolve until the anorectic patient can make her own constructions is much to be desired. The anorectic's reach for simple certainty leads her to insights that are about as accurate and helpful as her nostrums for physical well-being. "It sounds like . . ." says one of my patients. "So it would seem that . . ." says another.

6. Intimations

In trying to keep psychoanalysis intact, Freud found himself having to reject those aspects of his own theories onto which other theories could attach and then, with seeming seamlessness, modify. Of the many instances of this (involving Adler, Rank, Stekel, etc.) two were perhaps the most costly: Jung's work on the racial or collective unconscious, and later Melanie Klein's work on the nature of unconscious fantasy. Freud's "dynamic" unconscious, which was comprised of repressed feeling and fantasies, was, with repression and infantile sexuality and the Oedipus complex, a keystone in the architecture of his theories. Anything that threatened to vitiate it was, understandably, anathema. Jung's unconscious with its archetypes and Klein's with her elaboration of infantile versions of the archetypical oedipal representation and part object elements were tearing apart the centrality of the individual's particular life experience in the ontogenetic past. Early Freud, the Freud of *The Interpretation of Dreams* (1900), for example, recognizes unconscious fantasies in a way that the later writer of *The Unconscious* (1915a) does not. He wrote:

> The *unconscious processes* pay just as little regard to *reality*. They are subject to the pleasure principle; their fate depends only on how strong they are and on whether they fulfill the demands of the pleasure-unpleasure regulation. (1915a: 187)

and:

95

The content of the *unconscious* may be compared with an aboriginal population in the mind. If inherited mental formations exist in the human being—something analogous to instinct in animals—these constitute the nucleus of the *unconscious*. Later there is added to them what is discarded during childhood development as unserviceable; and this need not differ in its nature from what is inherited. A sharp and final division between the content of the two systems does not, as a rule, take place until puberty. (Ibid., 195)

and:

The system *unconscious* contains the thing-cathexes of the objects, the first and true object-cathexes; the system *Pcs.* (preconsciousness) comes about by this thing-presentation being hyper-cathected through being linked with the word presentations corresponding to it. (Ibid., 201–2)

But preserved even here are the two key concepts to be picked up later by Klein (M. Klein 1928, 1930, 1945), Segal (1957), and Heimann (1950): "mental formations" and the process of symbolization encapsulated by the term "word presentations." It can be seen that diversions of attention from the linkage abridge the realization, keeping it from being established in the first place (what Freud sometimes referred to as primary repression), or de-realizing it once established.

Freud himself elaborated this connection:

It is probable that thinking was originally unconscious, in so far as it went beyond mere ideational presentations and was directed to the relations between impressions of objects, and that it did not acquire further qualities, perceptible to consciousness, until it became connected with verbal residues. (1911: 221)

Freud was to discuss this again in *The Ego and the Id* (1923).

I wish now to add the idea that the "relations between object impressions" in the original unconscious are twofold and both require their own realizations; or more precisely, the impressions of *relations* between objects is twofold. They concern the the states of mind in which Self and Other are conceived of as constituting a *Pair*—beyond that, still shadowy, a formation of assumptions for the *Group* as a species; and a *Couple* of part-objects—beyond *that*, still shadowy, assumptions of *Coupling* in a libidinous sense. Both of these states need to find realization. I regard these as unself-conscious organizing principles in the service of motivations, in much the way Bion did of his group basic assumptions—that is, as antagonists either to reconcile or to use in an offsetting system of checks and balances.

Freud's elevation of the "word"—more broadly, language, may be too reflective of the fin de siècle Vienna. Klein's emphasis on people's intimations of *relations* between objects seems to place the emphasis more accurately. What was for Freud a fairly abstract description of the mind at work establishing and disconnecting linkages was portrayed by Klein and her school as activities, all of which had meanings concerning who was doing what how, to whom, where, and what would happen next. Repression and projection were filled with theoretical meaning to Freud as befits the observer; to Klein, they were animate acts as experienced by the participant. Bion's reference to knowing as K and (minus) $-$ K, which in a state of mind describes repression and in a state of affairs describes simple projection, or projective identification, articulates this. In the beginning was not so much the word as the keeper of the knowledge—a jealous god, who at Eden gave so much consciousness as to inseminate self-consciousness and at Babel disconnected the links of universal discourse and at Thebes provided his promethean fire stealer so much arrogance that know-it-all Oedipus knew himself right into perdition, confusion, and plague (Bion 1963).

In the *Pair*, under the selection principle, the "task" is to better and further the species' chances of surviving into future time. Three elements seem to need realization: one is about time, the second about who and what we are, the third about further or better. The last can conveniently be abbreviated simply to "-er." Thus: what is time? what is we? and what is "-er," or better yet, "er-ier"?

At the base of these realizations would have to be a mental process of comparison and contrast that would have to be capable of making at least three distinctions. Such a process would have to be able to divide and split time from space-time—and thereby now from later, later from after, and after from too late. Since survival is at stake, feelings would have *premonitionally* to provide an affective gauge—sundering dread from hope, hopelessness from despair. And then these from closure, completion, rapture, and bliss.

The closest we get to "best" (an approximation that takes place in spatial terms) and the closest we get to that point in time at which André Green (1986) calls "when the no-longer parts from not-yet" and the closest we get to the greatest of the unities of the Us, a kind of 3-D representation—the greater the rapture, the more pervasive the bliss. But if these are the intimations, what are the realizations?

These realizations, I suggest, are the product of a lifelong search. Like a latter-day Diogenes, we trudge the world round to discover the goodness of fit between what there is and what our intimations tell us must be there—somewhere, at some time, in some way. Of course a certain kind of madness would result from being unable to rest with approximations. Like the Pavlovian dog who is given a shock when trying to eat from a square plate but is allowed to eat in peace when the plate is round, and goes mad when the plate is an octagon and bites its own tail instead, there is an ongoing dialectic between what is discovered and what is sought.

Realizations are in flux. One might compare them to the preliminary sketches that painters use to work out their visualizations of the final canvas. Some fold right into that final realization; others, often fine visualizations in their own right, do not allow themselves to be subsumed precisely because they are too good; they have taken on a life of their own. They may become a nugget of a later realization or its very integuments. Or they may have done their time as realizations that cannot be surpassed or extended, but simply are.

Realizations of our intimations do something more than merely map the fathomless fog. They afford us a release from utter anomie. Durkheim (1933) used this word in contemplating the relation of the individual to the community; I wish to expand on it to describe the relationship of the individual to his two or perhaps several communities. Of these, one is the *Pair*—and going on from there, the *Group* and then the species. Another is the "community" of intimations and their relationship to the "community" of realizations. Though the word may be to some opprobrious, I wish to identify these "communities" as bred into the species. As latter-day Diogeneses, we are armed with identa-kits or with shoes: we are filled with unfilled images to bring to the identa-artist for filling in; we are the prince in *Cinderella* looking for the foot that fits our slipper. Alienation from either of these communities brings anomie and death.

Without good, sinuous ties, the individual will perish, whatever his success in the *Couple*. Rat babies that are not licked succumb to death; human infants who are not held and touched also perish. In the psychoanalytic community we have known this from Spitz and Bowlby, but it hardly needs telling. Not only is a species pruned by predator and ecology, the species weeds its own; each individual is built with an intimation concerning his own mortality; he has to a degree to be brought into life (some more than others). If he is not, his body systems begin to fail. He ages prematurely; he dies young. Among baboons it seems that males have similar physiologies when they become part of the hierarchy. Then those successful in domination become healthier; those unsuccessful become sicker. The hippocampus changes. Different hormones or the same hormones at different levels are secreted. It is as if the role in the social order is internalized. Put another way, one can ask whether the natural disposition to die off for the good of the whole is once again raised and the initial dread that this individual is not destined to be among the elect is brought up again. Not to be among the elect, not to be "in that number"* is to live falsely and on borrowed time. Winnicott's elaboration of "the false self" describes this condition perfectly, for in his delineation the false self is an imposter, begging, borrowing, wheedling, and conniving to be spared just one more minute. Like Freud's version of the "exceptions" and of Richard III in particular, the false self hasn't the decency to die and therefore lives alienated from his intimations, a psychopath to himself and a psychophant†-cum-sociopath to his fellow beings (Freud 1916). The entitlement that is well known to inhabit such souls comes from the fact that they are among the almost-dead. They are filled with envy of those who are among the chosen, as one might expect; and their envy, their gnashing and wailing, takes a Dante to describe. In their pestilential passion to despoil and denude, they are trying only to get their

---

* As in "When the Saints Go Marching In."
† Primo Levi's word (Levi 1990).

own back, quite as Esau tried. Or, like Joseph's brothers they steal their brother's coat to hide their tattered birthright. This is the selfsame birth*right* that Oedipus also lacked; they too suffer from survivor guilt.

Freud's rendering of the Oedipus myth highlighted the story of the *Couple* in a triangle and the pity and the terror of castration. When read in terms of the *Pair*, the story's other features come forefront. These entail the neglect of prophecy on the part of Jocasta and the shepherd, for which read intimations, the assumption of the false self in the metamorphosis from being Prince of Corinth to being King of Thebes, the indifference to the perils of miscegenation as embodied in the sphinx, the failure to hear the prophecy contained in her riddle, and the agricultural hurt to all when the hunter-gatherer fails to extend himself to the planter-sowers. In this reading Laius, Jocasta, and Oedipus each reap what in their envy they sowed—namely the dreadful fate of seeking false realizations for the intimations of the species, the social *Group* and the culture. —*click!* goes each approximation as it meets and fits a realization. In his consideration of the Wolfman, Freud made a point of footnoting that the nexus of each such meeting reflects one, then another, then yet another realization for the intimation of the primal scene.

For first takes are ungainly. They require experience and the relative absence of turbulence (as Bion called it) to find a good fit between preconception and conception. Poorer realizations are driven out by later, better ones except when the more primitive versions remain a better fit for the current state of mind (or affairs) than successive ones. The personification of Iraq in Saddam Hussein is reminiscent of the Shakespearean world where Clarence and York were not duchies so much as individuals. In such a realization the phrase "naked aggression" could only be iconic. Thus employed it could simulate the bad, hated father, once the "Willie Horton" figure, now Saddam, having his will of mother-Kuwait. As contrasted to our own bird who was safely in his bush, pillage, rape, and dismemberment of women and children placed the bad primal scene safely elsewhere. "Elsewhere" means not only that it was removed from us and our *Group*, but also that it was removed from being a state of mind onto being one of affairs.

Without such intimations there would be an ontogeny that was mindless. But humankind and perhaps other species have got it genetically into their heads that they should take on some of the duties involved in the preservation of our species. In Kantian terms, this means that the categories precede the experience, and give the ideational and sensuous data of the experiential stream a shape and pattern for relations internal and foreign while at the same time the data give shape and thrust to the categories. As the vertex changes, the same bits in the data stream form one kind of information and implication and now another. The deconstruction of the *Couple* version of the Oedipus myth reveals the "same" pieces ordered in *Pair* and *Group* terms. Insofar as these two categories are unaware of one another, binocular vision, as Bion used the term, cannot function. There is but figure and ground and, reversed, figure and ground. Only when the relationships between figures and grounds are espied is a new category available for thinking. "Binocularity" might be an example of the outgrowth of such a meta-category.

From this line of reasoning it can be seen that the psychoanalysis of an individual must introduce awareness of not only the contents of the categories but of their often obfuscated relations. It is in this sense that psychoanalytic treatment, in its "systematic study," in Hartmann's (1959) words, "of self-deceptions and their motivations" alone can display the relationship between intimations and realizations. But the analyst's capacity to do this will depend on his or her experience with these matters in his or her own analyses. For example, on the matter of so-called "birthright envy" alluded to previously, none of the features are foreign to us: to the contrary, it is clear that the compilers of the testaments knew of it, as did Shakespeare. But as we reconstruct the events for our patients, how shall we put it to them? If we believe that envy is secondary to maternal deprivation, we tell that story. If we believe the envy is corollary to the discovery that the ownership of the breast lies with mother, we will put it that way. And if we think that babies come into the world more or less unsure of their rights to endure, propagate, and survive, and it is that which fuels envy, we will put it that way. But the data are not secure. Construction and particularly reconstruction of conjugate events are hard won. In considering the problem Meltzer (1978) put it simply. Freud, he said, used his archaeological simile to imply a layering of later communities and their structures and objects upon earlier ones, whereas for Bion such layerings bespoke signs of attempts to seal over primitive catastrophe. I have found it helpful to make a distinction between construction and reconstruction. The latter, as its name implies, refers to realizations once formed: construction refers to realizations that, when briefly juxtaposed, induce so much anxiety as to be at once undone. This leaves expectations, like loose ions, looking for realizations to which to affix. And it is these mutant bondings that create bizarre and unique relationships.

A construction concerning envy may indeed appear to take place in respect to the infant's ongoing relation to the breast. An interpretation concerning the mouth's wish to get its own back, even if it has to destroy the breast, the mouth, or the breast-mouth link in the process, would seem to be perfectly adequate. But such an interpretation is inadequate when one asks the question: what is it that makes envy such a prominent feature of the relationship? It is easy to see why the infant might want to own that breast or others just as good—the many reasons may stretch from sheer convenience to admiration to greed. But attention must be given to the inverse of any construction, what Lacan is often occupied with:

> I think where I am not, and therefore I am where I think not. . . . I am not, wherever I am, the plaything of my thought; I think of what I am wherever I don't think I am thinking. This two-faced mystery is linked to the fact that the truth can be evoked only in that dimension of alibi in which all "realism" in creative works takes its virtue from metonymy. It is likewise linked to this other fact that we accede to meaning only through the double twist of metaphor when we have the unique key: the signifier and the signified of the Saussurian formula are not at the same level, and man only deludes himself when he believes that his true place is at their axis, which is nowhere. (Lacan 1949)

and:

> A book that does not contain its counterbook is considered incomplete. (Borges 1964)

What I take Borges and Lacan to mean when they draw attention to the nether, side, real, and counter worlds is that for every realization there are intimations left unrealized but by no means dormant. Figures like Freud, Klein, Bion, Sullivan, and the like illuminated so much as to leave vast, almost impenetrable—almost unnoticeable—shadows. Bion's approving reference to Freud's letter to Lou Andreas-Salomé (E. Freud 1961, ltr. 172) in which he stated that "I have to blind myself artificially" was an attempt to look beyond the construction to the unreconstructed reconstruction. There is something here of Theseus and Medusa and his need for the mirroring shield. In the instance of the infant's envy, this might lead to the question of whether, without the breast, the infant feels ill-equipped in a universe where it is fitness that matters. Beyond the story of the *Couple* reflected in traditional renderings of envy is a story of dread in the *Pair*.

"You came into the world feeling maimed and bruised," Bion reports Klein said in her analysis of him. Of himself he says:

> My analysis pursued what I am inclined to think was a normal course: I retailed a variety of preoccupations; worry about the [his] child, the household, financial anxieties. . . . Mrs. Klein remained unmoved and unmoving. I was very glad she did, but that did not lead to the abandonment of my grievance. I suppose, reconsidering the matter I expected to be supported in what I considered to be very moderate affluence. Why and on what grounds I thought the community required my continued existence is a puzzle, especially as I am not now to be eligible in any society—socially or militarily. Melanie Klein, however, was not easily led away from her awareness of a universe that is not subject to the needs and wishes of human beings even when they came to her for analysis. . . .
>
> I was assiduous in my psychoanalytic sessions. When I was given an interpretation I used very occasionally to feel it was correct; more usually I thought it was nonsense but hardly worth arguing about since I did not regard the interpretations as anything more than the expression of one of Mrs. Klein's opinions that was unsupported by any other evidence. The interpretations that I ignored or did not understand or made no response to, later seemed to have been correct. But I did not see why I regarded them as any more correct than I had thought they were when I refuted or ignored them. The most convincing were those that appeared to be harmonized with what I knew, or what Mrs. Klein said, about my personality. . . .
>
> . . . [As] time passed I became more reconciled to the fact that not even she could be a substitute for my own senses, interpretations of what my senses told me, and choice between contradictories. I did not

become more amenable to her views but more aware of my disagreement. Nonetheless there was something about that series of experiences with her that made me feel gratitude to her and a wish to be
independent of the burden of time and expense of money and effort
involved. At last, after some years, we parted. She, I think, felt I still
had a lot to learn from her but she agreed to the termination—partly
no doubt through the realization that enough of WRB was enough.
(Bion 1985: 67–68)

There is an interplay in this reminiscence, of *Pair* concerns—
community eligibility and entitlement—and of *Couple* themes—
the nursing of grievances, the dig—"even when they came to her
for analysis." But these do not merge except in the interpretation
concerning Bion as bloodied even before birth, which plainly he
remembers as mutative and helpful. The interpretation does not
quite touch on his enduring anxiety concerning whether he is hero
or coward—the early dread that he was not to be among the
chosen was probably not quite allayed by Mrs. Klein being Kleinian. He suffered from the intimation that he was not meant to be
in the face of compelling evidence to the contrary—evidence re-
cited by his habit of listing all his memberships and honors: D.S.O.,
B.A., M.R.C.S., L.R.C.P. Mrs Klein accepted him, but "enough of
WRB was enough."

Bion's wife, Francesca, was dismayed to think that her husband's recollection of his sins was going to be the last thing we
would hear from him of himself; nevertheless, though she showed
us more of him through his letters to her and the children, this
was indeed the case (personal correspondence). It is not uncom-
mon for people who find the intimation that they are outcast and
that their best efforts are only impostures to try on a realization
of guilt instead. But confession and penance do not serve false
realizations because they become parts of the imposture—elements in the falsity of the realization. Bion had ultimately to
investigate the group, join it, move away from it, move back.

As I have myself argued, so also does Meltzer (1978):

But it is not quite clear what position Bion adopts regarding the
essential relationship of group mentality to individual mentality. In
the earlier papers where the postulate of a proto-mental system was
put forward as a tool for examining the observations it seemed likely
that the two systems were quite separate but with a linkage. This

linkage seemed to be forged in the unconscious at a juncture of narcissistic organization (though Bion does not directly suggest this) and the
basic assumptions that are in abeyance at the moment and held at the
proto-mental level. In this psycho-analytical re-view he brings the two
together by way of the Oedipus conflict and the concepts of primitive
splitting and identification processes at a part-object level (Bion, Experiences in Groups [1961], p. 162), "On the emotional plane, where
basic assumptions are dominant, Oedipal figures . . . can be discerned
in the material just as they are in a psycho-analysis. But they include
one component of the Oedipus myth of which little has been said, and
that is the sphinx."

Here is an instance where one suspects that the special qualities,
sphinx-like, of Bion have obtruded themselves on the material, but he
insists that this is inevitable where the group includes anyone with a
"questioning attitude." The fears thrown up by this attitude "approximate . . . to very primitive phantasies about the contents of the mother's body" and sets in motion defences "characteristic of the paranoid-
schizoid position." The pairing group is consequently seen as bound
closely to the primal scene at a primitive level, the dependent group to
the breast relationship as partial object, the fight-flight group to paranoid anxieties connected with splitting-and-idealization. Consequently
a continuous spectrum of degree of disturbance now is seen to link the
basic assumption group to the work group and "the more stable the
group, the more it corresponds to Freud's description of the group as a
repetition of family group patterns and neurotic mechanisms." This
has the appearance of a climbdown from a more radical position. The
emotional colouring of the basic assumption group is no longer a
manifestation of valency but can be described with the words used for
individual emotions, for "there is much to suggest that these supposed
'basic assumptions' cannot be regarded as distinct states of mind"; by
which he means distinct from one another but also from the individual
mentality, probably. Again the equivocation sounds like a climb down
in the face of the intimidating impact of the psycho-analytical basic
assumption group.

If viewed in this way the brilliance of Bion's rapprochement to
Freud's views is quite disturbing. . . . In this way group and individual
mentality are brought absolutely together as merely "special instances" of one another (p. 169), "The apparent difference between
group psychology and individual psychology is an illusion produced
by the fact that the group brings into prominence phenomena that
appear alien to an observer unaccustomed to using the group." That
sounds a very sophisticated apologia and recantation. The impression
is reinforced when Bion asserts, "I have been forced to the conclusion
that verbal exchange is a function of the work group" and that the
basic assumption group communicated its valencies and generates its
unanimity by "debased" rather than "primitive" methods, that is, its

efforts lack symbol formation and are more in the nature of actions than communications. And here he brings in the myth of the Tower of Babel, which he will come back to twenty years on. (Meltzer 1978: 15–16)

A fairly unmistakeable impression results from taking these two papers, the Re-view and Imaginary Twin, together: namely, that psychoanalytical training has had an oppressive effect upon Bion. It is perhaps one of the great limitations of this sort of training that the personal analysis takes so long to "recover from," to use a phrase Bion used in 1976 in his lecture at the Tavistock Centre. In this regard one should note that all of Bion's major publications came after the death of Melanie Klein in 1960. (Ibid., 19)

The upshot of Bion's retreat, if so it was, left him unwilling quite to take that next step which I am here taking: to wit, that basic assumption *Group*s are a realization of intimations in the basic assumption *Pair*, which in turn has the valency Meltzer thought was ultimately lacking in Bion's "re-view." In the state of mind of the *Pair*, driven by the selection principle, identifications and projective identifications are the activities of choice and bear the same compelling "numbing sense of reality" that Bion said affected the participant observer of *Group*s:

Now the experience of counter-transference appears to me to have quite a distinct quality that should enable the analyst to differentiate the occasion when he is the object of a projective identification from the occasion when he is not. The analyst feels he is being manipulated so as to be playing a part, no matter how difficult to recognize, in somebody else's phantasy—or he would do if it were not for what in recollection I can only call a temporary loss of insight, a sense of experiencing strong feelings and at the same time a belief that their existence is quite adequately justified by the objective situation. (Bion 1961: 149)

Since transference is a function of the *Couple* (being libidinous in its tropisms, functioning out of the valencies of the pleasure principle, with *Coupling*s and copulations as their medium of exchange), its "manipulations" take the form of courtship. This is true whether the *Coupling* eventuates in love or war. A shift from this is indeed discernable to the analyst or to anyone else who does not reciprocate with a countering, a transference of his own.

When a *Couple* agrees that the commodity of their interchanges in the world of affairs might fruitfully be one of mutual transferences, they are in so doing establishing a *Pairing* within which *Coupling* can take place. Bion's pairing group, it will be recalled, was one in which the participants put a full stop upon *Coupling*, which might produce an actual baby, and instead sought the realization of a new messiah.*

I merely locate this intimation where it belongs—in the selection principle, the realization for which is the perfectly evolved specimen: the ideal, the er-iest ultimate fit.

The—*clicks!* of realization are quite different for the *Pair* and for the *Couple*. In a single encounter with something or someone, several realizations can and often do take place: "She is beautiful" may be one; "she is desirable" may be another. Referring to the third party, "s/he is my rival" is one; "s/he is one of our/my sort" are others. The realization is a function of how one pays attention, more accurately to what one pays attention, because the world is not a One and Only True World (a Bionian "O"). It is a world-as-experienced adventitiously—now in one state of mind, now in another; sometimes discovered, sometimes invented; sometimes perceived, sometimes dreamed. The *Group* offers support (and good company) for certain realized versions of the world:

"Man!"
"No-no, dear, that's *Daddy*."

Alternative deployments of attention when used freely serve each realization to build up maps and memory conjunctives: "Daddy-man" sometimes in *Pair* with me and Mommy, sometimes *Couple* and rival. Watch bad! Death if in *Pair*; castration if in *Couple*. Watch good! Friend if in *Pairing*, lover if in *Couple*."

The only protection against the imprinting phenomenon is preconception. (The concept of imprinting has it that a phasic ontogenetic readiness exists. Erikson [1950] espoused this view in his

---

*Kafka's parable concerning the messiah applies here. Because he is a hope, "The Messiah will come only when he is no longer necessary; he will come only on the day after his arrival; he will come, not on the last day, but on the very last" (Kafka 1935: 81).

life-history steps in which things such as trust either happened—
click!—or did not.) The only protection against being species *un*-
specific is preconception and predilection.

   In her work on preconception, Spelke (1991) and her colleagues
have corrected Piaget in important ways. In one study, three-
month-old infants are shown a ball and a barrier. Judging from
how long and intently they look, they do not remain interested
long when they are shown the ball going over, under, or around
the barrier. But when the ball appears to go through the barrier
the infants' attention is intense and lengthy. Spelke reasons from
this and other observations that infants of this age expect solid
objects to navigate around solid barriers, but do not expect them
to go through them. This is an instance of preconceptions met and
not met: met they constitute a conception because the expectation
is complemented with the experience; unmet they constitute a
novelty, a curiosity, a wonder, or a horror.

   Whatever the merits of this critical-moment view (now or never),
it is plain that at moments there has to be a readiness in a category to become pregnant with an encounter—for the two to form
a conception. The encounter-er can be discovered (in the perceptual realm), imagined (in the ideational realm), or invented (a
function of both). This is like a self-advance camera in the hand of
a child. Any exposure could record anything, each successive exposure might record anything to add to that.

   Dreaming enables the dreamer to juxtapose the various selective realizations and refashion them into new (and old) associative
bundles, new realizations. Little discussed is the phenomenon of
the dreamer running out of dream, running out of symbols for
further realizations. The quest for re- or de-realization that prompts
the dream has run through its supply of symbolic icons. This
occurs in states of strong inhibition when attention is riveted to
observations or formulaic configurations: a sort of dream-by-num-
bers dream, like the formulas for plots of B-movies. Or it happens
in creative states when the old simply no longer applies and the
new is as yet an intimation with nothing yet to link up with.

   When that attention is not free—if it is being used selectively
to undo or prevent certain realizations, erasing links as fast as
they are made, then there occurs something like this:

P, when he travels, always goes to a tall place in the area from which he can make a tour d'horizon with his camera. He brings back a 360° diorama of the place, each photo seamlessly abutted to the next. He thus captures the whole perimeter (of mountains, sea, etc.) which he can then reconstruct for his pleasure and presumably that of friends and relatives. This ritual is organized to keep any intrusive object from getting on the recorder and interrupting the sequence. Though it is by no means obvious from this story, the intrusive object is P's mother's "castration," later, mastectomy. The focus on the perimeter and not on the center of the scene also represents an effort not to let the primal scene recur. These efforts, because belated, use the new record to screen against the resurgence of the old, which travel stirs up. But the old has, of course, already happened— P's film has a thousand and one recordings of it.

In associating, which P, naturally, is reluctant to do and "does" by various kept-quiet "systems" of likings and order, there is the constant breakthrough of the grotesque—as if his slide-show montage of mountain views suddenly revealed an elbow or a pubic mass, Oedipus' sphinx.

There are early dark wildernesses that he recorded and linked with preconceptions to form realizations, the language of which, visual and ideational, he has now long forgotten.

A dream: a man, a torso: a man from the waist up, naked. He has a hernia or something punching out the skin in or around his belly button. He is putting on a show, doing contortions. He pushes this thing out and then takes it in. Now he moves it. He presses on his belly button and then whatever it is sticks out of his mouth. Coming out of his mouth it could be a piece of feces, a penis, or a baby. Then he covers his mouth and it pushes out from below again. Like a cuckoo clock or one of those cuckoo clocks where one figure appears, disappears, then another comes out in its place.

So the images remain there for the contortionists. P's photos are aesthetic approximations of scenes that as a youngster he could fashion only crudely. P is himself the result of nine prenatal months of improvement (in one phase of which the idea of a tail had merit and succeeding phases when it did not), thirty years more or less of postnatal work. His successive series of selves are all fashioned as improvements on their former function and structure—sometimes done with such urgency as to be the product of revo- rather than evo-lutionary procedure. These selves are designed to bear no resemblance to their earlier drafts. The earlier drafts show themselves as deliberate absences, uses of 90° or 180° where much less might have done—as if the tail had not merely to be suppressed but its very partial emergence countered by an enlargement of wing bones.

Being Ψs, we are accustomed to riffling through this photo album of the past, seeing the chubby baby turn into the slender child who takes on puppy fat at nine and at eleven seems to be all nose—outgrowing these characteristics, however, by age seventeen. There are also the massive discontinuities in which the child no longer "takes after" the child who is fathering and mothering him. In psychoanalysis, we have to reintroduce those children: "Age 4, please say hello to age 5. Age 5 was very troubled by what you gave him to work with, 4; and 5, 4 feels you turned your back on his intentions about being five and the way even being grown up ought to be, and that you ruthlessly imposed your own will on it. So naturally you will feel uneasy with one another at first. I'll stay, just in case, act as translator. You, 32, please also stay and help your forebears make (realize) some kind of nonmurderous exchange." 4 months will sooner or later plunge into the act. What happened to his or her realizations in the throes of succession?

> P at 28 is newly in a love affair in "real" life. In "analytic" life P is just reexperiencing the events of a very early version of the primal scene that was very exciting, frightening, and infuriating. For example, P can't wait to have sex with L[over], but when they are engaged in sex, P feels murderous and does something to interrupt it. P and L then stalk moodily about the house, still neglected children, now also thwarted parents.

The sexual activity itself also shows great disagreements between the "personalities" involved both in P (and therefore inevitably in

L), and who does what and with which and to whom, and how and for how long. These "personalities" are conformed around realizations. As once these realizations were shopped for in fantasy and encounter, or both, in order for intimation or preconception to reach the mental domain (if only promptly to be repressed or edited, split, sundered, condensed, displaced, etc.), now it has to be rediscovered and its fragments glued together.

P at age 20 and in the second year of his analysis became nearsighted and needed to wear glasses. This was physiologically quite idiopathic and psychologically puzzling until P was to recall that a carved wooden box of discarded and keepsake eyeglasses was kept on a dresser at the head of his crib. Ever since he could pull himself up to stand he would look through these and watch his elder brother and sister with whom he shared a room. But as it turned out what he could see in eyeglasses was not the spectacle he sought. He went from eyeglasses to binoculars, finally purchasing a telescope with which at last he could watch sexual acts at a distance.

At length, like the separate slides on a stereopticon, the current set of images converged with the early one and the slightly blurred close-up from his crib and the telescope became one.

Memories of the actual intercourse began to be remembered partially, but at night P would dream that he was blind and all around him was black. Though during these months P enjoyed a "normal" sexual relationship, it didn't have the excitement value of his scoptic encounters. This disappointment led him to quiz his wife closely on *her* previous sexual engagements, all of which he had known of, but each of which, in the current re-realization, stimulated a great deal of jealousy. In the face of such jealousy, P's wife balked at yet further tales, so P began jealously "egging" her on toward an affair. He wanted a close-up and present tense of a primal scene of which he could be part. As this became more deeply felt and recognized by him, he and his wife, on a visit abroad, had the concierge of their hotel arrange a sexual performance for them to witness. However, their anxiety throughout this show was such as to prevent them from enjoying it: it had been set up such that it was known they were watching: indeed they were invited to participate. But of course nothing could match the Brobdingnagian experience of the original realizations, and this caused P a great sense of loss and a fiercer envy of his wife as the woman in the lovemaking. The blacking-out in the dreams combined envy with falling asleep; the blindness combined castration and a refusal to look. Alongside all of this was the intimation that new babies were being fashioned in the parental intercourse that might confiscate his rights to live on.

Early conceptions have a good deal of power in so far as they are closer to first predilections. People need the time and latitude to grow out of this. These early conceptions either evolve or lie layered as in Freud's metaphor, outgrown before they are grown out of, and thus living an enduringly questing life of their own. The older child forgets them, but not they him.

This of course belabors the ego: nothing it can later find for the earlier formed conceptions will be good enough. Indeed the ego enviously staves off possible rival realizations as a wife might a mistress. The eventual consent to employ words, language, and speech as realizations marks a real concession: it is in this sense Freud and Bion valued the word.

The continued "life," first of intimations and then of realizations, produces a state that absolutely requires choice. Choice, however, means the renunciation of greed. Greed is an intimation in itself that functions within the *Pair* pushing against the *Couple*'s wish for now and soon again. Not so simply, greed cries, not so soon. Wait for better. Let not good be good enough. The threats to greed are the appetites, which in their nature can be satisfied.

Hope travels with greed. It seems to promise a time and event in which both pleasure and beauty can be satisfied at once and in the same realization. It opposes itself to desire, for desire pulls the trigger and discharges lust and longing; yet for that very reason hope needs desire to consummate its own longings.

This takes us back to the fail-safe of the original preconception and its need not to—*click!* and lock onto boots like Lorenz's (1966) ducklings. It must, as best it can, keep good, in the pleasure principle sense, from surrendering to better, in the selection principle sense, before it can reach best. Once best is known and then either found or relinquished, this need to wait and find better realization holds pleasure-taking in bondage.

Inter-cut, in the cinematographic sense, with representations of what has been mentally conceived are representations of what has not been: preconceptions without realization—proto-configurations of absences that are present: no-things. These inhabit the domain of unconscious or proto-conscious fantasy; they are part of the slide show, but they show up like transparencies: they are hallucinatory in nature; in dream language we might call them archival dream fragments awaiting the day-residue with which to meld and lead to a realization. Bion called some of these Beta elements, awaiting transfiguration into Alpha status in order to become mental: he thought that these elements had the status of *da sein*—things that needed transmutation or else they stood about in the thinking streams with everything else bumping into and off of them, causing turbulence and turmoil. When one blinds oneself to the detritus thrown up by the absence of what one expected, one gradually becomes aware of the shape and order of the expectation. This is not quite the same as reading between the lines; perhaps it can be thought of as what would be there were the lines and their spaces not there.

> P : First you tell me to talk of and not about what I experience. Now you tell me I might hold off even with the "of" to see what then occurs. But I am damned if I will do so. That leads to madness. Of this image. Oh God, I Can't Stand This.

A certain amount of sputter takes place—fussing, fuming. What is it that *is* OK? Is this it?

The dialectic of selection and pleasure take their disputations into the dream life as well.

P recalls his first wet dream; it was of a girl far less enchanting than he wished. Pleasure stole the night from hope.

is amidst the primal scene. As a result he cannot make sense of his new relationship. No matter how he thinks of himself and his new woman friend, it doesn't make sense. He wants to be the only one to make love to her, and he is. He wants her to bear his child, but she is more than willing. He feels nothing he can produce is worth anything, yet she admires him greatly and shows him off to her friends. It is imperative that she select him and when she does she becomes quite the wrong person: he does not want membership in that club.

P is also in the primal scene, which he knows to be a failure of his, for his mother told him so. Accordingly he stays quite drunk most of the time, because that state of being seems best to approximate the one he is in most of the time; this enables him to feel more sane and at one with himself. Sober he feels drunk. At times when he is very, very drunk, he takes photographs, often of the same object, often of an old, derelict building. Something is bound to emerge: it is like leaving the lens open so as not to miss something growing, changing, or dying. His lens is open; he washes his sand-papered irises with booze. What will emerge? Could anything be worse than already knowing?

The appetitive, recurring requirement of the pleasure ego or *Couple* are in their natural quantities. Whether to restore homeostasis or to propel the sluggish uncertain selection-ego or pair-formation. The nature of the impulse is attuned to attaining a peak Uhm-oh!-Ah. . . . The selection ego is in some people bestirred by the rising of the estrus sap. But it is more generally greedy for things which, though presented qualitatively, can be acquired quantitatively. There is, of course, no sharp line of delineation between these. As Aristotle noted in his *Poetics,* when speaking of the particular requirements of miniatures, the domain has its own exigencies. But certainly sheer quantity is not enough to convey the implication that something more must excite the utopian imagination. But on the other hand,

> Big thinkers are subject to big obsessions. Their eyes are fixed on the positive evidence. Their busy minds expand theories, extrapolate hypotheses, and invent logical structures, perhaps scenarios, even plots, at stroboscopic speed. Paranoia [becomes] the only secure guard against delusion . . . a double focussed awareness of symbol. (Adams 1989)

7. Realization

D. Marcus Beach, a poet and philosopher, though as yet unpublished on the present subject, finds realizations of no small beauty. He is quite mad but he does not seem altogether to mind it. Neither does he especially resent that sane people think him to be psychotic. He does, however, insist that perceiving things differently than other people does not disqualify the validity and worth that inhere in his unique access to meanings and intents. Not long ago I received from him a small treatise on his researches in response to some of my own work, including my paper, "Beyond the Reality Principle" (Boris 1990), which he felt represented me beyond the usual openness of traditional psychoanalysis. I think his studies of himself provide a most helpful guide to how realizations come to be formed; the relationship between intimation and realization takes the form of a quest, a pilgrimage, a crusade even, when it is not taking the form of a revelation, a suddenly-it-hit-me, an "Ah-ha!" an "Oh-ho" or an "Uh-oh." He writes:

> And for the madman himself, the arrival of insanity is always apocalyptic; the familiar world does, in his consciousness, come to an end. In its place another world, however temporary, springs into being with all the vividness, and with all the tight though invisible logic of any Book of Revelations. The words—the symbols—he finds in that new other-world can be brought back and interpreted in *this* everyday realm, which he continues to inhabit despite its sudden ending in his consciousness.
>   The relation of Original and Final is also a travelogue, this time

through time. It represents intimation as having occurred and realization as yet to come. In this structure Realization looks backwards to creation. The past informs the future: original sin shows the path to redemption; Paradise lost the way to Paradise regained. In these theologies as in scientific cosmologies, there is a Big Bang when everything explodes and the universe is formed out of the chaos; life is formed; man is formed; consciousness is formed. The same script of first principles applies.

It does not matter whether the originology features Vishnu floating on his back producing Buddha, or a state of perfect equipoise being invaded by one small disturbing speck that irrupts the vacuum and produces the bang; or an oceanic narcissistic state gone "phutt" when the infant discovers the otherness of the Other. These are but different realizations for a confluence between what once was and must become once more. The Beginning and the End have the same characteristic: stasis. Before and After have the same condition: perfection. Between them lies struggle—revolution and evolution. The species go from the perfection of the original conception to a destiny of which the nature will be signalled by no further need to change, develop, and evolve.

Spelke (1991), from her studies of earliest infancy, makes the observation that it is in the nature of these intimations to guide what can be experienced from among worlds and realms of potential experience that we barely know what we do not know. She suggests, for example, that as human beings we are oriented to think and notice the relationships among middle-sized bodies to the extent that thinking about large bodies, like stars, and small ones, like subatomic particles and waves, does not come naturally to us. As I hope I have shown, the scripts for science, art, religion, and nature tend to have the same plot lines; such realizations are governed by the preconceived nature of the intimations.

This does not reduce to "we find what we look for" but it does say we are much relieved to find what we have been a long time looking for—namely, what that perfection is that we are in some sense supposed to look for, where we find it, and how we know when we have it.

Idealization is so frequently a trait of infancy and thereafter that its defensive functions have been the object of much study (cf. Morrison 1989). But at its simplest, idealization rests on a denial that that is no more and no less than this and this no better than that. In respect to such a stasis, one can go two ways: one can resign one's self and simply be, or one can deny the impoverishment of possibility and recapture hope from the depths of despair by turning from discovery to invention. Inventiveness provides one with newer and better realizations. And these in turn enable one still to become and no longer bound (only) to be.

The one intimation that one might think cannot be undiscovered is death, which as time passes travels closer. In the joke: an old man lies dying, his beloved daughter at his bedside, his beloved wife in the kitchen from which there emanates wonderful aromas. "Be a darling," the old man says to his daughter. "Ask mother to give you some little noshes for me." The daughter returns. "Mama says no—that it is for after." Now he has realizations concerning "after" and "later."

Freud wrote:

> It is indeed impossible to imagine our own death; and whenever we attempt to do so we can perceive that we are in fact still present as spectators. Hence the psychoanalytic school could venture on the assertion that at bottom no one believes in his own death, or, to put the same thing in another way, that in the unconscious everyone is convinced of his own immortality. (1915b)

There is a way in which this is true. One of the intimations of the selection principle is lineage. Our own narcissistic personal life becomes irrelevant after the raising of our own progeny, unless or until the grandchildren come into the picture. Now they are to be the incarnations of ourselves and our *Group* (read species). It is they now who extend us through later to after.

But there is a way in which only the intimations of death galvanize the quest. As Dr. Johnson said, "The prospect of execution doth wonderfully concentrate the mind."

"But all of memory or anticipation is like this," Freud goes on to say. "After a certain age, we look back or forward upon ourselves from the perspective of an onlooker."

Winnicott partly disagrees: "In the total unconscious fantasy belonging to growth at puberty and in adolescence, there is *the death of someone*" (1986: 159, emphasis his). Elsewhere he adds:

Population has to be thought of another way, because we can no longer leave it to God, so to speak, to kill everybody, though of course we can have a war and people can kill each other off that way. If we're going to be logical, we're going to talk about a very difficult subject, which is: what babies do we kill off? (Ibid., 204)

My own view is that there is, upon psychological viability, whether before birth or after, an intimation of whatever death is. We apply this intimation to the Self until that stage or age arrives when we regard others as other than ourselves. This dreadful apprehension might be characterized by adding to my words, "Now is," those of Beckett, "—Now not."

"There is the death of someone," Winnicott says, but *of whom?*

I have taken this digression to set up what Professor Beach has written. The very rich material is likely to immediately call up metarealizations on the part of those who read it. These realizations mainly concern the *Couple*, and so the anxieties of love, hatred, and jealousy in the primal scene. But were we artificially to blind ourselves to these, realizations concerning the *Pair* will emerge as stars emerge when the sun goes down. Recalling that preconceptions precede and in part determine experiences, realizations in the *Pair* for love will be an outgrowth of "she walks the ground I worship."

Regarding Beach's writings, then, let us take our lead from Beckett's words: "that alleged life then he had had invented remembered a little of each no knowing that thing up above he gave it to me I made it mine what I fancied skies especially roads especially...."

From *Windows of Insanity:*

Early one morning, before the other patients had entered the dayroom, I engaged in an unusual and memorable "conversation" with my devout friend, Sonja. I myself was in a semi-delusory state of mind, and the objects around me therefore seemed pregnant with significance. Sonja was still acting out her fantasies, and she carried with her a plastic bag full of personal belongings which, for her, possessed special "occult powers." She began to arrange some of these items on a large, round table, whereupon I became fascinated, picked up some object at random, and placed it alongside the pattern she was forming. Sonja responded by setting down another of her "sacred tokens" beside my talisman. We were both hooked on the "dialogue" which had begun. I collected, from around the room, certain objects which bore consummate significance for me, and the two of us engaged in a "game," taking turns putting items on the table in positions that gave them further significance in relation to what had already been laid out. The game went on until Sonja's bag was empty and the table was covered with two interlocking symbolic arrays. What struck me afterwards about this curious "conversation" was, first, the totally engrossing mood it had created for both of us and second, the fact that not one of the "moves" had meant the same thing for one as it had for the other. Not only were the "denotations" of the items different for each of us, but even the "connotations," so far as we knew, did not overlap. The game had been like a bit of dialogue in a play of Chekov's; deep personal feelings had moved right through the expressions of the other without establishing contact or common ground. And yet, at the same time, the interplay had a coherent form. Each move meant *some*thing —and something for each of us. We were developing our own private thought, our own delusory systems; and if we did not "decode" each other's motions, we nonetheless shared—indeed, created mutually—a common pattern of play, the game itself as it took on form. This mutual form, this shared activity, brought us into a sort of intimacy, and we respected each move the other made, even though we gave it a misinterpretation or at least an alternate interpretation. In our isolated "devoutnesses" we communed perhaps more closely than many "conventional rituals" allow their participants to do, for we shared a potent sense of understanding and we participated freely. "I came in here for a big reason," Sonja had told me, and who can say that, as she manipulated her personal symbols and incorporated mine into her fantasy, those reasons did not deepen and enlarge? Our unlikely "conversation" had clarified and developed my own. (Beach 1991)

There is in this a hint of parallel play, of children playing side by side not with one another so much as to one another. They converse, but they do not speak. They are enacting the *Pair* version of being so identified that they can converse without needing to speak. Their conversation enacted less the contents than the structure of meaning—"the game itself as it took on form." The "devoutness" of which Beach writes is used to express a communion with what Sonja calls "the big event," and Beckett called "that thing up above."

In writing this section Beach has invoked the narrative genre: Once upon a Time, or In the Beginning was the. . . . Of narrative, Trilling writes:

It is in the nature of narrative to explain, it cannot help telling how things are and even why they are. . . . But a beginning implies an end with something in the middle to connect them. The beginning is not merely the first of a series of events; it is the event that originates the events that follow. And the end is not merely the ultimate event, the cessation of happening; it is a significance or at least the promise, dark or bright, of a significance. (1972: 135–36)

So the form follows the function: this is a religious tale, written in the religious vein of devotional matters. It is an assertion of hope ("Each move meant *some*thing—and something for each of us"), of charity and faith, his to hers, hers to his "deep personal feelings [that] had moved right through the expressions of the other without establishing contact or common ground. And yet. . . ." Thus the *Pair* shared hope where otherwise there might have been anarchy, chaos, and babble. Or the emergence of the state of mind *Couple*.

The first insanity . . . came upon me while I was conducting a seminar of ten students in their first year at the university. In my daily life I had been growing "higher and higher" for several weeks but was fully under control when the class began a two-hour discussion of Doris Lessing's *The Four-Gated City*, a novel in which insanity is one of the central concerns. For the first hour, the class proceeded smoothly, yet I felt a strange quiet—a hush—upon all our words. When we stopped for a coffee break, the students began talking of a controversial poster someone had, that morning, hung in the hallway outside. I went out to look at it and seeing it brought to a conclusion the process that was already underway in my mind: the violent image "put me over the edge."

The poster depicted a mob of women; the surface of the paper represented a glass window, and the mob, fiercely shattering that window, appeared to be coming "straight out of the picture," about to attack the viewer. My mind, now in an altered state, attributed to the poster a reality it did not have; I felt myself to be in immediate danger, and I cast about me for some sort of magical protection.

Earlier that morning, I had posted on the door of my office a sticker reading "Ecology Now," and that door happened to stand at the far end of the hall, facing the offensive poster. The two symbols opposed each other, each with its special potency, the one threatening and the other beneficent. I sensed that it was the function of the ecology emblem to keep the violent crowd of women at bay, and I believed that it had the power to do so.

With this mortal tension in the background, I returned to class. As I walked through the halls I was acutely aware of the people . . . ; their movements seemed . . . almost a cosmic dance. Picking up the rhythm of such chance encounters I entered my seminar room and at once began the second hour by reading out a notice about a Halloween party to be given the next week by another of the seminars. It was during this reading that my delusion came upon me in a specific and overwhelming form. It occurred to me suddenly that the notice I was reading actually constituted a message in cypher, and with that realization I became aware, as I thought, of its true though hidden meaning. Between the lines, the sentences said: "This world (the universe) will come to an end in one hour unless a symbol can be found which embodies a value having the special power to save it." I took it for granted that my students—indeed, everyone existing—had grasped this "true state of affairs" at just the moment I had perceived it myself. The notice of an ostensible Halloween party was serving as a sort of universal announcement. A crisis had emerged and there was no time to lose. I precipitously embarked on my share of the task now at hand, my personal role in the "game of survival" being played the world over for dire and cosmic stakes.

. . . My first venture was to propose the "saving value," love—the polar opposite, as I now see it, of the hatred expressed by the mob breaking out of the poster. I spoke of the various kinds of love, ranging from attraction between the sexes to universal affection and benevolence. I connected love with creativity and individual talent by going around the semi-circle of students, telling each one in turn what I had noticed of his or her abilities and strengths. At some point during this lecture on love, I was distracted by an art magazine lying on a nearby table. I picked it up, opened it, and, upon seeing the Alhambra and the Egyptian pyramids on facing pages, was instantly gripped by what might be called an intense "cultural claustrophobia."

The pictures wanted liberating. They required adequate space in which to express their own full meanings, for those meanings seemed to me both immediate and real. Furthermore, each picture carried a set of social values which had, at some time and place in history, proved productive and viable; and each picture, therefore, could be a valid bid in the urgent search for "a symbol which would save the world." And so I thereupon engaged in feverish activity which on the surface appears destructive but was actually according to its motivations, part of my constructive endeavours: I tore the pages out of the magazine and cast them about on the floor. Each page, thus given liberty, decreased the "cultural claustrophobia" which had come over me and, more important, made available to whatever Powers were overseeing the "contest for the world's existence" another alternative for "the saving value."

While I was thus pursuing, in my private manner, the theme of love and civilization, a further recognition entered my mind as suddenly and as authoritatively as had the original "decoding" of the message contained in the Halloween announcement. Bluntly, it was this: This game is a trick! No single value, or set of values, can save the world; none ever has once and for all. The solution to the puzzle is not to find a new symbol or myth but, on the contrary, to *demythologize,* as completely as possible—to strip away all the falsifications carried by symbols we conventionally adopt. And it also came to me immediately that my own clothing, which covered my actual form, consisted of just such "symbols" and bespoke the "myths" of my society. The surest and most efficacious way of continuing the contest upon which the fate of the universe depended was therefore to demonstrate "demythologizing" in the manner closest to my own being: to take off my clothes and thus discard the "illusions" of my society in which I, like everyone else, had encased myself.

First, I emptied my pockets and tossed away my pipe and tobacco. Then I disrobed. I do not know what I talked about while I was removing my clothes, but I do recall that I threw each item as far from me as I could; it was essential to distance the demythologized self from the remnants of its cultural cloak of delusions. When I had finished I noticed my wristwatch, and I remember saying: "Ah, I forgot to take off time." The students tell me that I placed the watch with gentleness on the floor in front of my feet. Looking back, I sense an appropriateness in that gesture. Would not the *ultimate* demystification be precisely the removal of time itself? But do we desire to sacrifice time? Without it, there could be nothing at all—no developing reality on which to found the many personal and social appearances which, as time goes on, prove to be false or inadequate. If we must take off the symbol of time, let us by all means preserve it carefully.

Soon after my disrobing, the students began to file out of the room, singly or in pairs. One young man stayed behind and helped me collect my clothing, which I put on without haste. As we picked up the loose coins I had scattered around the room we exchanged, as I recall, our favourite paradoxes. And that, too, seemed appropriate because, in my mind, the whole hour—the quest for the symbol that would prevent annihilation—had been based upon an antinomy, its first term buried in the Halloween notice and its second term contained in my disrobing. For the salvation of this vast universe, the only meaning which will do is that which has no meaning whatsoever. The very notion of value rests on such a paradox.

Beach describes intimation rather as other writers and artists describe in*spir*ation. Beach hears the tap-tap-tapping of the intimations, but these have failed to evolve from what Bion called Beta- to Alpha-elements. For Beach, these are stimulated by an encounter with a woman exuding hostility and menace. He despairs of the realizations that begin to form; he hates these, they frighten him. He has to find an antidote. After some struggle he finds a nullifying realization in the "Ecology Now" poster. With it holding the fort, he has a brief respite, which he puts to use by stripping off any and all realizations.

> Bluntly, it was this: This game is a trick! No single value, or set of values, can save the world; none ever has once and for all. The solution to the puzzle is not to find a new symbol or myth but, on the contrary, to *demythologize*, as completely as possible—to strip away all the falsifications carried by symbols we conventionally adopt.

Now he need no longer attempt to *de*-realize the persecuting insistence of the intimations with counter-myths. He demythologizes all symbols, his own good ecology myths as well as those represented in the poster of the women. By considering this in *Pair* terms we can see the intimations that drive the realizations as expressive of issues at the heart of natural selection:

> [E]very genotype is a compromise between various selection pressures, some of which may be opposed to each other, as for instance, sexual selection and crypsis or predator protection. (Mayr 1982: 589)

> Altruism is usually defined as an activity that benefits another individual (the "recipient") to the seeming disadvantage of the altruist. Haldane pointed out that an altruistic trait would be favored by natural selection if the beneficiary was sufficiently closely related, so that his survival benefitted the genes which he shared with the altruist. For instance, if there is 1 chance in 10 that an altruistic act would cost the life of the altruist, but the beneficiaries were the children, siblings, or grandchildren of the altruist, with all of whom he shares more that 10 percent of his genes, selection would favor the development of altruism. This particular form of selection has also be designated as kin selection, and the fitness which refers to all the carriers of the same (or similar) genotype is known as inclusive fitness. Haldane's rather simple theory has since been elaborated by Hamilton, Trivers, Maynard Smith, G. C. Williams, Alexander, West-Eberhard, and many others and has become part of sociobiology. (Ibid., 598)

> In many cases success simply consists in becoming different or more different, thus reducing competition. Darwin *(Origin:* 111) saw this clearly when he proposed the principle of character divergence. It promotes continuous change, but not necessarily progress. Indeed, it

has induced endless phyletic lineages to enter evolutionary deadend streets. (Ibid., 533)

These are of course scientific realizations of the intimations of the data. I have earlier called attention to the framework of science as itself a realization of intimations, such that scientific realizations are very akin to religious and artistic ones. Beach's urgent concerns reflect hostilities on an almost cosmic scale, so he too moves from religion to science in his attempts to offset the dark struggles he envisions. For Beach also has had bred into him the idea that he carries a responsibility for the welfare and perfectibility of the species:

> "*And time will actually have passed*, for we can remove its insignia but never step out of its ever-embracing actuality."

Muriel Spark, in *The Comforters* (1957), meditated on the experience of intimations becoming realizations:

> "How do you know the words come from the Blessed Virgin?" Caroline persisted relentlessly. Mrs. Hogg moved her upper lip into an indecent smile. Caroline thought: "She desires the ecstasy of murdering me in some prolonged ritualistic orgy; she sees I am thin, angular, sharp, enquiring: she sees I am grisly about the truth; she sees I am well-dressed and good-looking. Perhaps she senses my weakness, my loathing of human flesh where the bulk outweighs the intelligence...."
>   ... Just then she heard the sound of a typewriter. It seemed to come through the wall on her left. It stopped, and was immediately followed by a voice remarking her own thoughts. It said: On the whole she did not think there would be any difficulty with Helena.
>   ... A typewriter and a chorus of voices: "What on earth are they up to at this time of night?" Caroline wondered.
>   ... Then it began again, the voices: Caroline ran out on to the landing, for it seemed quite certain the sound came from that direction. No one was there. The chanting reached her as she returned to her room, with these words exactly:
>   "*What on earth are they up to at this time of night?*" *Caroline wondered. But what worried her were the words they had used, coinciding so exactly with her own thoughts.*
>   And then the typewriter again: tap-tap-tap. She was rooted. "My God!" she cried aloud. "Am I going mad?" (37, 47–48)

In Spark's reconstruction, the inconclusiveness as to which is intimation and which is realization echoes an impression of cannibalism in the *Couple:*

> Caroline thought: "She desires the ecstasy of murdering me in some prolonged ritualistic orgy; she sees I am thin, angular, sharp, enquiring: she sees I am grisly about the truth; she sees I am well-dressed and good-looking. Perhaps she senses my weakness, my loathing of human flesh where the bulk outweighs the intelligence. . . ."

This is quite lively. But a deadness enters in with the repetitive reproduction of the words typed, sung, and spoken. One generation is just like the previous one, a theme taken up once more in Spark's *The Prime of Miss Jean Brody.*

As in the state of affairs, so in the state of mind: Oliver Sacks (1990) writes, quoting Bartlett:

> Remembering is not the re-excitation of innumerable fixed, lifeless and fragmentary traces. It is the imaginative reconstruction, or construction, built out of the relation of our attitude towards a whole active mass of organized past reactions or experience, and to a little outstanding detail which commonly appears in image or in language form. It is thus hardly ever really exact, even in the most rudimentary cases of role recapitulation, and it is not at all important that it should be so. (47)

Of his own thinking he goes on to say,

> It is characteristic of a creature, in contrast to a computer, that nothing is ever precisely repeated or reproduced; that there is, rather, a continual revision and reorganization of perception and memory, so that no two experiences (or their neural bases) are ever precisely the same. Experience is ever-changing, like Heraclitus' stream. This streamlike quality of mind and perception, of consciousness and life, cannot be caught in any mechanical model—it is only possible in an *evolving* creature.
>
> Darwin provided a picture of the evolution of species; Edelman has provided a picture of the evolution of the individual nervous system as it reflects the life experience of each individual human being. The nervous system adapts, is tailored, evolves, so that experience, will, sensibility, moral sense, and all that one would call personality or soul becomes engraved in the nervous system. The one result is that one's brain is one's own. One is not an immaterial soul, floating around in a

machine. I do not feel alive, psychologically alive, except insofar as a stream of feeling—perceiving, imagining, remembering, reflecting, revising, recategorizing runs through me. *I am that stream—that stream is me.* (Sacks 1990: 49, emphasis mine)

With this last observation, no one could agree more, I think, than Beach:

The following summer, while I was on vacation and immediate pressures were off, I once again "went over the edge." For a week or so I had been gradually moving toward another delusory world and then one evening, without anticipating the event, I committed an act which took me beyond the second taboo. My father had died a few months before and I had received his ashes which were contained in a plain cardboard box. I kept them on a shelf in a closet, awaiting an opportunity to scatter them in a patch of woods he had enjoyed. As I sat that evening, with my thoughts drifting at random, I suddenly found myself engaged in a makeshift ritual I did not at the time fully understand. As if caught by automatic movement and without planning or even deliberating on what I was doing, I moved the box from the closet and cut a small square hole in the bottom of it. Into the hole I carefully inserted a plastic replica of a mermaid, one of those tokens that are hung on the rims of glasses in lounges and bars. The mermaid, which took on intense symbolic meaning for me, represented my mother who had died years before; she had been born under the sign of Aquarius (a water sign) and had loved the ocean as my father had loved the woods. And, as the plastic mermaid "partook" of my mother's being, so the ashes in the cardboard box still constituted for me the being of my father. My ritual act, without premeditation and *gaining* significance as it proceeded, was contrived to reunite my parents. It became, as the action developed, much more than an idle symbolism; the spirits as well as the emblems were present for me and, once the mermaid was lost among the ashes, the two spirits blended with each other or, I should say, became one. What appeared on the surface to me an irreverent gesture was in fact, in the actuality of my growing insanity, an integral way in which my own spirit could join into that union and thus hold communion with theirs. By the next morning my delusion of "transubstantiation" had increased; having begun my "meddling" with the departed and having found it refreshing to my spirit, it was easy to continue the fantasy. I placed the box in the middle of the living room floor and enlarged the aperture I had made the night before. The container of ashes now stood as a sort of memorial monument, but a monument having a special power to transform what it contained into "living spirit. . . ." And, in my vision, the domain of the dead was not

remote from the physical world I still inhabited but rather interpene-
trated it in some manner I could not fully comprehend. I had fleeting
impressions of the connection from time to time, and the monument
itself seemed to stand as a permanent link.

This belief in the two parallel realms, at that time an unquestioned
certainty in my dislocated mind, guided my actions for several days.
Through the opening in the box I sent various "talismen" to my parents in the alternative domain. Yet the donations were more than
talismen; I was convinced that a replica of each item I inserted would
immediately become available to my mother or my father, and my
task was to select offerings which would assist them in their present
spiritual activities. For my father, for instance, I put in a block from a
mathematical puzzle which I believed would allow him to gain victory
in a contest which presently engaged him and bore not only on his
continued existence but also upon this world and upon my own mun-
dane destiny. For my mother I put in a rose I had plucked in a neighboring garden and, as I did so, the sense of "transubstantiation" grew
so strong that I found myself eating a handful of petals rescued from
the flower. They were, so to speak, the "host" in a special family
Eucharist, and their taste seemed to give me freshness and strength.

Nor was the passage of the "spirit" and its magical embodiments
one-way; if I contributed bits of this world to my ancestors they, in
turn, were constantly sending offerings to me. I spent hours looking
through family photographs; each picture seemed to come alive as a
living episode, quickened by the "spirit" from the alternate realm, and
I wrote on the backs of the photographs phrases and quotations which
came spontaneously into my head and which thereupon became efficacious parts of the encompassing "spirit" which my ancestors, from
their secure yet adventurous positions in another but interlocking world,
were freely extending to me.

After three days of intense symbolic activity centred around the
monument I arranged to enter a hospital and, once there, my concern
turned from communication with another realm to reorientation within
this present world. I spent a good deal of time studying the announce-
ments and clippings posted on the hospital bulletin board, believing
that each item was a sort of map and would tell me something about
"where I was and what I was doing." By looking closely I could make
out, on each map, my own current location. Yet a problem remained:
how could I determine *where the map itself was positioned in the world?*
This was my chief puzzle and, to solve it, I required the assistance
(which by now I could rely upon) of the ancestors in the other realm.
For none of us, with our limited perspectives, can know our exact
relation to "everything else" unless some agency from a more containing "universe" supplies us with the information we require.

And so I began to interpret *all* objects as if they were maps—and, in a sense not totally remote, many objects in a mental hospital are, in some way, guiding charts. I had the vision that the hospital was a ship at sea and I called upon my mother and my father—all my ancestors —to inform me just how my environment of maplike objects were meaningfully placed on the ocean those maps themselves pretended to represent. Little by little my course in orientation progressed and, eventually, I returned to an "ordinary" state of mind. Yet, even then, the sense of union—or of significant exchange—between myself and my forebears left in me an undercurrent of joy—the feeling that the world as we know it is somehow a "transubstantiation" of something still more encompassing stayed with me for the remainder of that summer. Are not Love and Death the best—perhaps the only—landmarks we have by which to orient our lives? And once we accept this fact, are not Love and Death precisely the terrain within which we must orient ourselves? Human navigation through life requires a certain sleight-of-hand. Can we therefore afford to reject *any* magic, whatever its sources that can help us with this tricky but inescapable business?

Once the mates have more or less met one another's realization —have walked upon the ground each worships—a "tricky business," indeed—they are ready to reproduce. But they will also want the "best" for their children; that is, their loving wish and their charge. They will want the best obstetrician, the best pediatrician, the best caretakers—nurses, schools friends, camps, colleges, and clubs. Then the best marriage to the best mate and then the best for the children of that mating—all also tricky choices. Like will seek like and the model will be More of the Same or As Different As Can Be. Somewhere there is a jet-black Greyling, a Platonic ideal, an Ur, an O, an Om, a God-head—an er-iest.

But who knows what these are—except for knowing they are there? Pins and needles of intimations tickle the soul—but who goeth there? Does the sphere of plasticene contain more than the snake made of the sphere, the taller, thinner glass more than the squat fat jar? Again and again the experimenters show their young subjects that both contain the same, but the children don't like just-the-sames. Their pulses are set for more and less, and as any child can tell you from the several cultures Piaget and his co-workers tested, taller is better than shorter and lengthier is better than all rolled up. Bigger *is*—and it looks like *that!* But he hadn't set out to measure preconceptions; his own "bigger" were improvements in conceptualization. But do predilections go away? Piaget's did not. Looking at infant behavior (Spelke 1991) through another twist of the kaleidoscope yields an abundance of new questions.

8. On Influence

Of the several themes in D. Marcus Beach's manuscript, perhaps the most reiterative are those of influence and being influenced:

> One morning, after a night of dark fantasies, I awakened with the Voices in my ear. They warned me urgently that I was in great danger and must leave the city immediately. And so, instead of fixing breakfast and going to daycare, I drove in some haste to a town about fifty miles away and, following the direction of the Voices, parked in a run-down section outside the main residential area. For most of that day I wandered aimlessly around the streets, feeling deeply—and frequently reminded by the Voices—that under no circumstances was I to return home. Giving a false name I enquired for a job in several auto-part stores and at a small factory. I felt myself to be a displaced person or "tramp," and must have acted the part for the business proprietors did not welcome me. But still I kept on seeking employment, for Doctor Zee's (Beach's therapist) admonition to cease sinning by "getting back to work" must have been fermenting somewhere within me. I persisted in my futile efforts to establish myself there on the fringe of a neighbouring city.
>
> The most memorable "symbol" of that day I spent fleeing from my former identity and from mortal sloth was a malformed half-wit whom I encountered on the street. He seemed to me at once a curious "objective correlative" materializing the state of mind—disabled and partially insane—which I knew myself to be in. The half-wit had a striking, though distorted, countenance; he was crippled, and his wanderings appeared to have no object. He seemed to navigate by some power I could not apprehend. He was there by my car where I parked early in the morning, and he crossed my path at many corners throughout the day. Late in the afternoon I found myself walking behind him and,

tired and alone, I continued following him. He led me back to my automobile (I am not certain I could have found it without him) and, as if this "sign" or "omen" had some special efficacy, the singing Voices ceased and left me in silence. Collecting myself I made a decision of my own, entered my car and began the drive back home. The half-wit continued, with his swinging gait, on down the street. "Where," I recall asking myself, "does this man eat and sleep? For perhaps my lot will resemble his."

Out on the highway I found myself extremely fatigued. Changing my plan I pulled in at a motel, intending to stay the night. And it was there that the full—or the fully exaggerated force and weight of Doctor Zee's condemnation fell upon my shoulders. As I stood in the office of the motel, making arrangements for my stopover, the Voices suddenly returned and announced to me, with great force, that I was the Anti-Christ. They sang with a sinister insistence and I immediately believed their words—or rather, I judged that I could not take a chance on their being wrong. They went on to inform me that anyone to whom I spoke or whom I looked squarely in the face would share my own fate, that I would damn them to eternal punishment as I myself was damned by virtue of having been chosen as the Anti-Christ. I cast my eyes downward and stood in silence—for how long I cannot say. But in due time the manager of the motel, seeing that something was wrong, called in a policeman.

I . . . believed myself to be an evil power with a supernatural ability to destroy others, and it was not until I was in the policeman's car that I raised my head, spoke, and was relieved of the persuasive Voices.

The policeman drove me to a local hospital where I was sufficiently recovered to be denied entry, and then returned me to the motel. After speaking with the manager, I hired a taxi to drive me back to my own city and, once home, the Voices did not return that night. I slept soundly and with strange, almost loving, recollections of the crippled half-wit who seemed, in my dreams, a stronghold of health and sanity amidst the dislocations of the world. (Beach 1991)

In his essay "On the Origin of the 'Influencing Machine' in Schizophrenia" (1919), Tausk writes about the source of those "alien . . . hostile Voices" that Beach heard:

Many patients consider the cause of all these alien or hostile sensations of physical or psychic change to be simply an external mental influence, suggestion or telepathic power, emanating from enemies. My own observations and those of other authors leave no room for doubt that these complaints precede the symptom of the influencing apparatus, and that the latter is a subsequent pathological development. Its appearance, as many observers state, serves the purpose of an explanation for the pathologic changes that are felt as alien and painful and dominate the patient's emotional life and sensations. According to this view, the idea of the influencing machine originates in the need for causality that is inherent in man; and the same need for causality will probably also account for the persecutors who act not through the medium of an apparatus but merely by suggestion or by telepathy. (34)

. . . In some cases it may be stated with certainty, and in others with strong probability, that the sense of persecution originates from the sensations of change accompanied by a sense of estrangement. These feelings of persecution are ascribed to a foreign, personal interference, "suggestion," or "telepathic influence." In other cases, the ideas of persecution or influence may be seen entering into the construction of an influencing apparatus. It is necessary to assume, therefore, that the influencing apparatus represents the terminal stage in the evolution of the symptom, which started with simple sensations of change.

If we take into consideration the view held by Freud and myself that in object-choice the mechanism of identification precedes the cathexis proper by projection, we may regard . . . the development of the delusion of reference preceding the projection (namely, onto a distant persecutor in the outer world). The identification is obviously an attempt to project the feelings of the inner change onto the outer world. It constitutes a bridge between the feelings of an inner change without external cause and the attribution of these changes to the power of an external person, a kind of intermediary position between the feeling of self-estrangement and the delusion of reference. This rounds out especially well, and substantiates psycho-analytically, the concept of the development of the symptom, up to its crystallization in the influencing machine. (Ibid., 37)

If the selection principle is to work it has to have influence: we have to be moved toward and away from actions. We get a take first on this, then on that, ever searching for a goodness-of-fit between intimation and realization. "Goodness of fit" was a concept first brought into prominence by the Gestaltists as an activity that governed mentation, but it was plain even in that concept that there was a kind of *striving* involved in the search for fit and closure. In a broader sense it has been part of Plato's philosophy in which our restlessness with the real reflects the jittery edges the real has with the ideal. Hume and Kant also saw the real as approximations to an ideal of sorts. Nelson Goodman (1978) calls this attempt to search for realizations "worldmaking." He describes it as follows:

With multiple and sometimes unreconciled and even unreconcilable theories and descriptions recognized as admissible alternatives, our notions about truth call for some reexamination. And with our view of worldmaking expanded far beyond theories and descriptions, beyond statements, beyond language, beyond denotation, even to include versions and visions metaphorical as well as literal, pictorial and musical as well as verbal, exemplifying and expressing as well as describing and depicting, the distinction between true and false falls far short of marking the general distinction between right and wrong versions. What standard of rightness then, for example, is the counterpart of truth for works without subjects that present worlds by exemplification or expression? (109)

The welter experienced by Beach and described by Goodman is the condition we might call greed. That is, each recognition given our limited supply of attention (energy, resources) reduces the potential by one. Each such reduction is experienced as a little death (or, to restore this to its context, *un petit mort*). But were it otherwise, there would be nothing to fuel the quest. The pleasure principle is often easily enough satisfied by sheer polymorphous perversity.

P has a dream concerning polymorphous perversity: balloons are being twisted into shapes; each configuration causes respective swelling and reduction; these in turn affect the color of the balloon; it is erotic and induces orgasm.

Proximity serves desire. In fact, proximity serves desire so well that it can positively endanger future generations:

A male has sufficient sperm to inseminate numerous females, and his investment in a single copulation is therefore very small. A female, by contrast, produces relatively few eggs, at least in species with female choice, and may furthermore invest much time and resources in brooding the eggs or developing the embryos and in taking care of the brood after hatching. She may lose her entire reproductive potential by making a mistake in the selection of her mate (for instance, by producing inferior or sterile hybrids). (Mayr 1982: 597)

When looked at in the broader perspective of the *Group*, the problem of random breeding based on propinquity shows up even more clearly. There are characteristics of entire populations, such as aberrant sex ratios, rates of mutation, distance of dispersal and various other mechanisms favoring either in-breeding or out-breeding in natural populations, and degrees of sexual dimorphism. Such differences among populations, say the proponents of group selection, can be established only when an entire population (deme) is favored over other demes because it differs in its genetic constitution for the stated factor. Studies of the fitness of the isolated individual are supplemented by studies of kinship selection, inclusive fitness, reciprocal altruism, parent-offspring relations, and so forth. The study of the evolution of plants and animals is enriched by the study of their coevolution. (Ibid., 595)

In his work on the Influencing Machine, Tausk (1919) brought into the psychoanalytic vocabulary the special features of what Klein (M. Klein 1952) was later to call "Projective Identification," namely those of wanting to gain, locate, or disperse influence. He writes:

The main effects of the influencing machine are the following: (1) It makes the patients see pictures. When this is the case, the machine is generally a magic-lantern or cinematograph. The pictures are seen on a single plane, on walls or window-panes, and unlike typical visual hallucinations are not three-dimensional. (2) It produces, as well as removes, thoughts and feelings by means of waves or rays or mysterious forces which the patient's knowledge of physics is inadequate to explain. In such cases, the machine is often called a "suggestion-apparatus." Its construction cannot be explained, but its function consists in the transmission or "draining off" of thoughts and feelings by one or several persecutors. (3) It produces motor phenomena in the body, erections and seminal emissions, that are intended to deprive the patient of his male potency and weaken him. This is accomplished either by means of suggestion or by air-currents, electricity, magnetism, or X-rays. (4) It creates sensations that in part cannot be described, because they are strange to the patient himself, and that in part are sensed as electrical, magnetic, or due to air-currents. (5) It is also responsible for other occurrences in the patient's body, such as cutaneous eruptions, abscesses, and other pathological processes. The machine serves to persecute the patient and is operated by enemies. (Tausk 1919: 33–34)

To these portrayals, Bion added the observation that such influencing was not simply a matter of omnipotent fantasy, but an ongoing activity between one person and another. From this it followed that the analyst must find or regain the mother's "capacity for reverie." The ordinary defenses against such openness to the influences of projective identifications were, he wrote, those which Klein had described as the paranoid-schizoid position toward experience. In the analytic consulting room, Bion further noted, these were to be found in the organizations the analyst imposes on the influences being created and projected by the patient, among which were the analyst's use of memory and anticipation, those twin impositions of his or her desire. This desire he distinguished from sexual desires in the analyst's transferences: the latter, he noted, might ordinarily be made conscious in the analyst's own analytic work; the latter, he suggested, might be protected from realization by the collective efforts of the analytic *Group*. The *Group*'s unconsciousness made individual unconsciousness unnecessary. Therefore the individuals comprising the *Group* could be quite aware of their practices without attributing to these practices any significance other than normative. The great value of the *Group* accordingly was its influence, or if one prefers, counter-influence on the patient's ability to use his projective identifications freely—really, one should say a counter-influence on patients' being able to use *their* influencing machinery. All of what I have been saying can be illustrated by small examples such as: "Oh, she is probably a borderline," or, "With a mother like that . . . ," which reveal the ordinariness with which the perturbative impact of the patient or patients' influence on the emotional and psychic life of the analyst or analytic *Group* can be defused.

There is so far as I know nothing "wrong" with such use of countervailing influence, except in so far as our *Group*, the psychoanalytic *Group*, is in most other ways dedicated, even devoted, to assisting their clients toward finding realizations of what they experience and, even more, what they don't quite experience. We generally accept that our patient's capacity to experience what he experiences depends in some measure on our capacity to do so also or first. When "saturated" (Bion's phrase) with the identifications that link us to our particular *Group*, we are that much the less able to offer reverie to what the patient can sometimes only intimate. Bloom (1973) wrote of the "Anxiety of Influence," the term he used to describe how imperiled artists feel lest they open their mouths . . . and an impersonation appear (see Feiner 1988;

1992). Joyce, who was of course a particularly gifted "impersona-
tor," wrote passionately of the artist's need to find his own voice,
in fact his need for exile. Most artists speak of the characters or
painting taking on a life of their own, as dreams seem to. There is
both a welcome and an unwelcome aspect to this experience.

In trying to trace this matter of influencing and being influenced we cannot but come up against the very matter into which
we are attempting to look. We quickly see how we use influences
to offset influences. It is as if to resist influences even just long
enough to study them is so dreadful that one can only escape the
clutches of one set by hurling one's self into the arms of another.
That is the problem for both the patient and the analyst *Groups*.
As we allow the patient more and more to have his way with our
thoughts and feelings, we naturally fear him more. The idea of
maintaining at the edges a presence of our own seems more and
more feckless. Soon we will be hearing what the patient wants us
to hear and saying what he wants us to say. A takeover is in
progress and it may have qualities of a hostile takeover. A battle
for the hearts and minds of the people is under way, and we, it
turns out, are the people.

In transference terms, this is the wrangle of every *Couple*. In the
words of the limerick, they argue all night as to who has the right
to do what and with which and to whom. Gifted with polymorphous perversity and burdened with no little greed, no sooner
have we achieved forty-four than we want ninety-six! No sooner
are we ascendant, arcing, and triumphant than we want the utter
voluptuousness of absolute and abject surrender (Ghent 1990). But
there is something besides that, and it comes not from the *Couple*
but from the *Pair*.

Pairs are founded on mutual identifications; two people become
a *Pair* by developing what George Klein (1975) referred to as a
"wego." Freud, of course, regarded identifications as a second
resort, and to an extent so too did Melanie Klein. Naturally there
are identifications and identifications. There are those that preserve the difference between subject and object, moving the relationship to the internal arena, where it can be conducted symbol-
ically and at any time of the day or night. And there are those
where the intent is to remove the differences between subject and
object, the better to meld the two. In his work on groups Bion took

note that this kind of relational formation was a basic assumption, innately shared, part of man's being and heritage as a social animal—the only remaining question therefore is which of the three or four realizations these assumptions might take. In his customary review, he added that these assumptions came into being as something juxtaposed vis-à-vis the primal scene.

On the other hand, I do not suppose that identifications such as those employed in *Group* or *Pair* formation are secondary to defenses against or reparations for irreconcilable differences in the *Couple*, though they well may be used as such. People will fashion a *Pair* or *Group* if their *Couple* needs are being gratified elsewhere or in good portion; in the event of too much frustration, the members will go into reverse, and try to use the others in the *Group* for coupling purposes while finding other Others to fashion *Group*s and pairs with.

Since nature is parsimonious, her eithers and ors must always serve several purposes. The *Couple* is surely necessary for mating and reproduction: the different genders must find one another and of their differences make merry. But to know no bounds is to remain oblivious of whom one shares the species with. The *Pair* and the *Group* and beyond them the species must command one's affiliation. We must be open to their influence, particularly as to our identity. If we are not, we might be subject to imprinting like Lorenz's ducklings and end up a Wellington boot. These dual necessities of biology, rooted in us, I suggest, in the forms of the pleasure and the selection principles, are plainly capable of conflict and harmony. In the pleasure-driven *Couple*, each member may wish quite ruthlessly to use the other for predatory purposes, or parasitically, as an *ongoing* source of food or place for waste disposal or as an object for sensual gratifications of every careless sort. But the call of the species is much more civilized than our own id-ish impulses.

But if we were to save everything for later and look only for the eugenic best, would we ever get around to mating? By the time one reads and re-reads the menu, hears all the specials, asks plaintively if what one had last time that was so good will ever be served again, one could be too old to take on one's choice, let alone conceive. Fortunately hunger intercedes enough for something to look good enough. But in doing so, hunger's wish to mate is inimical to the wish to mate perfectly; the wish for perfection must be appeased too. This can only happen when a sense of sequence comes into the picture. From sequence comes time and with time a sense of the future and a whole new time/space in which to distribute priority.

Future time, so essential to the selection principle, becomes a figure who is part and parcel of every event. "Soon," "later," and "after," though such neutral words in Freud's psychoanalytic thinking—in which the reality principle is vested in the ego, that wise counsellor to the schoolboy id—are subsumed by the term "delayed" gratification and are more accurately represented by those bad stepmothers who make one fall into brambly sleep. Icons for time—the clock without hands, the melting watch, the many labors or feats or proofs—are also icons for clinical depression. Delay can be friendly only in so far as there is a robust belief in time's open arms—or failing that, space's possibilities. For this to occur, space/time has to be split. The creation of space *and* time provides new applications, but loses the enormous potential that space/time had. Though it permits the evolution of appetite, it undermines the state of greed.

In contrast to appetite, greed fosters the search for eugenic ideals, opposing these to desire's quest for an every- and an any-one. Often those desired, while propinquitous, are not quite in and of the species. As we watch Beach dematerialize as a result of Dr. Zee's rebuttal of projective identifications concerning his illness, he no longer knows to whom to run. In resuming greed, he has gained hope, but he has lost appetite. And without appetite he cannot be satisfied. He is reduced now to finding out who and what he is by seeing who recognizes him. This is portrayed by his hope that passages from the Bible will rise up and meet his words. So wide open is Beach to being defined and discovered that it would beggar the imagination to think this a simple projection of his own wishes to influence and control, though these most certainly are in evidence. Under Dr. Zee's prompting, Beach puts aside who and what he thought he was and lies fertile to an "annunciation." The need to recognize and to be recognized is present in all species. It is the only way individuals do not lunch upon one another. Even at the cellular level such distinctions are imperative, lest the immune system turn upon the self system and not the alien invader. Among mammals, when the mother licks her newborns she imports to them a smell and perhaps a taste that not only enables subsequent recognition, but identifies them as Us-creatures.* Human infants appear † to attain both voice and image recognition of their mothers almost from birth (cf. Beebe and Lachman 1988; Brazelton and Cramer 1989). Professor Beach, having gone unrecognized by Dr. Zee for what he thought they thought he was, is flummoxed. He awaits instructions. Perhaps he has come to the end of his signifiers, too; after "Zed," who then— Dead?

André Green has this to say regarding what I believe to be Beach's plight:

> Just as God made man in his own image, the paranoiac makes the object resemble himself. It was inevitable that we would turn to the idea of a mirror's surface—or even better and closer to Freud's theory —to a projector and screen. Narcissism allows the ego to be unified. In other words, the transition from ego instincts to narcissism occurs through the constitution of the ego's protective plane as a reflecting surface. The narcissistically cathected ego tries to become an object to the id by attempting a seduction. It takes on the characteristics of the ideal object. The narcissism gathers its energy from the desexualiza-tion of the instinctual drives which come from the id and which the ego appropriates. Since the purpose of this narcissistic seduction is for the ego to model itself after the ideal object, it seems logical that this reflected and reflecting (projected and projecting) narcissism will con-stitute a protective screen upon which a homologous image of the other will appear. The cathexis of the other will project at him the image of the ego and, in turn, the other will project this image onto the ego, reinforcing its deception. In paranoia this cathexis bears the mark of homoeroticism, a unity of subject and object based on each having the same sexual appearance. We must add, however, that such a cath-exis is sublimated and narcissistic. In other words, there is a relation-ship of narcissistic identification between the ego and the other through their mutual projections. This protective current is duplicated by an introjective current, the other absorbing the ego's projections and vice versa. To the protective screen on the surface of the ego corresponds another protective screen located outside of the ego in the mirror

---

* "... and mark it with B/And put it in the oven for baby and me."

† The marks of this recognition are taken to be increased interest and these in turn are measured by slowed-down videotapes and computer readings of the way the infant sucks the bottle. The infant sucks the bottle more ardently—faster, harder—when he hears a recording of his mother's voice.

formed by the other. The situation is alienating in that neither the ego nor the other can locate each other because the image is constantly bouncing back and forth between the ego's internal mirror and the other's external mirror. When the paranoiac becomes aware of this, he no longer knows where he is, he is no longer sure of the efficacy of projection, the split loses its effectiveness, he depersonalizes. (1986: 95)

". . . [H]e is no longer sure of the efficacy of projection . . . he depersonalizes." He withdraws the attention which ordinarily makes people and events three-dimensional, for such attention is part of the quest for objects. He must now put himself in the way of objects, and seek new influences. This opens him so widely that he is likely to be a camera without f-stops, so open that there is no image to project and no "musculature" to project it with. I disagree with Green's formulation concerning sublimated homoeroticism and narcissism as primary, for I regard those qualities as belonging to the *Couple*. When we do see them, as we do, we are seeing sexualized versions of efforts to *Pair*. The *Pair* requires mutually vicarious interchanges, based on sympathetic imagination, in order to make themselves ever more alike; to achieve this they must, correlatively, filter out their differences by not paying those differences much heed. But when differences become obtrusive in the way they did between Professor Beach and Dr. Zee, their therapeutic alliance, if there was one, is smashed to smithereens. The pleasure ego may well take up the *Pairing* that failed, in that way secondarily giving the act and the meaning of the acts the erotic tinges Green supposes are primary.

The danger of such openness in the *Pair* is that an imprinting may take place such that the first object recognized may be taken to be—may fill out and saturate the category—*Mother*. If imprintings do not wholly imbue the category, they will exist as realizations alongside of other realizations and compete with these for later re-realization. On the larger scale the dialectic is between whether objects should be regarded as new recruits to the aims of the *Pair* and *Group* or as fresh provender for the aims of the *Couple*. The evolution of appetite from greed accompanies either alternative: appetite develops with a made choice. The aphorism concerning the having and eating of the cake applies. The cake, strictly speaking, is not a cake until its relationship to the self is determined. The cake that is ours and the cake that is for eating revisits the infant's dilemma about the breast—shall he take from it and receive its bounty, or shall he rather own it and enjoy its capacity to manufacture? While this greedy predicament prevails, there can be no such thing as a good breast, for the providing and the to-be-owned breast both deprive greedy wishes. The unchosen breast is empty of milk and absent of other *Coupling* sorts of experiences. But by the same token, it is richly engorged with hope—that selfsame hope of which Sir Francis Bacon wrote "makes a good breakfast but a poor supper."

"Only by remaining a hope does hope persist," observed Bion (1961: 151–52). Yet fast upon an encounter with a realization of the hope vested in the *Pair* there is triggered an affluence of desire. For when the imago implicit in the *Pair* is satisfied, the *Couple* is required and/or released to go forth as quickly as it can and consummate the arrangement.

As Mayr (1982) observes:

> It is well known that the mating drive in the males of many species is so strong that they display not only to females of their own species, but also to females of related species. If the females were equally lacking in discrimination, an enormous amount of hybridization among closely related species would take place. Since hybrids are ordinarily of considerably lower fitness, natural selection will favor two developments: First, any genetic change that would make the females more discriminating, and second, any characteristics in the males that would reduce the probability that they be confused with the males of another species. Such characteristics are designated isolating mechanisms. (98)

Mayr notes that earlier, in 1942, he had

> called attention to the fact that the conspicuous male characteristics sometimes were lost in island birds when there were not other closely related species on the same island. The loss of these characters was apparently due to a relaxation of selection for the distinctive isolating mechanisms. (Ibid.)

The inhibition of the procreative drive pending the approximation of the object to the preconception and later the series of realizations developed from the template of preconception paradoxically facilitates the release of the drive. *The readier and more assured the capacity not to choose A, the easier and quicker the capacity to choose B*. Though sexual selectivity involves this procedure, so too do feeding and parenting, eliminatory and aggressive actions and interactions. In all of these, inhibition until the "right" conditions are present makes for greater ease of release once the "right" conditions are present. In my paper "On Hope" (1976), I suggested:

> For myself, I find it reasonable to put forth, not as a substantive analogy but as a hypothetical construct, that preconception in man may be a residue of Darwinian processes of natural selection such that hope's effect upon desire can be viewed as having a species-specific survival value in carrying out nature's blueprints for man. Hope holds desire from taking its any old course of least resistance and it keeps desire from static satiety by calling it to "finer" possibilities.
>
> In proposing such a construct I do not intend in any way to minimize the role of man's social universe; quite the reverse. The categories, as I mentioned before, are only partly full. They bear a format and a structure. Because man is born into a social order, the values, ideals and sanctions of that order importantly shape his hopes, aspirations and expectations. But neither should it be forgotten that the social universe was no less born of man: he shapes and reshapes it, even while it does him.
>
> By regarding man as the shaper of his social universe and not exclusively as its product, one is in turn able to see beyond the unique differences between the pre-programmed creatures of simple reflex and those whose categories are left gaping and needed to be filled with the contents of the culture. Cultures, thus, may differ widely, but they are alike in that they must contain versions of a we-they, good-bad, true-false, lovely-ugly organization of experience: thus no known culture is without a religion or a kinship system. (144)

The emptiness of truly empty categories is perhaps beyond imagining. No matter his periodic desolation, Beach is never without some "contents" for his "containers." Indeed, he is frequently staggered by what seems to flow so naturally, really so inevitably, into his categories. A man so sensitive as unfailingly to take note of his own processes, he becomes, as he is bound to, almost entirely aware of the implosive force of experience upon him and in particular that experience for which his emptier categories yearn in their quest for completion.

Such is the allure of the *Group*.

P is disturbed by the hum and buzz of Ψ's computer. P feels that when it whirs P should shut up. Although P is interested in Ψ for possibilities of *Coupling*, the sounds of the computer or printer seem to proclaim that Ψ is on to higher, better things, like writing articles or books for the *Group*. P proclaims this situation crazy, knowing that Ψ's full attention is at P's disposal. Nevertheless P's own adherence to the *Group* would be offended were Ψ not involved with the *Group* represented by the computer. The "alliance" would suffer were Ψ at this point to show ignorance or disdain for the *Group*. So P lies silent, except to say, "This is weird, this is so-o crazy."

P is easily influenced. And resents it.

9. Selection and Choice

P : Once, it was during the missile crisis, I think, I was walking down the avenue of an unfamiliar city. I felt lonely. More, I felt out of place. I thought, "What if the missiles come and I am here, to whom or what shall I go?" I looked about me and it was as if certain people became 3–D. "I shall run to *them*," I thought. But who were they? They were the people in tweeds. "My kind," I thought. I then imagined what I thought lemmings might feel, because I have no reason to think that people in tweeds have the inside track on survival, nor do I think those in three-piece suits know less. All the same I felt, "If I must die, it would be better not to be among strangers."

P : At last I got home, away from the dreary, tiring day. I took off my work clothes, thinking to take a shower and relax. In the shower I became aware of feeling horny. There is a kind of body cream my wife uses and I sometimes use that if I am going to wonk-off. I thought, "What the hell?" But I felt, "Christ, I will be the only one doing this." Then I thought, "Well, fuck *them!* They don't have to know." So I grab my dick and started wonking. But it was as if my dick had gone over to them. It didn't want to be seen with me, I was an embarrassment to it. It shriveled with shame. I said to it, "Look, goddamn it, who the fuck's in charge here." But it was no good, I felt like outnumbered.

P : I hate the national anthem. I don't mean the song, but that you can't go to the ballpark and not stand up while it's playing. I always try to be there a little late in order not to get there until it is over. Yesterday I was going with this friend. "Hurry up," he keeps saying. So I told him. So he says, "So then don't stand up." So we get there and we're in time. Right away he's on his feet. I think, "Good, let him stand for the two of us." But this doesn't work. He's no longer the two of us, he's one of the rest of them. And with him gone, I can't not stand up. I feel as if everyone is staring bullets into my back. I feel like a wad of used newspaper. I try to make myself feel smaller still. No use. I get up as unobtrusively as I can. I just kind of slide to my feet. I still feel the eyes in my back and stand very still, careful not to move. When the anthem is finally over, I kind of slump down, maybe like I was already shot. I sit down, careful not to look around, meet any eyes. And he's looking at me like what's the matter? But he stood up so he doesn't know and if he doesn't know, how'm I supposed to tell him?

These are individuals taking reference from their reference *Group*. At the moment it would seem they are each, in the phrase of Riesman, Denney, and Glazer (1950), "other-directed." And in being oriented to the other they are forbidden from going to the "inner" source of direction. As one man asks his penis, "Who's in charge here?"

It's a good question, for it leads to three sets of distinctions: (1) self and other; (2) *Pair* or *Couple;* (3) inner and outer. Where are the boundary lines? How are they established? What is their dynamic?

R. D. Laing (1971) makes a distinction between inner and outer. He uses as his example a person spitting his or her saliva into a glass of freshly drawn water. The saliva, before expectoration, is good and is me. The water before being spat into is good and not me. But upon the invitation to drink down the water containing the saliva, people generally feel great repugnance. In being expectorated the saliva has passed from me to being not-me. It has been experienced as foreign, even alien; a waste product. It has contaminated the water. Xenophobia has grown up around it. It is an instance of the bad not-me's.

During the 1990 exodus from Iraq, amidst appalling starvation, fatigue, and stress, the various nationalities (Kurds, Greeks, etc.) set up and protected their toilet areas. Though warned by health officials of the risks of contamination to the food and water supply, due to the proximity of sewage and camping areas, the various *Groups* nevertheless did nothing to distance the sewage and went about as before. It seemed that while bodily waste had to be separated from the "I," it nonetheless had to go into a We-zone that was plainly different from a Them-zone.

This is a xenophobic distinction entirely shared by peoples of different cultures, by a "We": "We agree that the waste materials we produce are a nasty business, but better ours than yours. Yours undoubtedly contain a toxic virulence that ours lack! Ours is Not Me; Yours is not Us."* Lewin (1951), in developing his field theory, portrayed differing (national) character groups by placing surrounding lines around the individuals of these cultural variants. Very private people had a thick wall close in. People who were open within a group (like good friends and family) but were rather self-contained beyond such intimates had a thick wall some distance from the center. These lines also separated degrees of us-ness according to context—the work place; the family; acquaintances and friends. The implication was that the field was not infinite, but divided up a given capacity into areas (this being the basic premise of all systems for model-making, my own on selective attention, for example). Lewin, like Riesman, did not concern himself with the "inner" fields that are at the core of psychoanalytical models, but one may easily extrapolate the boundaries for the field describing a man's relations with his neighbors, an equivalent set of boundaries to describe a man's relationship with his inner objects, and theirs with one another and with him. Lewin's innermost circle was the person himself: we need merely replace the person with that unit people refer to as their "self."

Freud's aphorism concerning the man with a toothache being unable to fall in love was a distillation of the thinking he devel-

---

*There is a similar distinction made by the populace about Congress: we all agree that Congress does its job very poorly because of everyone else's representatives.

oped in *Mourning and Melancholia* (1917). The idea was that a loss experienced in an outside-of-me ring was re-sited into an inside-of-me ring from which the relationship was continued, adding now a fantasy concerning the individual's power to move his objects around as if they were chessmen and not people with a will of their own. Thus not only were the boundaries movable but so were the objects that resided within those boundaries. Freud contrasted this sort of re-siting with an ability to let go of the dead or gone object by relinquishing it and fall in love or hate with quite a new person. The obstacle to this was the transference, for in the transference the original object is relinquished but not the relationship. A new object (or objects) is brought in to take the place of the original in the old relationship. In a discussion of bulimia, I have written of the torment visited by the patient on his or her objects by the patient's efforts to keep them on a string, pulling them hither, casting them yon, never allowing them to rest in peace: and the talion anxieties this stirs up (Boris 1988). In a note in the epilogue to *Sleights of Mind* (forthcoming a), I wrote of the anal features of such a relationship.

> In the face of a nameless dread, even something so otherwise dire as catching on to specific anxieties and particular defenses is an attractive alternative. Indeed, even to merge the dread natural to the *Pair* and the *Group* with anxieties inhering in being a member of a *Couple* and so with specific libidinal interests, may seem to a child quite helpful. A phobia and counter phobia may seem more manageable than a dread, in much the same way a no-thing may seem more helpful than a nothing.
>
> One such possibility for transfiguration of the experience of dread—of something being out of one's control and quite possibly arriving with the speed of an express train—is provided quite early on in life in the form of the question: Who controls defecation—the fecal mass, or the sphincter? However, the many other issues contingent for people in this regard may well obscure this one. Those are, first, the use of the anus as a prehensile organ in quest of recapturing the absent or fickle nipple; and second, the excited embattlement in the interpersonal aspects of the training situation over penetration, possession of product and production, rights of access and the terrain for deposit. (A flurry over the "paper-work" is usually a sure sign of this last conflation.)
>
> However, the alarm that, in one's identification with the White hat

of the sphincter one may not be able to control and manage the Black hat of the feces is for some people an anxiety paramount over the others. Spontaneity of bodily functions is associated with being subjugated, and every effort is made to quell the natural rhythms and activities of the body. The peristaltic inexorability that brings the mass to the point where it must be evacuated seemed accordingly persecutory in the extreme. It seemed to rule them, as self and alive, with its relentless time and tide. And when it did, it was they who felt like so much shit and their feces which were rampant and triumphant.

As this issue comes into the transference, it bears a particular characteristic—a two-position situation: either the patient is in control or the analyst is: either he or she felt like shit and the analysis was a vast intestine which would deposit the patient out no matter when, or the analyst is and they were. There are no two ways. Patients otherwise frugal found it at these times no expense at all to come irregularly or late, for if he or she could not control the end of the session (as one who suffered anorexia put it to me), she could at least control the beginning. For the analyst to accept such treatment is worrisome to his patient, a matter of agreeing to be treated like shit, and thus a source of great guilt, which could only be compensated for by alleging that the analyst rather is treating the patient like shit. Not to take such exercise in dominion, however, seems a palpable indication that the struggle for hegemony is indeed interpersonal.

The difficulty arises in the tendency for the infant and young child to treat the feces as if it were a person, to have and to hold or to evacuate and to discard, until death do them part. This means that the feces are considered to have a potential life of their own, and that they can and may (comes the revolution) reverse the designs of the sphincter. Some children lose interest in their feces as their interest in other people grows, and thus the object relationship gravitates to the Other as object. But other children absorb themselves with their feces, and employ them as a transitional object—and sometimes, in service of envy, as an object from which there will be no transition. Endgame.

Ordinarily when matters are drawn into such enduring and particularized struggles, the struggle is a counterfeited one, mobilized to keep the real tensions from finding their way into the analysis or the analyst and patient from noticing them. This struggle however only counterfeits being counterfeit. It is fake in that the analyst has to impersonate a part of the patient, while being made to seem (and feel) like another person—the bad intrusive mother—in the matter. But the deep sense of aggrievement and hatred are not. Rather careful sorts of interpretation are necessary to return the conflict to its base point—the patients fear of and alienation from his or her own natural processes.

Because the "field" is delimited, there is no shift possible without a sort of Newtonian compensatory shift coming into play. In "Interpretation of dreams, interpretation of facts" (Boris 1989, forthcoming a), the "economics" of the interplay of such actions on objects appear:

> Semi-truths guard us from whole truths which are nothing but the truth, but also keep us from them. Psychoanalytic theory informs, but it also conceals what might be knowable beyond it. . . . there is the problem of how to go forward—how to see matters afresh. Freud's great light throws a great shadow. We have then the possibility of increasing the light, of extending it in all directions, of attempting more, seeing more and getting better at it. But amiable as such increments are, do we know more of the truth, if there is one—more of the X—or only more of the psychoanalytic truth? If we know more of merely the psychic truth, we increase the light, but also the density of the obscuring shadow. The void is held at bay by the cheerful light of the campfire, but so too is what else might be out there. Paradoxically facts hide truths as well as fictions do, and sometimes better; even, as we saw earlier, fictions reveal and illuminate truths as well as or better than facts.
>
> Both are equal in their potential for conveying pain and hence fright and for protecting us from it. When one piece of either feels too menacing, it needs to be replaced so that the experience can be reconfigured. Either can replace whatever bit is being excised or needing transfiguration. The only requirement is that it fit seamlessly into the fabric in order that its counterfeiting presence go unnoticed. Once again, it is the use of the idea that must engage us. Fact or fiction, one no less than the other, can transform an unbearable experience. Each can be used truthfully or otherwise.
>
> . . . What kind of knowledge does one want? Know the truth because the truth will set you free? Or elaborate a fiction, since the fiction is the font of hope and possibility?
>
> . . . The epistemological question of how one knows what one knows surely comes into play; for though the child cannot read the future and know what Mother *will* be, he has every reason to know what he knows about Mother so far. Shall he continue to know what he knows or should he doubt it? Should he replace bits of it or give emphasis to other bits, so to change the reading? There are, here, two sources of knowledge. He remembers Mother, and he perceives her. The two must correspond, or, if discrepant, at least be justified in some way. If he proposes not to know what he knows, what of his perceptions? If he proposes to see Mother differently, what of his memories?
>
> . . . Ego-psychologists may argue Kleinian attributions of ego mech-

anisms to the infant. And Neo-Freudians may introduce cultural relativism to the Viennese delegation. And the children of the information age and of the neuronal sciences may adduce their new facts and figurations. But all agree (hence the bitterness of the dispute) that there must be a better and a worse *and it must be factual.*

As with dreams so with facts, as with beauty, so with truth, as with inner, so with outer, as with one, so with many, as with discovery, so with invention, as with conscious, so with unconscious, as with *Couple,* so with *Pair: each exists at the expense of the other, each exists as an alternative to the other, each functions to modify the other,* to provide freedom and choice and relational possibility—within the shifting adaptational parameters of one another's constraints.

Such states of mind are comprised of uses and re-uses of realizations, which is to say the employment and reemployment of the relationships (verbs) one is having with the data (subjects and predicates), such as they are. The cortex, the ego, man, god, big bang, etc.—these are nouns, not verbs. They invite the questions that inquire of their own nounish origins: for example, "Who made God, then?" or "What was the status of the universe prior to the big bang?" or "How does the ego get its energy?"

Consider now the relationship between Selection in the *Pair* and Choice in the *Couple.* Following Edelman's model, we have a partly formed, partly realized bundle, expressed by and expressive of the DNA, what I (following Kant) have conceptualized as empty categories, and Bion as preconceptions and premonitions. Here I have used the words "intimations" and "realizations" in the hope of underlining the *motivational* dynamics that propel the paradoxical dialectic between paradigms. I have linked up states of mind with states of affairs following Lewin's concept of a dynamically shifting field. To emphasize the dialectical nature of the formation of the fields, I would rather call them fields of force.

Of these forces, one is in the *Pair,* and it involves selecting and being selected. The initial realization of selection is in the formation of identity.

Identification is both a fantasy and an act (really a series of acts, bound together by their mimetic goals). The fantasy is that self and other are as if one. This can but does not necessarily bespeak a sense of fusion of bodies or of personalities. It is often very well satisfied by the mutual sense of being a *Pair* in the sense that the two- (or three- or more-some) is "one for all, all for one," that the identifications are mutual.

The other is in the *Couple* and it is called choosing and being chosen.

One can readily see the considerable room for confusion between these categories since so often they work so much together. For example, the newborn of a species have to be recognized as being of that species in order for them not to be used, themselves, either as prey or as rivals in predation. This is selection, and the more the newborn is able to fit into the newborn category of the species, the better off everyone is. But not every newborn is selected into the *Pair*, before or even after being born:

> P : This is not my baby! He (or she) is nothing like me, nor does he have anything of his father about him. I don't want him. Throw him away.

> P : I'd like to have his children. I'm sure he'd make an excellent father to them. But his features look so, so overpowering to me that I am afraid he will stamp them with himself. For example, he is six-six. Now what would I do with a little girl who was going to grow up over six feet? Tall people feel different about themselves, they see things differently. . . . That's funny, I meant to say, not just the view they have but that it is *their* view and I feel it is different from ours.

It is not just that the "runt of the litter" cannot compete with its sibs for food; it is sometimes neglected when it comes to receiving the grooming with its commingling scents that mark the family as the Family. When the litter moves, the runt is not moved along with the rest. It is as if it no longer smells right to the mother.

The selected being is—only then—chosen or not chosen. The configuration, it will be recalled, now changes. Whereas in the *Pair* the third-to-nth are agglomerations of the *Pair-Group*, in the *Couple* the third-to-nth is a triangle or sets of triangles, of which those-who-are-two comprise the primal scene and the thirds are the odd ones out, dead, or in danger. The assumption—intimation —native to the *Couple* is that it takes two to find pleasure and satisfaction. Two what? Two *whatever!* Thumb and mouth, breast and mouth, hand and genital, genital and genital, Self and Other. Each one gratifies and takes gratification from the other.

In reflecting on the process of differentiation between mother and self, Hoffer (1950) noted that Self gets two sensations out of a thumb-suck, the thumb and the mouth, while from a breast-suck, the Self gets only the mouth plus milk. If this is so, what is lacking cannot be ascribed to sensation alone, nor do we live by food alone. The something extra is reciprocity.

The great value of oneness is that it affords satisfactions of a vicarious kind, satisfaction via identification. In this respect the individual can employ the *Group*'s capacity for specialization of function and division of labor to qualify for pleasures he cannot himself directly enjoy. The New Englander's fascination with the Red Sox is a case in point. They bat for us, pitch for us, field and steal for us—they play our hearts out. When they win, we win with them, and "high-five" one another; when they lose . . . we do not cry alone.

What vicariousness is to the *Pair*, reciprocity is to the *Couple*. A reciprocal relationship truly makes use of and so celebrates all the differences the *Couple* has and can muster. Yin/Yang. Freud felt that when this reciprocity broke down in a relationship the slack would be taken up by identifications, like the resolution of the Oedipus complex. But there are indications, some by Tausk quoted here, that Freud at least sometimes thought identification *(Pairing)* was primary. My own view is that because linearity of time is one of the *Pair* concepts indigenous to the zeitgeist of psychoanalysis—one of *its* er-iers—neither may be primary.* All the same, relationships do break down and as they do they excite those predilections that had lain latent to use the now-surplus "mate-

---

*My own use of dualities is another such emotional predilection—or is it premonition? One need only consider the range and number of typologies available for use—Wednesday's child, Aquarius, morning person, Apollonian, Type B, Bear, Hysteric, etc.—to see the appeal first to the *Pair*, then to the *Couple*, that these divisions have! Each division knits the *Pair* closer, each creates fresh objects for the wish to *Couple*.

rial" for their own purposes. But to fully understand this, it is of the first importance to remember that the relationships are what change:

> When the theory of object relations was at the beginning of its development we were at first led to describe the interaction of the self and the object in terms of internal processes. Not enough attention was paid to the fact that in the phrase "object relation" the word "relation" was the more important. This is to say that our interest should have been directed at what lies between these terms, which are united by actions, or between the effects of the different actions. In other words, the study of relations is that of links rather than that of the terms united by them. It is the nature of the link which confers on the material its truly psychic character which is responsible for intellectual development. This work was postponed until Bion examined the links between internal processes and Winnicott studied the interaction between the internal and the external. (Green 1986: 47)

It has been easy to confuse descriptive terms such as Bowlby's Attachment/Separation/Loss (1969) or Mahler's Separation/Individuation (1968) and even Klein's Paranoid/Schizoid and Depressive Positions (M. Klein 1952) as events rather than ways of relating and re-relating experience. Such confusion has given us nouns where verbs should be. Since there can be no no-relationship, we must be prepared to think of relationships competing for material with which to link up and unlink. This is approximately the state of affairs in respect to choosing and selecting and being chosen and being selected. All imply power * as the ability to exercise choice. As John Barth put it in one of his novels, *the key* to the treasure is the treasure. Being chosen means that one has the capacity, in one's own turn, *to* choose. And it is in this that choice and selection veer wildly apart.

   P : Are you seriously asking me to do the impossible? My thoughts, images, sensations—what have you—happen much too fast for me to put them into words. I mean, I get the idea— that I shouldn't pick and choose—but now you are accusing me not only for not saying everything, but even for what I do say. Maybe I'm just not cut out for this.

* With Alfred Adler, that exile from classical psychoanalysis.

The point is well taken. P's declaration exemplifies his dilemma, if one reads "cut out" as having more than the conventional meaning. It is bad enough, P feels, for Ψ to select from among what P communicates, but now—and what does Ψ have, that s/he dares impose selection upon P?-P himself may not choose. Yet he must select. Nor may he really select, for what comes to mind of his experience is . . . what comes to mind. Precious little choice does he have about that short of reciting a mantra—perhaps White Elephant, White Eleph. . . . The Purple Rhinoceros of what comes to mind *chooses him.*

Beach feels similarly chosen by the forces that emanate from the posters on opposing doors outside his classroom; those forces of good and evil require him to "search for a 'symbol which would save the world.'" There is no other choice but to respond to protect himself.

If Edelman and Erikson are correct, the process of being the recipient of selection pressures starts at conception or perhaps even before (i.e., many sperm are called, few chosen, many ova likewise), and certainly by infancy. Evidence of preconceptions appears in the research on infants: an experimental paradigm (Kellman, Spelke, and Short 1986) involved the observation of infants four months old while they watched stationary and moving objects and visible and occluded objects.

> Adjacent contiguous objects lying in the same plane were seen by these infants as one unit; those separated in depth were seen as two objects. The major conclusions of this work suggest that very young infants see the world as made up of spatially connected and separately moveable "objects." Infants do not seem to recognize textures in precedence over unitary systematic relative motion and do not tend to classify objects as uniform in substance or regular in shape. They do not respond simply to surfaces or sensation. It is not clear whether infants are born with the notion of an object—but if these observations are confirmed, it is clear that vision and relative motion can lead to a primitive categorization of things that move together as "objects." By and large, the continuity properties implied by motion carry over into these capabilities of categorization. (Edelman 1987: 252–53)

Choosing is a function of the *Couple*. It too takes place in a field of "continuity properties" of which one is desire and another is rivalry. These are symbolized by the primal scene plus One. This configuration is of the nature of an intimation: where there is, was, will be a twosome, they will be copulating in some fashion; that is what *Couple*s do and what *Couple*s are for. And what *I* am doing and what *you* are for. And, where there are Two, there are Three. Never One-or-More, always One, Two, and Three.

This intimation takes on a series of realizations: Melanie Klein described youthful ones—ones that Bion, already quoted, refers to as "primitive" versions of the primal scene. These persist and live side by side with later realizations: they do not altogether replace them. The intimations fleshed out with image, sound, bodily sensation, emotion may not find any final realization until the individual can construct or chance upon fresh material that can further flesh it out: "So *that's* what it is!" The "what" can be a painting or a scientific finding; it can be an H-bomb or the *Ode to Joy*. It can be finding a partner and getting dressed up to see a play or getting undressed to be in a play. It could be anything—or no-thing. When it is found or discovered it completes the realization, and a sensual act leading to repletion can take place. The melody is heard. The anxiety in the primal scene is over who gets and loses what. Triumph in the *Couple* means loss of the "other *Couple*s," just as the loss of anything to appetite devastates greed and pierces hope. For whenever a choice is made, a relationship is realized, and other relationships with that person and with others are lost to other realizations. If the child wishes to *Couple* with one breast, it loses the other, with the parent of one sex, it loses the other.

Among the realizations of the state of mind Freud called the Oedipus complex are these: the child wishes to lose his penis in order to copulate with his father, fears its loss in a talion sort of way, welcomes its loss as a means of decreasing his anxiety and his guilt, welcomes its loss so that it need not stand in the way of using his father's penis with which to satisfy mother or to placate her vagina for *its* loss of father. Although these are only a fraction of the many realizations the primal scene takes, if they are pulled inside-out, all their reciprocals come into prominence.

P : I am afraid that if I tell you what I feel you will say it is just some kind of variation on penis envy. But what I feel and have always felt, since I began noticing its depth, is that my vagina isn't deep enough.

Ψ: [thinks how shallow he is and wonders if that is why he is left out of the fun.]

It is hateful when two people are having a better time with one another than either would have with you.

P : When you said just now "the ties that bind," I began remembering my mother's nipples, how long and so pink they got when she was nursing. I think now that the next time I saw them they were the pink tongue of dogs and then the penis of a dog going in or coming out. What would a dog's penis taste like —ugh! I am now thinking of that dream in which I stuck my tongue into the vagina of that young adolescent girl—and she tasted so acrid and chemical? I seem to be of about a hundred minds!

On the face of it, this last is plain statement: apprehension requires realization; realizations, counterrealizations. Anxiety, writes Bion, is a mental pain, a non-sensuous effect (Keats's "Pipe to the spirit ditties of no tone"). Carefully looked into, an anxiety attack (an adrenalin rush) is indistinguishable from an abrupt onset of love, rage, or fear. How the attack is interpreted depends on the signal value it has been given. Freud's concept of "signal anxiety" (1925) noted that we came to anticipate apprehension—but was this the wish to apprehend or to be afraid? It threw a switch that diverted our attention from what might evolve next. The signal signaled anxiety (eagerness, apprehensiveness) ahead! (which meant behind) by calling so much attention to itself that it was able to be riveting: *nothing* comes next, not even, especially not even, the no-things. In this way it is like fascination or obsession.

In moving again toward a delusory world, Beach becomes fascinated by the "ritual act . . . contrived to reunite my parents," and the "transubstantiation" he feels. He is "caught by automatic movement" as he puts a plastic mermaid, the symbol of his mother, into the box containing his father's ashes, "the being of my father." He becomes intensely involved in contributing "bits of this world to my ancestors [and] they, in turn, were constantly sending offerings to me."

Desire and its *bête noir* jealousy would remain very simple were it not for its *Pair* equivalents being so often barely indistinguishable.

Concerning the *Couple:*

"I want you to be as happy with me as you are with others, happier! Let there be just you and me. And, if we must have Three, let it be Baby." And, "Damn you, s/he's mine, it's me s/he wants! And I want him/her and mean to have him/her."

Concerning the *Pair:*

"I want to be as happy with you as you are with others." "I want to be as happy with you as you are with me." "I want to be as happy with me as you are with me—or as you are with yourself."

These are neighboring statements, which express envy. They belong to the *Pair* and issues of being selected. The *Couple's* concerns are with reciprocity, the key element of which is the asymmetry of desire. But because selection and choice must coincide in the nature of things (the nature I am here supposing), choice and selection are so nearly of a piece that they are not easily distinguishable.

Part of the difficulty appears to stem from the mind's relationship with the brain. In certain fish, for example, the hippocampus attains more cells (even while enlarging those it has) when the fish in question has achieved social dominance. As a result, its gonads enlarge, and its libido enlarges accordingly; it mates more frequently and fights more aggressively.

However, on an occasion of lost confrontations, the same fish goes into reverse, losing coloring, size, gonad enlargement, hormonal balance, libido, and hippocampus cells. The role of brain activity and size as a juncture or mediator of all this is of course "predicted" by Edelman's selection theory. What remains unclear is at what point and from what collocation of "information" the state of affairs becomes susceptible to also becoming a state of mind. This is not so much a question regarding the cichlid (Angier 1991) as it is of where and when such states of affairs are made manifest in changes in mind, perspective, and outlook in people. That as human beings, we know in some sense more than we know we know—for example, that there are categories and procedures for so-called autonomic functions that operate in feedback loops of varying memberships but of which consciousness and self-consciousness are *not* members—is well established. These customarily operate outside of the wavelengths of ordinary attention. By dint of training that spectrum can be widened or narrowed, such that conscious attention can link up with blood-pressure levels, oxygen metabolism, and so on through biofeedback loops of which self is a member. This contrasts strongly with the haplessness shown under stimulus deprivation conditions and those in which there are neither ways to think or time to use the ways there are.

In the ontological evolution of what is called Self and Myself, lines—lines in the sense of boundaries, lines in the sense of links, and lines in the sense of conduits—must at once accommodate shifting sands and resist mirages. Edges must appear and, when the need is for different edges, they must disappear. The convergence of the feelings of hope that accompany the quest for the perfect or nearly perfect mate with those of desire as it yearns to be set free culminate in an explosion of everything falling into place. Just so.

The Yellow River people of New Guinea do not leave the circle of their huts after someone has died, and particularly not at night. They feel very strongly that the dead feel hurt at being dead and are bound, therefore, to feel the greatest envy of the living. Accordingly neither do the living wish to taunt the dead with their liveliness, nor do they care to have the curses and spells of the envious dead harm them.

   Their attitude toward illness is rather similar to their attitudes toward death. If someone falls ill, it is assumed that he will in time regain his health. If the illness persists, it is, they feel, being motivated, so the ill person is walked or carried around the village to learn whom he might have offended. Some may feel the sufferer engendered no animus, quite the contrary. This is believed to be of therapeutic benefit. Others may recall incidents when the ill person spat beetle nut husks almost onto their property area, or walked by without returning a greeting. To these accusations the sufferer is asked whether he wishes to make a reply; he is, indeed, urged to do so, especially if those accompanying him on his pilgrimage feel his accusers' insult or hurt to be grievous. If he too feels ashamed or guilty at what he hears, he will apologize, often to the rejoicing of all. At journey's end it is expected that he will soon recover.

If still he does not, then those offended are considered to be internal to him. As in Hamlet, these are ghosts so wounded that they cannot rest and will not let the ill person rest. For healings of this sort ceremonials are organized in which the wounded party and the sufferer can have it out and make their peace. The internal dead person is played by those privy to the ceremony. They hurl accusations of every sort at the ill person and he hurls back his own. Presently the accusations and counter-accusals seem to narrow to but one or two of an especially bitter nature. Now the chief enters and explains each party to the other, while castigating each with their failure to forgive and forget. "Look how much time has been taken, how short we are of meat, how the crops have been neglected. And all because you did not understand that. . . ." The dead are told to reconcile themselves to being dead. It is no fun, but it is their job. They have to make room for the young, who in turn will make their way for their young. Nursing grievances is a poor substitute for life, so they should spit out the grievances. And as to the sufferer, he or she is chastised for paying attention to these disgruntled ghosts: "Have you nothing better to do? What is wrong with your life that you must take up with ghosts?" (William Mitchell, personal correspondence)

Remaining unselected but alive means that the individual is himself a no-thing. Unable to walk upon hallowed ground, he feels half dead and burdened with a variant of Original Sin. If he is to alleviate that deadness he will have to do things that make him feel alive. In the interests of parsimony he will be bound to choose those activities that put him at risk. (If what he does makes those who do not share his dread feel envious, so much the better.) Vaclav Havel describes this feeling with clarity:

In Kafka I have found a portion of my own experience of the world, of myself, and of my way of being in the world. . . . One of them is a profound, banal, and therefore utterly vague sensation of culpability, as though my very existence were a kind of sin. Then there is a powerful feeling of general alienation, both my own and relating to everything around me, that helps to create such feelings; an experience of unbearable oppressiveness, a need constantly to explain myself to someone, to defend myself, a longing for an unattainable order of things, a longing that increases as the terrain I walk through becomes more muddled and confusing. I sometimes feel the need to confirm my identity by sounding off at others and demanding my rights. . . . Everything I encounter displays to me its absurd aspect first. I feel as though

I am constantly lagging behind powerful, self-confident men whom I can never overtake, let alone emulate. I find myself essentially hateful, deserving only mockery.

I admit that superficially I may appear to be the precise opposite of all those K.'s—Josef K., the surveyor K., and Franz K.—although I stand behind everything I've said about myself. I would only add that, in my opinion, the hidden motor driving all my dogged efforts is precisely this innermost feeling of mine of being excluded, of belonging nowhere, a state of disinheritance, as it were, of fundamental non-belonging. Moreover, I would say that it's precisely my desperate longing for order that keeps plunging me into the most improbable adventures. I would even say that everything worthwhile I've ever accomplished I have done to conceal my almost metaphysical feeling of guilt. The real reason I am always creating something, organizing something, it would seem, is to vindicate my permanently questionable right to exist. (Havel 1990)

Balint in his 1968 study of the nature of the thrill takes excellent note of the dynamics involved. From the *Pair* point of view there is this aspect to the thrill that needs to be repeated: I am not one of those whom life has welcomed, but rather one of those who must offer to die a thousand deaths to live as many months. Each little death is at once my penance and my reprieve. Each risk is a down payment on a bounty to come. Since I am among those who have scant right to live and flourish, I lead an already forfeit life. All that has happened is sheer luck. But when it comes down to others' rights and my luck, what do I have to lose?

The Voices tell Beach that he must die at least one death:

The following day the Voices again insisted, with relentless repetition, that I was the Anti-Christ. They repeated the former condition that looking at or speaking to any other person would betray them and deepen my own guilt, and they added a further explanation: I, the Anti-Christ, must fulfil my doom by committing a definitive act, and there were to be two alternatives. I must kill another or kill myself. If I chose to kill myself I would descend to the *Tenth* Circle of Hell, which was being prepared especially for me. If I killed another, a choice which could lead only to still more abominable crimes, I would, when finally defeated, descend to the Eleventh Circle—or the Twelfth, or the Thirteenth, depending upon the extent and nature of the new offences it would be my destiny to invent. Hence the dice were heavily loaded, but what were most at stake were my own life and future.

That afternoon I went for a long walk, averting my gaze from every passerby, but the exercise did not calm my mind nor drive away the persistent Voices. As I walked they spelled out for me, in painful detail, the two possibilities and the tortures which would result from the one or the other. My morale cracked and, when I returned home with the Voices singing loudly and accusingly, I screwed up my resolution and made the selection. Self-death was the obvious choice; it had never really been otherwise. It seemed to me patent that the deepest duty of the Anti-Christ was *to rid the world of himself.* In this way, perhaps, the Final Judgment could be averted and, certainly, the suffering of the innocent would be diminished. I began to cut my wrist—slowly, carefully, with intense deliberation. But I could not bring myself to go very far with the job. I discontinued—and cowardice was added to the accusations the Voices were hurling into my ears. After a moment or two of frustrated pacing, I compulsively put a can of Lacquer Thinner to my mouth and drank down what I could.

Immediately on completion of this act the Voices changed. Their singing lost its sinister insistence and became joyous. They instructed me to read the Bible immediately. As I took down my Oxford Reader's Bible from a high shelf, three words (which had come singly into my previous nightly fantasies) converged in my mind and seemed to indicate a unified and pertinent meaning: "conversion," "chastening," and "exorcism." The words somehow flowed together and, in doing so, named what was happening. I took the large Oxford volume on my lap and opened it at random. Fortune placed me in the Old Testament apocrypha in the midst of the "Book of Esdras," and it struck me even then that this scripture—or rejected scripture—was highly appropriate, for the episode I was living had about it, so to speak, something "highly apocryphal." And I was, after all, an Anti-Christ in the milder sense—someone objecting, or trying to object, to Christian mythology and searching for images that would move beyond it or, more simply, out of it. It was not the Bible which gave the moment a magical quality but the fact that I had turned, by chance, to what Christian authority rejected. I *sensed* that I was on the right track.

I then began to read where my eye fell and, after an overwhelming craving, I put down the Bible, went into the kitchen and consumed all the salt I could find in the house. Shortly thereafter I vomited. Realizing now what I had done and was doing, I called an ambulance. At the hospital a nurse bandaged my wrist and a doctor informed me that eating salt had been exactly the right course to follow.

Frightened by Dr. Zee's words—for they have given him a realization that he is not ill, as he had thought and thinks, but a laggard—he is desperate for a category. In his predicament as a man without a category, he is in something of the position of the Ancient Mariner and other souls destined to wander from country to country: *"Where is what isn't?"* he seems to cry out. Feeling increasingly de-selected, de-realized, the conviction grows fast upon him that he may be one of the unchosen, the ones whose destiny is that they must die. As he wanders the broad steppes of categories, he begins increasingly to feel that early death is the realization that best fits him. Only when he finally learns that the salt he has swallowed is the best thing he could have done for himself is there another realization.

To this madcap rush along the fast lane there is a particular quality that unmistakably indicates the motif of the *Pair*. That is, what one accretes is ever more (and more) of the same. This compulsion arises from greed—more, more, more; again, again, again. Unlike *Coupling*, which begins with appetite and can therefore end with repletion, the object of the more-of-the-same drive is ownership. Completion: a complete set; the last one of its kind; and the best one of its kind.

Oh, if you think *that's* something, look here.

You think you're special, well lemme tell you this, you're a dime a dozen. A nickel.

Husband : What he says is that he has had—you know, slept with—every woman in this apartment house except for one. And until he has her, he isn't moving.
Wife: I bet that's that stuck-up Mrs. Greene in 5E!

When choosing is regnant, the problem of a different sort of pain arises. One can hurt. One can get hurt. And yet one is in a kind of free-fall. Here is the right person; at last we can do it; so get ...* out of the way. This is the juncture at which patients experience their signal anxiety—fears of falling, fears of flying, and dreams of cars without brakes, dreams of edifices crumbling or of the ground disappearing; fears, too, of getting stuck, in, into, and by.

And yet, as Beckett puts it, "The Quantum of Wantum is not

---

*The elipses are important. They contain a range of links. It might be: so get your ass outta here, or get the fuck outta here, or get your x outta here before I x it. In the *Couple*, there is the enduring expectation of a Third who is already part of a primal scene and whom the narrator is proposing to replace.

negotiable." A projection of "Wantum" requires, in the *Couple*, a reciprocal agreement on the part of the other to allow more than his own portion of Wantum to be discovered in him or herself. The other, that is, must identify with the projection of the first and act concordantly: "This is what you want, isn't it?" "Oh yes, yes."

A further step in the transfiguration is encompassed in Freud's work on the homoerotic element in projection (see Green 1986) in which "I love you" becomes "You hate me." The replacement fantasy attached to oedipal triumph makes the victor feel quite guilty (but not guilty enough to stop). Usually the sense of loss of one's beloved rival, the feeling of being bad and the shame of being found wanting are not so great as to have to be so exhaustively transfigured.

> P was a "renter." He had not yet found a woman to own, lock and stock, piece and parcel. Every time he saw such a lock and stock, he sighed with dismay. He knew in an instant how he wanted it, draped this way, curled that. But he could not bear to let her know of his degraded status—that which was inherent in his being a wanter. P liked the bosom and was fascinated by the vulva. As to the former, he had found a way of opening his focus so that he could get an eyeful without appearing to be looking. If he felt that he might be seen to be looking, he took off his eyeglasses. (At the point in the analysis when the subject of how he felt about being gripped with sexual desire at all arrived, he declined to wear contact lenses, even though this caused him to travel to his sessions in less convenient ways.) Regarding the vulva, he was able to reciprocate his partner's wish for cunnilingus with great agreeability and, if required, the patience of a saint. But since the wanter was her and the provider himself, there could not be much joy in the lovemaking. So, instead, P would construct possibilities for what he called "recreational" sex. This weightily multidetermined realization (e.g., creation and re-creation) was managed by finding photos or films that bore features of his current partner and forming a cross-referenced "collage" of them. Once she was extant, he could masturbate to his heart's content, with her none the wiser. When he had her just prior to an actual meeting, he was sufficiently drained of libido to stand indifferent to his

own needs. When she was gone, he could take out his creation of her and assert his *droit de cuissage*. It followed that the best sex he had was with a woman who loosely tied him to the bed and took her will of him.

P finds the Wantum in someone else temporarily.

Part Two

Sessions

Introduction

Of the therapy of psychoanalysis, Heinz Hartmann wrote (1959): "Psychoanalysis is the systematic study of self-deceptions and their motivations." Such a study requires an Other because by definition the self-deceiving self has been so adept as no longer to track his own sleights of mind—one of which is precisely that he is attending to experience selectively. Since the patient's patiently constructed self-deceptions are ever in danger from one not so motivated as he, he will perforce in his life have had to construct the smoke and mirrors necessary to deceive others in direct counterpart to his own self deceptions. He will need to do that again (or still) in his analysis. So that even as he is attempting to communicate what is so, he will still want to do so selectively. Knowing this his analyst may ask him to freely associate, that or to "put into words whatever he experiences while in the session" or some such. And he will feel this to be a tremendous burden since so much comes to mind that he cannot possibly comply with the analytic suggestion. (The old "Ali Baba maneuver," after the rogue who hid himself and his thirty thieves by extending the "X" that marked the spot of their headquarters to every door in town.) The alternative plainly is for the patient to pick and choose—or to gabble forth rambles from which the analyst is then free to pick and choose.

Right off selection and selectivity are at center stage. One does not need to study the contents of the associations to see the tensions—they are all evident in the experience.

The motivations represent, in the first instance, man's adherence to an egoistic "pleasure principle" that wants, and wants what it wants here and now. In the second instance the motivation originates in man as a creature of his species, sub-species, *Group*, or *Pair*. For *also* in man's genetic endowment is the urge to select and be selected for advantage in sending forward only the fittest and the finest into the gene pool of generations to come.

When in the frame of mind of *Coupling*, one directs one's desires along the course of immediate gratification, no matter its cost or gain to the Other. When in the state of mind of *Pairing*, one directs one's desires to the Other only partially: *Coupling* instead with people not (wholly) in the *Pair* or *Group*, as indeed those *in* one's *Pair* or *Group would have one* do.

What one *experiences* of the potential pool of information, what one *knows* of one's experience, what one *knows instead* of knowing what one experiences—all these mental phenomena also precisely follow out, via the *selectivity in the use of attention*, the duality and dynamics of the motivations just enunciated. What we need to come to, then, is Hartmann's idea of "the systematic study" of these matters in the therapy of psychoanalysis.

In the modern history of western psychological inquiry (Charcot, Janet, Bernfeld, etc.), it became clear that altered states of mind produced altered states of the body and that people's states of mind could to varying degrees be altered by hypnotic trances. This had already been clear in the East and elsewhere, often as part of religious ceremonies and other ritualistic observances. That these alterations were motivated by some agency or another could hardly be doubted, but precise determinations of source and an exact determination of mechanism were not well understood or, at any rate, stipulated. Some agency, man-made or divine, replaced one state of mind with another and with it induced an impressive array of changes—psychological (e.g., memory and forgetfulness), physical (e.g., paralysis or its opposite), and physiological (e.g., blood pressure or oxygen consumption). What appeared to have minds of their own in the conscious, waking state turned out to be subject to the influences of God, self, and other.

Freud's own entry into the field was initially inauspicious. But soon he was doing what others had not; with Breuer he was thinking that one state of mind did not simply replace another; it repressed, or buried, it. Behind any given state of mind there was another one of which self and others were unaware. However, upon investigation, the two men began to see that there was a certain amount of traffic between these alternate states of mind. Sometimes one knew the other, sometimes not, but if not, one could sometimes be induced to remember the other by post-hypnotic suggestion. (Josef Breuer's [Freud's mentor and co-worker as well as the man who reluctantly wrote the theory chapter in Freud's *Studies in Hysteria*] retirement from this field of investigation arose upon his realization that the patient did not always heed such "suggestions": one of his patients felt herself to be quite in love with him and began to show every sign of experiencing a pregnancy that was to consummate "their" love; her doctor's suggestions to the contrary were unavailing. He then had to transfer the patient to Freud, thus marking for all time the phenomenon of transference.)

Yet the connective tissue linking one state of mind and another continued to seem discernable, providing one viewed the tissue as compounded of experiences at once real and contrived, present and absent, all woven together anywhichwayandhow. To make sense of such communications one had to know that bits were missing and the bits that were there were linked up in ways that obscured that anything was missing or anything substituted for what was missing. Real detective work was required, and, indeed, at first Freud played the detective.

There was a trauma (read, crime) and from the tattered debris left higgledy-piggledy behind, that event could be reconstructed. He would gather hints and fragments from the hypnosis sessions and then quiz (sometimes interrogate might be the more appropriate term) his patients on what they knew about this clue and that detail. What do you think of.... What comes to mind.... Hold nothing back....

The case histories read like detective stories; nothing escaped his attention. He prized open events that had occurred separately in time or place or in dream or actuality, but were told to him condensed into one. And in this he found memories—and such memories!—hidden in the newly revealed interstices. But his patients, having put together their one version of experience, were not so coolly absorbed as he in reconstructing the pain and anguish of the experiences thus concealed. They or "part" of them resisted his efforts, they forgot what they told him and he them. What once made such a hash of matters *still* and quite, quite actively made a hash of them—even, like Breuer's patient, a new hash. As there was no escaping this, however much hypnosis altered the state of mind, Freud deferred to the inevitable and, abandoning hypnosis and *its* sources of motivation, enlisted his patient as his Watson. Now the motivations for the original self-deceptions and the resistances by which part of the self still hoped to continue to keep itself deceived became the object of the analysis. Thus Hartmann's definition.

To reconstruct the trauma, or, so to say, crime, from the present, and much-transfigured versions of what the experience was once is a full-time job. But as it was, to turn out the original experience was not naively sitting there waiting to be found out. It, itself, had been much transfigured way back then. What the digging was to reveal were experiential events already transformed from what they were. So there was to be a vertical reconstruction from current experience to past. But then, having arrived at the past, there was to be a horizontal reconstruction from the past experience's contrivances to what the experience actually may have been. And that experience too may have had a past. And its past too had to be not merely discovered, but looked into for transfigurations which misrepresented it not to the self of the time and not only in the present but to the subsequent experiences of the past. And that was a job and a half.

But there is more still. There are the experiences which, because they were never experienced, cannot be *re*constructed. These "unborn" experiences, having never happened, can only be *con*structed. One constructs them from precisely *when they begin once again not to happen* in the present. This requires a different orientation, and a different kind of attention, the quest being for a different datum entirely.

Attention selects from the world of information certain experiences. These discoveries may turn out to be ones Baby rues. For example, Baby may discover differences between how he is constituted and how mother is—that she has the breast and he only a mouth unconjoined with her breast. Stacks of noticing how different it feels when she nurses him from how it feels when he sucks his thumb or fist or foot may be borne in upon him. If he is a greedy baby or is not helped to surmount or to make use of this discovery, he may experience as part of it an envy so intense as to be intolerable. He may then use his powers of attention to undo the discovery. He may change his realizations of differences in kind, for example, with an idea that embraces only differences in degree. We are the same: she is only more so. A world shifted over to differences in degree is a markedly different world. Imagine the discovery as to gender differences that will presently begin to intrude. If he and mother are the same, what on earth happened to her—or to him? And when and why and how? Homo means same; it is a way of refashioning differences that once barely experienced, experienced, as it were from the *threshold*, have proved to be too painful and frightening to endure. (Perhaps it is fitting that in some corners of society the groom carries the bride over the threshold on their first night together.)

These thresholds are encountered in the therapy of analysis. They are like the little man who wasn't there. Or, to use another illustration, they are absent from a series: 2 . . . 4 . . . 8 . . . What is missing? 6 or 16? The 6 is like something that has been negated. Freud's model of analysis as therapy would be onto it in a moment. It can be reconstructed. Sixteen, however, is another matter. Not having happened yet, it can only be like the proverbial color blue to a blind man. If the patient is to know it, he must experience it, crossing the threshold he teetered on but did not cross originally. A "more of the same" person can have an analysis all about his rivalry, acquisitiveness, terrors about losing things, derogations of those different from himself and his sort and ultimately come to his underlying depression. This is the depression that, like any hollow, marks the place where something was supposed to be but wasn't. For Baby as patient, that would be the breast he discovered he didn't have. But having come there, he has come back to the threshold. Will this time he manage to cross it and lead a life filled with authentic difference—the very differences he spent the first decades of his life trying not to notice? Now we are in a different analytic encounter. Familiar landmarks, such as castration anxiety, look very different to the child who has already lost "his" breast from how they look to the child who, by being weaned, has lost "only" the satisfaction he enjoyed from his mother's. His love of sameness makes for a different sort of love for his father from that experienced by the child who can tolerate differences. Indeed, the entire landscape is different.

And this is what makes the analysis so different—and so difficult. No longer is the analyst introducing the forty-year-old to the fourteen he was and the fourteen to the four and the four to the four-month; he is introducing the four-month to what he almost was, but wasn't. And four-month-olds need to experience a lot vicariously—"You first!" They "rid" themselves of noxious experiences by paying attention not to their own experience but to that of others. (That is often the power of the bond between grandparent and grandchild. The former, reduced to living less in deed, lives more in recollection; and the latter, unlike the generation that separates the two, loves to hear of the wonders and travails of life secondhand.) So too Baby as patient: he wishes to instill in the analyst certain experiences and then sit back and observe what happens.

The discovery of difference means that one person knows where he ends and the other begins. A boundary, however faint and evanescent, is discernible. Two beings appear with more or less regularity. Looked at from inside, that sense of boundary is but a single membrane; like semidetached houses, sharing one common wall. But it is enough to make a place where an I/me can gradually collect—and a place where not-I can also collect. Containers make for contents—and for the redistribution of such contents as one may wish to convey elsewhere in the form of gifts, or for that matter, of wastes to be gotten out of the container harboring self. Out of means into somewhere (or someone) else. In this connection the adage "Don't get angry; get even" takes on new meaning. Instead of being angry and helpless about what you are experiencing, make the other person experience it as well. Curiously, "as well" often turns out to be "instead of," and the once angry person, having achieved this objective, now feels calm and cool.

Such transmigrations are in the jargon called projective identifications. The "identification" tags the content as having been once experienced as part of self, the "projection" being the verb for the transportation. In the analysis of people who have not been able to tolerate certain experiences one feels that one's greatest use is to provide the somewhere else to stow experiences unwanted in the self: to be the waste container. But not *just* a dump site; that would *only* besmirch, sully, and ruin one and is only really useful for purposes of getting even. Rather a waste recycling plant, into which the gobs and fragments of unusable and potentially toxic experience, encountered briefly on the threshold, can be quickly sent for recycling: wash, dry-clean iron, and repair. And then brought back, now metabolized into something safe, tame, clean, and bearable.

This is the main use of the discovery of difference some people can make: difference is tolerated only in that it avails them of Otherness, a not-me which is yet a far cry from being a You.

As Freud began to take the transference more and more as an opportunity than a nuisance, he saw how greatly his patients wanted to employ their differences from him reciprocally. All the ways in which his analysands had felt unrequited in their lives came with them into the analysis: it was as if this time around they could achieve the perfect reciprocity that fate had denied them up until then. Indeed, Freud began to count on that to see right there in his consulting room what their fate heretofore had been. Indeed it is reported that with one patient he pounded the couch in exasperation, saying something like: "Am I so old and ugly now that you cannot bring yourself to have longings for me?" But in Freud's work the differentiations between the Me and the You had for the most part evolved into occasions in which the differences were tolerated even when the experience was one of frustration. Jealousy might reign and rage, but greed and envy did not hold experience to or destroy knowledge of differences—leaving only something so unevolved as mere Otherness. Classic or traditional analysis flourished with such evolved transferences, where the I was an I and the You was a You and always and ever the twain should meet. Indeed, Freud was well aware of how "healthy" his patients had to be if they were to be helped by analysis as he knew it. In a paper written as an appendix to his more well known paper concerning lay or nonmedical analysts, he visualized a role he called the *seelesorger*, in which psychoanalysts would not practice as psychotherapists, after the medical model, but rather as lay pastors to a community, helping out as small difficulties emerged, rather, perhaps, as he had helped "Little Hans" by conveying interpretations to the child through his father. (Having myself for several years attempted such a community-wide practice, I can testify both to the quite-solvable difficulties and the vast potential benefits of that version of psychoanalytic consultation.) But of course a set of practices devised for one population will not serve another unless the practices are modified, and traditional analysis had that in store for it as analysts increasingly worked with children and with people of a psychotic disposition.

Many members of these populations did not yield up the experiential data in their associations, dreams, recollections, or play—to which the analyst in due course could draw their attention. They set out, rather, to communicate through projective identifications.

The analyst was an Other in whom the patient provoked, created, and inculcated those experiences the patient felt in danger of having firsthand and directly. They gave him information, but it was he who was to have the experience. And if part of the experience was knowing of the experience, it was experiences of his that he perforce had to know of. It followed that the emptier he could make himself as a petri dish or container for the cultures his patient needed to grow *within* him, the better. It became increasingly obvious that what was required was a "by their *fruits*, so shall ye know them" perspective.

The datum for which psychoanalysis was in quest had moved. Initially it was intrapsychic. Being within the patient, it was gatherable by hypnosis and soon guided free association. Presently it was seen to be a datum observable between the twosome. It could be studied interpersonally and especially as recreated in the transference. Now, however, it was seen to occupy a position within the analyst. From this new position intuition arises not so much from what the analyst knows of the patient's experiences in the analysis, but of his own. Later, rather than always interpreting what the analyst *surmised* from the current experience, formulations that directly expressed the analyst's experience as, in Sullivan's term, a "participant-observer" in the pair became part of the repertoire (Sullivan 1953).

Now this was always true: no one can truly discern what another person experiences without exercising sympathetic imagination and empathy—without himself having the ability vicariously to put himself in the other's shoes. And it was already clear that the patient's transferences readily lent themselves to eliciting reciprocal or antagonistic transferences in the analyst. The custom, later the dictum, that every analyst should first have an analysis of his own was designed to augment his capacities to intuit his patients' experience and at the same time to diminish the effects upon him these elicitations were bound to have. He had to know what he felt in order to fathom what the patient was sending his way but also to keep himself from acting his feelings out with the patient in a way that kept both of them from knowing what they were experiencing. The difficulty was, however, not so easily cured. Everyone practicing analysis knew how difficult it was both to do and to succeed at; and everyone knew that individually and collectively modifications of technique and procedure had to be made. So how were these modifications to be distinguished from wishful enactions of countertransferences? Suppose one hugged a patient, or took his hand or cried with him? Didn't Freud himself give a meal to a patient too hungry to lie on the couch and do analysis? Presumably one's own analyst could scent out constructive modifications of technique, the takings of license that were driven by wish or fear; and then there were the supervising analysts who followed each session minutely.

But even so there were, as there are, problems. The obvious one is that presently the analyst-in-training is on his own to make what *deviations* from the standard he sees fit. For this Freud proposed the remedy that each analyst return every five years or so for further analysis. This does not seem to have been accepted as a general rule. The second sort of problem is in the inhibition to deviate from standard orthodoxy these rules impose. A patient needing "deviations" might not get them.

But it is the third aspect of the matter that may have been and may still be the most problematic. This is the way countertransferences get built into what is considered standard, and thus, as Bion pointed out in 1966, remain hidden from view precisely because they are standard. The intensity of some of the debates among analysts about what standard is or should be certainly evince the power of the feelings involved. The "discussions" in the British Society some years back; the legal suits, concluded only in 1988, between American psychologists and psychiatric analysts on the question of lay analysis that surfaced first at least in 1924 in the instance of Theodore Reik; the splits in such institutes as those in Boston and Los Angeles—all these quite baldly reveal the depth of the issues that "standard" contains.

Still it is openly in the nuances that the secrets are best hidden. An analyst may be alert to himself if he is often late for a particular patient. But what if he is often late for most of his patients? What, moreover, if his *"Group"* of colleagues thinks that being on time is compulsive behavior unfitting for analysts? What if an analyst uses a couch and schedules patients for fifty-minute "hours"? What if he doesn't use the ten-minute interval for himself, but schedules one patient directly after another? One answer to these questions is, "It's all grist for the mill." One does as one does and one helps the patient to learn what he makes of the experience.

Ψ: This is such an issue for you that it must have meaning; let us see what comes to mind concerning this feeling of yours that I . . .

P : But Doctor, I feel this is an issue of yours. It is you who—

Ψ: Yes, yes, it may be, it may be; but now, since it is your analysis, let us see about you. You have had such feelings before . . . ?

As a brief vignette, this illustrates practice of a certain sort. The problem is the patient's and he must look into himself if he is to learn what the analyst's behavior represents for him. The patient who can profit from doing this will profit from such an encounter. Those who cannot must have an analyst who does not ping-pong the problem of fault with them. That analyst may have to absorb the feeling the patient is trying to instill; he may have to feel guilty and mean. He may be unable to kick the problem into first the patient and then the past if he hopes to be able to identify what the patient rightly or wrongly is ascribing to him.

A session, any session, even sessions from which the patient is physically absent, is filled with information. As the patient and the analyst do or do not pay attention to that information, it becomes an experience for one, the other, or both (Modell 1990, 1991). As an experience, it can become known and noted. Together the two can piece together their experiences of the experience until it is fully felt, understood, shared, and remembered—at least so far as words can serve. What either the patient or the analyst says may serve to conceal or to reveal, to lay plain or to disfigure. Sometimes it is a line of chat designed to keep the analysis going, for the analysis itself is being used as an experience to forfend against other experiences, like having a breakdown or being poorer. Thus as the practice of psychoanalysis itself needs continuous review and ongoing evolution, so does the analyst, the analysis, and each analytic session. What were we *doing:* and who was doing what and with which and to whom. And why?

10. Session: Monday

Ψ has furnished a consulting room. In glass and chrome, Early American, or Berggasse 19, of course, but also as a playing field for very old and dear games—like "doctor," "house," or "Daddy (or Mommy) goes to work." But not *just* these games that *Couples* play. The analyst is a member of a *Group*, a species that began, perhaps, with Joseph (in whose tradition Freud saw himself), interpreter to the Pharaoh, or some other great explorer, healer, or scientist.

Regarding the relationship of analyst and patient in any one of such "games":

> No doubt the unconscious counterparts of such a vertex will have been laid bare in the psycho-analysis of the individual members, but this should not blind us to the conscious aspects of these vertexes. (Bion 1966)

That is, we may expect the analyst to know of the once unconscious sexual and oedipal designs that brought him into this line of work. But we should not necessarily expect that he will know the significance of his conscious intentions.

For those conscious aspects are and can remain conscious because they are characteristics not of analysts taken individually, but of the analytic *Group* to which the analysts belong. In the charter of each and every *Group* there is a section regarding mutual toleration, what Bion calls "blindness," which holds that serious defects in psychoanalysis are to be discovered elsewhere than within the precincts of any particular institute and society.

> There may well be vertices which are not regarded by the groups as respectable and therefore of which it needs to be unconscious. The group tendency would be to foster unconsciousness in other groups of these defects in itself while claiming their discovery elsewhere. (Ibid.)

It is by no means easy to give up the fantasies for which the psychoanalysis provides its practitioners a realization. When the sources for practicing analysis are the games of doctor, rescue, or reparation, sources that recapitulate the *Couple,* these are routinely "laid bare" as transferences awaiting a partner. But frustrations in the *Couple* have a way of drifting over into the *Pair.* "I understand you better than Daddy (Mommy) does!" easily transforms into "Psychoanalysis provides a form of understanding far deeper and better than any other." This intention also requires a partner. But the partner can now be another member of the analytic *Group,* namely a patient. All that is required for the furtherance of the plot line is a division of labor based on specializations of function. The copulative elements left out from this *Pairing* may circle hungrily waiting for a transference from the patient to join up with in the usual meaning of countertransference. But much gratification can be had in the playing of the strings in which differences are in degree, not necessarily in kind.

Poe's Dupin was able to "find" the purloined letter, not despite the fact that the police searched everywhere, but because of it. Since the letter had to be somewhere and the police had poked and pried into every conceivable hiding place, the letter had to be where the police did not look, and that was of course in front of their noses. Such sleights of mind require collusion—the "fostering" of consciousness and unconsciousness by the direction and misdirection of attention. The villain in the story anticipated that the police would undercredit him and set to expose every possible hiding place. He was safe so long as they paid him insufficient credit. Dupin's respect for the police was great. If they searched a place, he did not need to re-search it. If the letter wasn't where they expected it to be, which was in hiding places each more cunning than the last, they became even more cunning in their searches. Without much thinking about it, they believed their difference from their quarry was calculable in matters of degree. Dupin switched the mind set. The place no one would find the letter was the place no one would think to look for it: and this was right out in the open.

Once the analysis of the *Couple* elements is complete, it is as if everything is discovered—as if the debris left over from the digging required to lay bare the guilty secrets of the *Couple* just fell heaped about and did not precisely hide a hidey-hole.

"But the dog did not bark in the night, Holmes!"
"Precisely, my dear Watson."

These hidey-holes may be fronted-up as quite respectable "ian-isms" (as in Freudian, Kleinian, Sullivanian) even if more philo-sophically they contain deeply held emotional points of view on the human condition. In extension from the earliest games and their positions, some analysts, for example, are concerned with what the patient has been *put* through, others with what he has *gone* through, yet others with the procrustean bed the patient has *made* for himself. Within these theories of causation, there are assignments of *motive*—*not* motivation—that deal out ascriptions of inequity and/or iniquity. The important thing about these as-criptions is not that they are held but that unconsciousness sur-rounds their infusion via an ian-istic "school" into an institute for analysis, thence into an analysis itself.

The training analyst, finding his analysand's vertices congenial to him and his own "isms," may simply not think to investigate them with the diligence he might give to the outcropping of heret-ical "ianisms." To his trained ear, they may sound "normal and natural." There is always a process of fission and fusion in the selection scheme with which the individual, via his *Pairing* state of mind, imbues the *Group* with his responsibilities for being choosy on the one side and choosable on the other. This process operates from the basic level of attention itself. To attend to things from the *Pair* point of view is not to attend to them from the *Couple* point of view; to attend to things as belonging to us is to attend to *other* things as *not us*. If we are normal, they must be abnormal. It is abnormal for the Kleinians to impute so intricate a mental life to infants, especially as the nervous system is not yet myelinized; it is abnormal for the interpersonalists to think the intrapsychic to be so pervious to the kindness or unkindness of others; it is abnormal for the self-psychologists to extend themselves toward the grandiosity and fantasies of omnipotence of the young; psychoanalysis is unscientific and it is abnormal of us to think it otherwise.

Being part of the analytical *Group*, the analytic *Pair* is one of the systems by which the needs of the species can proceed. The analytical *Group*, for example, needs patients. To get them it must be "relevant": prospective patients also have their own theories about what went wrong and what it will take to fix it. Most psychoanalysts, for example, take their patients seriously. They think there is likely to be a great deal to them, each aspect needing to find its place in the assisted self-scrutiny of which the therapy of analysis consists. Many patients actual and (more so) potential do not wish to be bathed in such waters of concern. These worry them or make them subject to the derision or envy of their *Group*. In such a conflict in cultures, where is the analyst to find his other half (Boris 1971)?

The patient has his own theories, and he is sure to get on better with an analyst who shares these. A very great deal of time in any analysis is spent in the proselytization of views by both analyst and patient: there is a possibility that even as late as termination neither will feel that the other has come around. But what may be more to the point, what happens to the patient whose analyst lacks some of the realizations necessary to reconstruct those of his experiences that cannot find their way into *being experienced* without those realizations?

But far from being at termination, we are in the thick of things: P is just about to enter Ψ's consulting room.

The two are likely to offer one another a conventional greeting. Both are likelier than not to want hubbub and hurly-burly contained until patient reaches his chair or the couch, and both will have learned to count on their respective conventions and routines to restrain such potential for turbulence. The development of these small courtesies and their almost daily application rivets enough attention to make these transitions neither too revealing nor too exciting. The ceremonial repeated seems to say, "We both still know that today again we're here for business. These are our safeguards against both chaos and the abyss." If patient and the analyst must pass one another, say at the door or as each composes himself at the juncture of couch and chair, these ceremonies help against touching or hitting, embracing or murdering.

Insofar as the analyst can perform these rites mechanically and count on the patient to observe them as well, the analyst can busy himself with what he is here to do, and that is to find out who has arrived. The patient inevitably brings in with him the startlement of fresh being however familiar he (or the analyst) may seem. Not to recognize that is more than an invitation to chronicity: it is an insistence on it.

Being a brand new person is an imposition on another person who is trying to be good at things in order to get better at them. The absorption with good, better, and best is the concern of the *Pair* and the *Group* in respect to the selective advantage of their species. Differences in kind, on the other hand, represents rather the occupations of the *Couple*. The two needs converge when the species, psychoanalyst, is faltering in such a way that "new blood" may be needed. In this century some of the new blood has been contributed by the patients who previously were thought to be unworkable—very young children and psychotics. They selected from the pool of practicing analysts those who could stand the ambiguity and turmoil inherent in the encounter, at least long enough to evolve interpretations that could serve these patients well enough to keep the practice of psychoanalysis identifiably intact. We are still able to speak of "schools" of psychoanalysis. The fate of those whom Bion referred to as the "Mystics" is still unsettled. Mystics are alternative to the holders of received wisdom, the founding fathers and mothers. The latter keep the species intact and safe from hybridization. The former offer hybridization, often in the form of finding new analogs. The survival of a species requires both.

The perils of change and discovery will exercise a powerful effect. Examined for continuity, each party may find the other unchanged, even stubborn or stuck. That "discovery" may be so compelling as to overshadow any manifestations of newness. On the other hand, today's patient and today's analyst, however reminiscent they may be of two people each already knows, are also brand new and unmet. Today both are different and their differences come into being in the small plosion of their encounter.

To move away from the turmoil and shock of the new, both the patient and analyst will tend to contract their spheres of attention to the familiar: Oh, he is wearing that tie again; I see she has her hair up again today. Indeed, a book missing from the analyst's shelves or a new folding of the afghan may be startling enough for patient, causing him to glance twice at the analyst just to make sure. And yet in the patient's dreams, the analyst is never a settled state of affairs. The patient often dreams that time and familiarity are out of joint: that there are others present in the waiting or consulting rooms when the patient arrives; or that the analyst is different from usual. The analyst is by no means immune from such dreams either. Both long for a breakthrough, or at least a breakout. But when they dream these dreams they have prudently stopped much blood flow to the portions of the brain involved in motoric activity. During most dream-sleep, only the eyes move. The dreamers may imagine, but must lie still. They may look, but not touch.

P says he felt an anxiety attack coming on when in a crowd at the theatre last evening.

Ψ knows that anxious means frightened, but that it also means eager. He listens.

P : [Describes the fright.]

Ψ: [Where is "the eager?" He listens further. Some aspects of the story that might make someone else feel eager (the heady scents and revealing dress of the women; the presence of an important personage) are told with a particular emphasis on the negative. Ψ seizes on this remarkable fact. He draws the patient's attention to it.]

P : [Protests.]

Ψ: [Waits.]

P : [Wonders what Ψ is thinking in the silence that followed his protest. P renews his protest; he does not want the analyst's attention going in that direction.]

Ψ: [Remains silent. His silence says, "I told you what I thought. Either I was incorrect and must have more data, or I was correct and you don't want to have the experience that will ensue."]

P : [Adds to his experience of the evening, offering more data; he reiterates what he said, adding more weight; then P is silent, as if to say he has said what he has said, and it appears there is no use in talking; then he takes up with some aspects of Ψ's state of mind, such as his always assuming that P is like everyone else, or that just because Ψ likes theatre intervals, does P have to? And the like.]

Ψ: [Is listening to hear whether what comes next broadens the field of inquiry or narrows it. He knows that creatures commonly shrivel and make themselves small when they feel under attack or otherwise in danger. And he knows that if P broadens it, he is trying to give more data in hopes that more data may help to identify the source of his unease. In either case, the more P has to say on the entire range of the subject, which now includes Ψ, the more P will, by overhearing himself, learn of what he experienced before, during and after the experience of anxiety.]

This is psychoanalysis of a certain genre; and if the patient can make use of it, he will learn what alternative experience he wards off by resolutely experiencing only anxiety.

Anxiety, after all, is not easily distinguished from excitement: the same adrenalin rush, the same movement of blood to fight/flight tissues and organs, the same increased release of cholesterol from the liver, the same increases in blood pressure and heart rate, the same narrowing of the field of attention to the object; the same impulse to do something. That is why chemical agents, like beta-blockers, used to control heart activity and even angina, can be used to control anxiety. One's physiological state is, like everything else, open to interpretation. The patient is not lying when he says he felt faint or tight in the chest, began to breathe more rapidly and less deeply, therefore ipso facto anxious. Yet he might as easily and accurately be describing love at first sight.

Both Ψ and P are using formulas to interpret P's experience; P has one, Ψ another. There may be others. It is not clear how much we can extrapolate to ourselves from other species, but when baboon infants are unselected they undergo a stress reaction that

meets every physiological point of what epidemiologists say hu-
mans experience when "stressed-out," beginning with a severe
lowering of the effectiveness of the immune system and extending
on to hyperlipidemia, hypertension, and the rest of what people
die early from. And the patient may be coming to this as he starts
directing his attention from the evening to his experience of Ψ in
the session.

Let us now suppose that they presently arrive together at an
interpretation like this: P found the women attractive, but he
resented this, feeling such sentiments are what women and, for
that matter Ψ, expect men to feel. P feels that these important
personages, the women in their fancy dresses, and Ψ with his
silences, think that in the end P will roll over and give in to some
form of abject, even sexual, surrender. Such a prospect, however,
even as it enrages him, excites P; and he begins to feel an inkling
of fearful interest. P, however, seizes on the fear, for out of the
hubbub, it is the best compromise. It says, "You may have an
effect on me, damn you all, but it was only to make me fearful and
drive me away. I had an awful evening last night"—which is
what, upon lying down for today's session, he has said to Ψ.
Evening may have meant even-ing, as in getting even.

If P had stopped in for a nightcap after the theatre at his favor-
ite bar and had started talking about the crowd at intermission,
his bartender may have said, "Yeah, I can't stand the bitches
either; God's gift they think they are." And emphatically he might
have saved P a certain amount of time. And money.

Such empathy and insight can be arrived at formulaically,
without imagination, and they are helpful, no matter the source,
for those who can use them. The analyst may go further than the
bartender (or the hairdresser), because part of *his* formula is that
what happened at the theatre resumed there and didn't start there.
Those the patient encountered at the theatre were merely players
in a revival of a drama of his own construction—one that started
long ago.

The woman in the persimmon-colored silk shantung, of course,
plays Mother. The Important Personage plays both Father and Ψ.
The wispy little thing with the bare back is Sister. And P plays the
slight, shy child of three, hair tousled, eyes gummy from sleep,
hands in the waist of his seersucker pajamas as he comes into the

bright lights of the room. Was it a dream that awakened him? Yes, a dream, a dream of a very tall man and a woman with orange lipstick and the man is doing *some*thing to the woman, but everyone including his sister is standing around as if it is all normal and someday he too will understand and agree, but he doesn't, and he feels angry and he goes over . . . and he wakes up, and his mother says, "Did you have an awful dream? Maybe that movie you saw was too exciting." And he says to the villainess, "It wasn't exciting, it was scary."

But he doesn't argue very hard because there is something about the people in his room, who are supposed to be his family, but who look a little like the people in the dream; and he wonders, briefly, if the people in the room are only actors, which is an idea that scares him very, *very* much. "Too much imagination!" says the woman in the silky-looking dress. He feels relieved that that's all it is, and then the movie, the dream, the awakening, the play, the intermission, or the session ends. "Now back to bed with you. Give Mommy a kiss, that's a good boy. See you tomorrow."

"See you tomorrow," he says to Ψ, as he always does.

11.   Session: Tuesday

P : Hello.

Ψ: Hi.

P : If this were a book, I'd feel that I was here less than a page ago.

Ψ: [Odd, I have that feeling too.] What is the feeling like?

P : Well, familiar. Like I went to sleep and just woke up, and here we are again.

Ψ: And here we are again.

P : Yes . . .

Ψ: Just as you said we would be.

P : I said that? When?

Ψ: Before you "went to sleep" yesterday. You said, "See you tomorrow."

P : Oh, yes, that. I always say that.

Ψ: As if there might be some doubt.

P : Doubt? About what?

Ψ: You sound doubtful about what I just said.

P : Oh, no. I just didn't understand what there could be doubt about. No, that was just your imagination.

Ψ: Too much imagination?

P : Yes. No! Which one of us are you talking about? It irritates me when you get all cryptic like that.

Ψ: As if you begin to doubt me or you own senses?

P : I don't doubt you. For Christ's sake, I see you often enough.

Ψ: Could that be why you see me as often as you do—so that

I don't change in the night? So that you don't offend Christ by changing me around in your dreams?

P : When you said "Christ," I saw the Christ, where is it, in the Andes? That tall figure high on the mountains overlooking Rio. They say the women don't wear clothes on the beaches. That reminds me of that story. A kid comes home from camp. He says, "Guess what, they swim naked at my camp." So his friend says, "So could you really tell the boys from the girls, huh?" And the kid says, "Stupid! I just told you they don't wear clothes."

"I don't doubt you. For Christ's sake, I see you often enough."

As P may have hinted, this could be yesterday's session today. Yesterday P went to the narrative form to communicate; he told of his experience at the theatre. Today Ψ is helping to keep the experience in the room, but the same experiences that fueled yesterday's narrative are making themselves manifest in today's session. P, at age three, is having his say, as best he can. P is trying to help that three-year-old find the words for it that he didn't have at three. At three, P went to sleep "like a good boy" so as not to cause a ruckus among the rest of the family and to have a dream instead. At three, P woke up too angry, scared, and excited to finish his dream. At present, P is having another dream—of Rio and of camp. Ψ will listen to this and other dreams, like the one about the theatre, but today's analyst will bear in mind that P is still being a good boy, as that Important Personage, Christ, in return for watching over him, wants him to be. And he will also bear in mind that the dreams about camp and Rio are meant not to cause a ruckus in the consulting room.

P doesn't remember that night when he was three or the dream or what happened to make the ingredients for the dream. Or if he does, his memory will be like a yellowed photograph stumbled upon in an attic: "I remember one night when I was a kid waking up, maybe from a dream, or something woke me, I don't recall, and coming into the living room or my parent's room, anyhow some brightly lighted room, and my mother saying something like 'See you tomorrow' and putting me back to bed."

But *it* remembers P. *It* is trying to catch his attention like someone dressed for a party tries to catch a cab on a rainy night. But each time, P manages to divert it. I am not the only one ready with similes and metaphors; P also has an image for every occasion: theatre, anxiety, Rio, camp. Stuff about doubt and about imagination and who, Ψ or himself, is feeling what about whom. Indeed P is acting as if there is big trouble ahead, and not that the worst is all behind him. P is acting, that is, as if he is not yet three and what happened at three is not a memory but an anticipation. As such, he is anxious to prevent it. But what he is anxious to prevent he cannot say, precisely because what he is trying to prevent has already happened. He acts as if there weren't anything much to remember, but that is wishful thinking, even as his anxiety about something's happening is wishful thinking. Thus, as P lies on the couch, talking of Rio and camp jokes, trying not to make too much of a ruckus, he is trying to forestall something. His motive is identical to the one he had at almost-three and at three. P is older now, old enough to go to the theatre and buy a drink. Or is he?

Ψ treats him today as if he were three, only with a bigger vocabulary. P acts as if then is now, and despite remonstrances from Ψ, he goes right ahead talking as if then were now. It is almost as if Ψ were not talking to P who is, in fact (or is it in fact?) lying on his couch, but to some two- or three-year-old. He is talking as if P didn't feel himself to be there or were there in flesh but not in spirit. Ψ is talking as if P in spirit is more real to him than the in-the-flesh patient. If, as they might, they go on to talk about the differences between the genders, Ψ may continue to behave as if P didn't know and didn't want to know, and not as if P has had relationships with women and is possibly married and the father of two. For that patient is not the person who came in saying Hello today. Today Ψ is meeting with a rather little boy who is trying to re-prevent a catastrophe.

12. Session: Wednesday

P : Hi'ya.

Ψ: Hello.

P : Warm day.

Ψ: [Brazil? Cold heart?]

P : Well, let's see. . . .

Ψ: [See. . . . *Us* see: "where is it? In the Andes?" Let us go then you and I . . . etherized . . . table . . . -half-remembered . . . muttering . . . women come . . . women go. . . .]

P : I had a dream—

Ψ: [—I made a b.m. The go part of come-and-go.]

P : —But I don't remember it very well.

Ψ: [Half-remembered.]

P : Just a scene or two, really.

Ψ: [I saw *some*thing when I made a b.m. Just a seeing or two. Really! But I don't remember it very clearly. Do you? I wish you knew. I didn't want to know it by myself. It was about where women come and go, but I must have dreamed it. Where was the tall figure? What happened to the Mountains? Perhaps I only dreamed it. I hope I only dreamed it.]

P : I was sitting somewhere and I knew it was late but I was watching something, like a glacier or iceberg in the water. Something was going to happen, and I had a good view, you know like a good seat, say, in the theatre. And then there was a loud noise, like an ocean wave crashing. And I looked again, only it was hard to see, like steam or mist. Mist. But I thought I saw a piece of the glacier or what ever it was had broken off and was floating. Then I woke up, I think. I was at Lake Louise once, you know in the Canadian Rockies. And the contrast between the water of the lake—turquoise, sort of, or aquamarine —and the white of the glacier, though in places the ice was dirty. . . . Blue and orange are complementary colors. . . . But the blue of those glacial streams is something. Have you seen it? You must have seen it. . . . I don't know. There doesn't seem to be much to this dream, though I guess you would say there's more than meets the eye. There was another scene, I know that, but I'll be damned if I can remember it.

Ψ is tweaking at the pleat in his trouser leg, straightening the line of it, feeling the material between thumb and finger. This is, he notices, comforting to him. He likes the sharper edge he is putting in the pleat. More to meet the eye. But he calls the pleat "crease" as he is thinking about it. "Convexed pleat, concavéd crease," he is thinking. "Zeno is a Cretan; all Cretans are liars. . . ." Butt me no buts, And me no Andes, and If me none of your jiffy iffies. There is a way of taking the edge of the labia minora and pleating it, of the nipple too. (Excuse me, but are you young enough to drink here. This is for minors only.) Roseate. What Rosie ate. Let's put the X back in extra. Of course, if blue and orange are complementary, wouldn't persimmon be the complement to aqua? Persimmon is where Mother was when last we saw her at the theatre. Is Mother in her bath? Expiate. What the P ate. P ate the X and X marks the spot. He must have dreamt he ate her lower breast-and-penis."

"I'll be damned if I remember it." Memory, for the P, is the proverbial return to the scene of the crime, as if to remember is to do it twice over. Something happened twice over—or something that happened once must not happen again. How's he going to stop it, except by not remembering? It's aqua-vulva time, it's aqua-vulva time. For a close, *close* shave. Shaved her legs in the bath, mayhaps? Mishaps. Mist. And nothing must be missed, and nothing can be missed. Missing something? Wasn't it he—yes it was—who talked of woman's pubic hair, smudgy, dirty, can't see. Dirt on glacier? Ice-her is nicer but liquor is quicker. Bartender. So first the nipple and the breast the "Rockies and the Andes" go. And if *they* go *so-o-o cold*ly, what else can go wrong? The b.m. goes, out, out, but right off too, splash! and down the drain. Best seat in the house. I am sitting on the best seat in the house and I have your paper before me; soon it will be behind me. Someone said something like that, very amusing. From behind girls and boys are look-alikes. You have to see them in clothes. From behind all people are equal. Yon castle hath a pleasant seat, so don't, I beg you, turn around or rise from your bath, Primavera. What *else* can go wrong? Have you by any chance talked to the Captain of the Titanic!

P : I thought I would be late here today. I had to stop to go to the bathroom. Bowels. Usually I go last thing at night, just after going to bed. . . . I feel thirsty. Maybe because it's warm. When I leave here I'm going to have a cream soda, with plenty of ice. I've always loved cream soda, ever since I was a kid. I hated going for rides. But that was the big thing on Sundays, we would all take a ride. It was so boring in the back seat. The treat was if my sister and I didn't fight, we could stop on the way back for a cream soda. . . . I am thinking now of a sunsuit or sundress she had. Bare in back. I could see, you know, the little cleavage of her butt. I used to say "Oh, look at that. Oh, no you missed it." And she would swivel around to see it through the back window and I could see her bottom. She used to get awful mad, not, you know, about my seeing, I doubt she knew that, though maybe. But about me saying "Oh, you missed it. Too late." I know I should be associating to the dream, but nothing seems to be there, nothing about nothing. Well, maybe you'll be able to see something in it, I never could. But I know I said something about ice, and ice was in the dream. Oh yes, ice and cream soda. My father hated us to suck the ice after we drank the soda, you know how kids like to do. "When it's over it's over," he would say, "and I hope you are not hinting for more." But there *was* more there, down among the little ice shards, but you really had to suck to get it. Dig the straw in or shake the cup around. Christ, but that would get him mad. Sit there in the front seat stiff with anger. Big fucking stiff. I mean, if he didn't like us sucking ice, why didn't he buy us seconds? . . . But there was a swirl to cream soda. We used to call it suds. Kind of swirling and curling around the ice that would show through, like foam. I am dying of thirst. These memories, it's

like what happened is happening all over again. Excavation.
Pick and shovel. Preserved in aspic. What . . . ? Oh so soon?
Well, see you tomorrow.

There is so much Ψ *could* have said that it is not surprising he
said next to nothing (only "Hello"). As P said, a breakdown had
taken place in the night and the debris were scattered all over the
place. One could certainly see the signs of this reflected in the
analyst's own ruminative processes. Along with the substance of
the material, he was soaking up the sense that it consisted of
detritus. There was a hint of delirium in his experience. Toward
the end of the session he was probably able to see that the session
was being run backward, in a kind of fast reverse, from defecating
out to drinking in. P was getting back to something, but he was
also evacuating it as fast as he could. To a degree, he wanted to
make something of these evacuations that was more worthwhile
than what he was able to see in them and certainly more worthwhile than what his father, mother, and sister were able or disposed to make of them. But there was a sense in which he wanted
to make his movement after he went to bed: that is, *into*, as
analyst stood in for the others and for Christ. Having moved his
bowels, he could dare to have this dream, without fearing that it
would in fact happen. There was a certain suppressed rage in this
activity: having to do this ass-picking, shovel-it-out-work that is
called analysis. Get out of my asshole and give me something to
drink, you chilly prick. Get into my back seat and give me something nice, you creamy tit. But submerged in all of this is the cave,
which today is feeling like the empty place the nipple was after it
wasn't anymore. This is the icy empty place that so enrages P that
he wants to shit into it and even to break it off. For it has become
at once an empty container and one full of frustration and pain. It
is like the remains of the first and the unforthcoming second
cream soda. "Oh, so soon?" may have been the watchword for the
session.

That Ψ didn't have anything to say of all this may have been
his sense from noting himself at his own trouser pleat, that today,
more so than yesterday, was a day for action. Ψ could have said
some of what he thought was going on, but he risked two things
were he to have done so. The first of these is that what he said

would have been thought of by P as being countering actions: Stop sucking ice; move your bowels, etc. The second is that his talk would shut P up, and P was contributing a good deal of additional information to that contained in the dream. Why then should Ψ risk jarring P by telling him what he is coming closer to knowing on his own? The experience alluded to in the dream was coming unglued from dream language and reforming itself into the potential delirium that it was. This P was holding in abeyance by stimulating some of this delirium in Ψ. Ψ was kindly absorbing it, so that P could do some recollecting and re-experiencing on his own without being unduly frightened that "these memories, it's like what happened is happening all over again." Today Ψ is doing a lot of remembering himself. Perhaps that is his contribution to today's session.

13. Session: Saturday

As we know, P attaches considerable significance to his "See you tomorrow." It was his goodnight ritual with his mother, and, as we are beginning to notice, seeing has an air of impermanence about it. There is more and there is less than meets the eye, as he reminded Ψ he knew ("I see you often enough!") in the previous session. So we may not be altogether surprised to find that this incantatory farewell was not strictly speaking accurate. Today is Saturday, and there is no session.

Saturday is a good day for doing errands with the kids, working in the garden or washing the car, listening to the afternoon opera or taking in a football game. It is also a good day to reflect on the week. For in the absence of a session, one can sometimes better tell what did not take place that might have.

For example, P and Ψ seemed for the most part to know that they were officeholders in an analysis—a *Pair*. P seemed to know that he was to lie down, tell dreams and free associate, while Ψ seemed to feel that to let himself go into a stream of consciousness was not inappropriate. That he said nothing beyond a hello might have raised questions at other social or for that matter work occasions, but neither of the two seemed to be put off by this peculiarity. Nor did they act as conspirators in an event that secretly defied convention—no furtive nods and winks or secret passwords. They both acted as if what they were about was a natural, sanctioned activity, though if one were to think about it one would be hard put to think of where else such an activity is conducted. The confessional, perhaps, or in some sense a physician's consulting rooms. But P is neither being shrived, examined, nor counselled. Indeed there is no manifest sense of wrongdoing, illness, or deviancy about P. If these qualities are present at all, they are present in the setting and the conduct of the two parties to the doings. And yet, when together, neither seems to find his activities dubious.

True, P does not tell everyone where he is off to so regularly each week, and Ψ would not tell a soul he even knows who P is without the patient's explicit consent—and sometimes not even then, as when a phone message came to Ψ to pass onto P. Ψ and P know this about one another, though they have not really discussed such "ground rules." It is as if before they ever met P and Ψ belonged to a larger *Group* to whom the traditions and customs of something called psychoanalysis were known.

This *Group* is a curious one. There is no knowing quite who belongs to it and who does not. Some analysts, reading this, would not feel that Ψ and P were members of any *Group* to which they aspired to belong. (Some perhaps would not even read this!)

Then there is the community of psychotherapists who would be scandalized but not surprised that two grown people could indulge themselves in anything like what I have been attempting to report. They might well feel for P because anyone can get into the wrong hands, especially a person who is troubled. But as for Ψ, well, the less said the better. Psychotropic drugs, it is to be hoped, will soon rid the world of this cult and its preoccupations with sexual matters and its voodoo practices, which most people can't afford anyway even if there were statistics to demonstrate any improvement in functioning at all, which there aren't.

Meanwhile one does what one can with drugs and offers a kind of psychotherapy which, in contrast to what P and Ψ are doing, is neither elitist nor bizarrely wide of the mark. P had an anxiety attack at the theatre. All right, these things happen. The solution is to prepare P for going to the theatre and not having such an attack again, or if he is to have one, at least to manage it so that he doesn't lose the theatre from his life. "Whom was P with? Did he feel safe with that person? Is there someone he would feel safer with? How did he feel about the physical sensations? Did he feel free to tell anyone, to ask for help—to excuse himself and go to the men's room and hyperventilate into a paper bag? What *are* the patient's relations with people, anyhow? How, for instance, does P feel about being here? Was it difficult for him to come? Had he experienced any anxiety? What did he do? What helped? Has he felt anxiety since being here? When? What did it feel like? Why did he not say something about it? Was he worried about anything before he got here? Now, what was this play. . . ."

Among the patient's *Group*, there are many who would approve of his meeting with the therapist. He seems sympathetic, no-nonsense, and to the point. He does not seem as if he hoped to put a succubus-like IV into P and bleed him of his earnings and savings. Even P's wife, if he is married, may well be one of those who don't approve; people can share much, while decidedly not sharing a view of the putative value of psychoanalysis of the sort Ψ and P are engaged in. People who know that P is consulting someone sometimes ask him how much longer it will take:

"Um, well," P would say, "well, it's kind of complicated."
"But you do feel it's helping?"
"Oh, yes, sure, but, you know, it takes a while."
"Does he give you Valium?"
"Well, er, it's not that sort of, um. I mean they don't er. . . . It's more getting to the root of the problem."

And in saying that, P announces he has made a *Group* with Ψ. Even were P to ask about Valium the next time P goes to Ψ, he would half-expect to hear the unmistakable sound of the analyst's eyebrow rising. But even if he stalks right out of the office, so as to break a bit off that glacial figure, he will probably make his way back. This is obvious to both of them: they are co-members in good standing of a *Group* that, despite having lost a certain amount of its luster over the years, is their *Group*. Ψ, one hopes, knows that much is forgiven him in advance, simply as a result of being not who, but what he is. It is not so much a matter of belief or faith with which P endows Ψ and his circle, though these may be elements in the formation of the *Group*. It is rather a piece of the patient's identity, one not wholly shared by other members of his other *Group*s. Of the thousands of people who are told that psychoanalysis might help, only a portion can visualize themselves as an analysand. They hear this, and in their mind's eye they see a small man with a goatee and a notepad and a Viennese accent saying "so-o" to a figure embarrassingly recumbent on a couch. "You maybe vish to zleep viz your mother, hm'n?" And they think of the middle-aged woman slightly running to fat, with increasing varicosity, who is Mother, and they think, "Thanks but no thanks."

Penicillin helps, inoculations help, sometimes surgery helps, but much of medical practice consists of finding those people whom these can help, while helping the others wait out the time it takes to get better. Does what Ψ does help? He would like to think so, but the truth is he can't know what would happen if P simply waited. Is there a four-, five-, or ten-year placebo that some subjects could be given, while others got the real stuff? No, and moreover what Ψ does with P is different from what he does with others and others would do with P and P with others. The Scientific Status of Psychoanalysis is hopeless. Some people, as we have seen, couldn't be persuaded to become a P even in the noble interests of science. So forming a scientific control *Group* is impossible. (Research, however, remains to be done to see what happens if working psychoanalytically, like esteemed others do, helps provide an identity which is in and of itself helpful.)

Ψ became a patient (and may even become a patient again from time to time; one hopes so for his patients' sakes, if nothing more) at least partly in order to become an Ψ. He and other analysts have done something rather like what he and P have done in their turn, and Baby and Mother in *their* turn. They have agreed to divert certain demands from one another and instead to express these elsewhere. They have agreed to put the *Group* of participants in psychoanalysis ahead of sheerly egoistic desires. They have foresworn certain wishes to *Couple*, and have instead accepted the alternative of *Pairing*.

If Ψ thought that if or when P asked him for Valium or Prozac Ψ were to raise his eyebrow, P would quit for good. Ψ would have to have *his* head examined to see why he poured so much work and care into P. Ψ has to know that, when push comes to shove, P will continue to consent to join in analyzing his wishes, this one included. Thus their future as an analytic pair will survive despite the frustration both may feel at being unable as a *Couple* to gratify their wishes instead of analyzing them. This is an act of mourning that begins in babyhood and continues lifelong. The analyst's own capacity to stand and survive these daily acts of mourning was presumably facilitated by his analysis. In return he has received the training, authorization, and moral support to practice as a Ψ. Should P leave over the Valium issue, for example, someone senior to Ψ will say, "So he turned out to be a borderline, after all. Well, you did your best. Borderlines are always a risk. Listen, I saw someone the other day who might make an interesting patient for you. She's . . ."

As Ψ sits there in his reveries, having the audacity to work contrary to the standards and practices of the Valium givers, the Other Analysts, the Behavior modification, Reality, and Cognitive therapists, the psychotherapists of other persuasions, eclectic, electric, or orthodox, the counsellors, the couples, and the family therapists, it is that expectation of support from his *Group* that sustains him. It sustains him even now, as it does P, as they go about their weekends, confident that the analytic pair will re-*Group* on Monday to continue the investigations into the turbulence of the patient's experiences with being part of a *Couple.*

Let us end this examination of what goes unattended to and unsaid in their sessions on this comfortable note. But since what takes place in the *Pair* is of no less significance than what takes place within the *Couple,* we might ourselves feel more sanguine if presently further thought were given the matter. The transferences that go into the formation of the *Pair,* what is sometimes called the therapeutic or working alliance, go unnoticed by the precise set of agreements that make up the *Pair.* The agreement is to look elsewhere other than the *Group* of which one has been made a part, and to discover what our *Group* abhors not within Us but in Them.

The placidity with which the analyst and patient are comporting themselves is going unexamined. It could, as Freud said, go on like that interminably.

14. Session: Monday

P : Hi.

Ψ: Hi.

P : I am worried about this session. I feel the weekend has broken something—that I feel closed off and far away. . . . I have things to say, but nothing sounds, as I preview it, very real. I know I shouldn't preview it, but I do. [Silence.]

Ψ: Broken—Closed off—Far away—View—Shouldn't—Worried.

P : Yes, I see. I like it when you do that; it's like a word association test. Black—white, dog—cat. You propose: I respond. "Broken," let's see. . . . Broken. . . .

Ψ: [Speak for yourself, John Alden. And yes, I did, didn't I? Propose. Why couldn't I wait? What am I trying to do, giving him, as he says, this word association test? My, my Freud, how Jung you look today. What if he proposed? Mother may I marry you/ why "yes" my darling daughter/fix the limb on your little bush/ and lamb goes to the slaughter.]

P : . . . fix. Closed off—opened out. Near. Postview—look after. No. See after. Yeah, *see* after. It reminds me of those before and after ads. Me, before I lost weight; Me, after twelve weeks of Nautilus. Our house before the addition. Here he is as a baby—and here he is graduating! Pre and post. I sometimes wonder if there is anything to this premenstrual syndrome that they talk about? I don't know why I think of that except that T had her period this weekend. . . . She doesn't seem to mind, in fact she seems to like it that way. "Gushy," she says. I'm a little more squeamish. But I don't tell her that, in case it hurts her, you know, feelings.

Ψ: [There it is, now, again: "I *don't* know"—*you* are the one who knows. *You* know, *you* propose. I, on the other side, am tactful, closed off, know I shouldn't look. Above all, constructive. A matter of black and white. You black, me big, me grown up, me white. Me good fellow. Hate the sight of blood, I do. But would I tell the slaughtered lamb that? Not on your life. Would I tell her I like the sight of her blood. Not on my life. My postlife, anyway. . . . Something to say here? Not now: Trampoline. He projects—woosh, zoom—into me, I take it and boomerang it back. Already offered a proposal; better now to wait until he is finished. What is he using, by the way, in the manner of transport?]

P : I, uh, feel that this is boring you, that you are feeling, "I have heard this all before."

Ψ: I didn't want to feel impatient earlier, when I prompted you with the word association. I wanted to put or return the impatience to you.

P : Me? But I didn't feel impatient, quite the reverse.

Ψ: Exactly. A matter, one could say, of black and white or cat and dog.

P : I don't know what you mean.

Ψ: [Silence.]

P : I hate it when you refuse to answer my questions!

Ψ: It could be said that that wasn't so much a question as a something else.

P : All right. What do you mean?

Ψ: [He attends to me and gives me so little now to attend to in him. He is opaque now, as best he can be.]

P : This is awful. I can hardly talk. I feel blank. Am I angry? Yes. I am angry that you don't answer me. I feel humiliated when I ask questions you won't answer. I don't know how that feeling of humiliation is supposed to help. How is it supposed to be therapeutic? What am I supposed to learn about myself from feeling humiliated? Don't think these are questions; they are not. So don't bother not answering them. You know what this reminds me of? I'll tell you what this reminds me of—a blank wall. But not just blank, exactly, but negative. Like the iron curtain wasn't just a wall, it was an aggressive act. A blank wall could be like a canvas ready to be painted on or a blank page, like a new leaf. Filled with promise. But this is the opposite. Blank. Empty. Like blind, staring eyes. It gives me the creeps. I hate to watch blind people. They should all be made to wear dark glasses. You think there is an eye there and you look and there is, but it isn't. It's disgusting. It makes me nauseous. It makes me. . . ."

[P continues.]

Ψ is going to stay out of the patient's way for he feels the latter is on to a rather vivid experience now, one which he would be wrong to head off with interpretive commentary. P has "found" the "wall" in a place he can work with it. At first it was located in the weekend break, the broken thing that separated them. Then he located it in the analyst's failure to propose: to give him something to which to respond. For reasons that are unclear, this touched off a feeling of compunction in Ψ that later he was angrily to regret. Somehow P was able to instill in him feelings of being too Jung to be Freud. Ψ responded to this with a burst of bravado. The role reversal attempted by P, where dog and cat and black and white were also to change sides, was intolerable to him in that point in time. He very much needed P to take back what was intolerable, so that he could be spared that impatience of his own which linked up with and added to what P was insinuating into him. Happily for Ψ P agreed to do this. He took the wall that he had moved from being between them to being in himself, and while still complaining about it being a hostile and forbidding characteristic of Ψ nevertheless stopped trying to force Ψ to be alone with it. While leaving one wall in place, he began to take down that wall within himself that had made him so opaque.

This allowed the oppositions to look more like viewpoints and blindspots. The question of what was beheld and what was in the eye of the beholder could be reopened. Was it the blind eye that was so persecuting? Or was it that which blinded the eye? Was it the horrible absence where the eye should be or the horrible absence upon which the eye gazed? And which was responsible for the fear and guilt that followed? Who did it to the other? Ψ started off impatiently to make P look at things one way, *his way.* He knew, of course, that he had no business doing that, and whatever itch of his that needed scratching was not the P's responsibility. So having done it, he was mad at P.

P naturally called this to Ψ's attention by telling him that something humiliating was going on, but he forbore to tell Ψ that it was he who was humiliating himself. He turned a blind eye to this defect in Ψ, but was quite put out that once again he had to pretend to like someone else's gushiness. He was sick of having to feel black was white. It humiliated him when someone made him do it to spare the other the feeling of having been silly. But having done this, P went on to provide both himself and Ψ with the details of what was worse than blankness, namely absences where he had supposed presences to be. These he said were not possibilities for growth and development, but no-things that bore the marks of an active malevolence.

But whose? There was a considerable backing and forthing on this question, as if both realized its importance to each of them.

Was it important—indeed, was it a question, an issue? Looked at within the context of the session, there is no doubt that it was. But are we witnessing a variation of the *folie à-deux?* Are two people so enclosed with one another that they are developing a special culture and a private language? Even were others to read this session, would it be comprehensible to them? In the introduction to his book on attention and interpretation, Bion writes (1970: 1, *line* 1), "I doubt if anyone but a practising psycho-analyst can understand this book although I have done my best to make it simple. Any psycho-analyst who is *practising* can grasp my meaning because he, unlike those who only read or hear *about* psychoanalysis, has the opportunity to experience for himself what I in this book can only represent by words and verbal formulations designed for a different task. They were developed from a background of sensuous experience. Reason is emotion's slave and exists to rationalize emotional experience."

It may be that until his last sentence concerning the relationship between emotion and reason Bion is too sanguine. Indeed prior to writing those lines he had stopped using case vignettes in his talks and papers because he felt them to be misleading or to open him to misunderstanding, or most likely both. It is, at any rate, not clear to me that any practicing psychoanalyst would agree that the sessions we are considering are like anything he knows—or, if they are, as pastiche or parody only. Many, perhaps most, would feel something like one feels when one sees a pretty woman on the cinema screen who is outfitted with tightly drawn black hair in a bun, wearing oversized horn-rim glasses. But others might feel the portrayal, far from being a cliché, is far too real. It may confirm their worst fears: a man or woman sets up to be an analyst and proceeds to further debilitate some suggestible soul into a position not unlike the cult leader and his followers. The more the gobbledygook, the more arcane the activity, the greater the hatred and distrust from the normative community around it, the more the sense of being closer to the source and alone with the truth. Since there are indeed such cultist relationships based on an occult language and method of explanation—one thinks of the late Jim Jones and his *Group*—how can one separate what we have been reading from their activities and practices? For would they not also say with Bion, you can't understand unless you are one of us? Hearing or reading about us is not enough; you must become among us to truly know us?

Thus while some may revile what has been presented as not being psychoanalysis as they know and practice it, some may revile it because it portrays just the kind of mischief and charlatanism they always suspected. Both would disown what Ψ and P, however difficult they are finding it today, regard as a process with *bona fides* that will in time lead somewhere. More, P and Ψ seem to believe that there is sense to the nonsense, even if, at any given period of time, the sense is obscure to each of them. P has scolded Ψ for being cryptic; however, Ψ has declined to explain further, feeling P is misleading him by pretending to know less than he knows in order to prove that it is Ψ and not P himself who is withholding something or is defective. Yet this apparent mistrust of one another is contained; the treatment is not broken off for breach of contract or malpractice. They continue to work for all the world as if they are conducting an honorable enterprise of mutual benefit. So perhaps it *is* a folly of two. Should the authorities be notified?

Let us consider what we might tell them when they arrived. We might begin with the idea that Ψ, who is duly accredited and licensed, is nevertheless behaving parasitically—and quite oddly, to boot. He is taking money to sit around in some sort of Joycean-manqué stream of consciousness from which he presumes to derive "insights" into P. The insights he claims to be deriving have increasingly to do with a rather shopworn nineteenth-century idea concerning something Freud called "castration anxiety." Rather than simply coming out with this theory, and its relationship to P's anxiety attacks and other dis-eases, Ψ is spinning things out as if he expects P will understand matters and benefit from that understanding from this spun-out procedure. Ψ also appears to harbor an old Grecian idea, resuscitated by Freud, that there is a castration-death equivalency in the P's mind. If that equivalency exists, as it seems to have for Sophocles, Shakespeare, Goethe, Freud, and others, the idea is certainly not without interest. But is it Ψ's or P's? Is it there in P, waiting to be given attention, or is it in Ψ, who may wish instead to "discover" it in P. It is certainly in Ψ, that much we could report, and moreover the drift of this idea is not a Freudian one. Freud thought death so incomprehensible to the child that it could only approximate the idea of death via reference to a catastrophe the child did know, which was the fifty percent possibility of castration. But Ψ seems to be departing from this notion, at least with P. He is agreeing with Freud that the quirkiness of children has it that the penis is the presence of something of which the vagina is the absence. Piaget has also showed how uniformly children of a certain age will think that a serpent shape of clay is larger than the same clay rolled into a sphere or that a tall, thin glass holds more water than a short, squat glass even after they are shown again and again that the volume of clay or water is the same before attaining the shapes they are asked to compare. (He however shows no sign of agreeing with Boris [1976; also in forthcoming b], who has argued that the child's departure from the observable is in deference not to an immaturity of mind, but to the ascendancy of hope, which *wants* there to be betters and worses among shapes and sizes, such that bigger, taller, and longer are selectively better than rounder, shorter, and squatter. But this is not in itself sufficient to notify the authorities, though the idea somehow does occur.)

Ψ, to the contrary, seems to be on a drift whereby P has wanted to lose his penis to save his life, as one might sacrifice a piece in chess to gain an ultimate advantage in positional endgame play. He believes, it is beginning to seem, that P's ongoing preoccupations concerning loss and damage are such that the natural horror one might feel at such events have undercurrents, for P, of interest and satisfaction. Indeed, he is wondering if the "wall" represents the breast without nipple—the word "disgusting" that refers to eating and taste sensation may have nudged him further in this direction—as well as the body without penis. And he is wondering this as if P's spontaneous use of metaphor and image were not a poetically creative act but an encrypted sort of communication that his own meanderings and spasms of thought and feeling can decode. There is a Delphic quality to this reading of psychic entrails, which scholars have retrospectively seen to be a matter of using knowledge as power and the degree to which the knowledge is claimed to be arcane and closely held to be a matter of the degree of possessiveness involved in the holding of that power. Is this Ψ's game?

Ψ quite probably would not go quietly on the basis of these charges. Indeed, though his first line of defense would be privileged communication, he might, if pressed, ask why not level these charges instead against P! After all, he might argue, P is a confessed self-deceiver, who has come to him asking for help in exploring his unconscious reasons for feeling and behaving as he does. But the so-called "unconscious" is neither more nor less than a state of mind. What is unconscious today may perfectly well be conscious tomorrow. P, however, has asked to enter with him into a kind of collusion wherein P can plead innocent of the knowledge for which he, P, would otherwise be held accountable. If Ψ would kindly agree that there is an unconscious the contents of which one cannot by definition know, then he, P, will go through the charade with Ψ of "discovering" what is in that unconscious.

As to the contents *being* "discovered," Ψ would argue that not he, but P, decides what to say, what to hold back and when. If the authorities would like to read his notes of other cases, they would see that he says quite different things when he is told quite different things. Does this mean that he talks only to P about this putative castration complex of his? Of course not—because P is not the only one who has observed the impressive fact that fifty percent of the population are without. Is that not rather a male and chauvinist viewpoint? Yes, but it is P's, not Ψ's. But P denies holding the view that woman are inferior and that the phallus reigns supreme. And indeed the P one meets now may (or may not) hold this phallocentric view. But the present P may or may not be representative of the P who was once and did. However, in choosing from among the "associations" P provides, isn't Ψ making manifest a selective bias of his own? Even if one person says different sorts of things in a different sort of way, wouldn't Ψ have to admit that he does all the selecting as to what he notices and to what he directs P's attention? Ψ agrees that he "conducts" the analysis, but denies vigorously that he could or would hear the same thing in whatever was told him or say the same thing no matter which P. He adds that this might not be true, however, of P who rather systematically distorts what he experiences in particular directions. Indeed, Ψ concludes triumphantly, it is the exposure he has to P's very forces of distortion that allows him to note and bring P's attention to them.

"Distortion?" he is asked. "You are the mercury in the thermometer that merely submits to the other's presence? You have no biases of your own? You do not, in this conducting that you do, *bring out* qualities in P? Do you maintain that P would be the same were he to be working with a different analyst?" Ψ is irritated by this. Of course not, he answers. But the qualities in P that do *not* vary from person to person and situation to situation are the important things. And it is these that would show up with a different analyst because it is these that are invariants. And, as with P, so with other people, himself included: people have much in common, yes, the castration situation or fears of death, if one prefers. So, yes, he is bound to work with all those who consult him in ways that are alike because all who consult him have had, being all human, experiences common to humanity. And yes, each is different, himself included, in the biases and proclivities that they have. He has taken the time and trouble to study his own, as even now P is also doing. Having done this in his own behalf he would like to think—no, this is too modest—he confidently asserts that his distortions are less compulsive than P's and are less likely to show up repeatedly and invariantly from person to person and situation to situation.

But he doesn't acknowledge at least one repeated bias: he is a psychoanalyst and, being one, is bound to see what P says and does in ways peculiar to psychoanalysis. And isn't the Freudian view or at any rate the psychoanalytic view, like the Marxist view, just a particular lens through which to view phenomena? Indeed did not Ψ scold himself in the very session so recently past for being too Jungian? Or does he blame all this on P too? And as for saying, yes, I am a psychoanalyst, as P knew and knows, and am bound to look at matters in ways peculiar to the field; and as for saying I didn't choose P—he chose me: does Ψ mean to imply that he explained all of this to P and P chose freely and not with his usual bias or "invariants," as likes to call them? And speaking of choosing, did Ψ choose psychoanalysis because of its beauty as a science and a craft, or did psychoanalysis as a field happen by any chance to rationalize "invariants" of Ψ's own, which, now being Ψ, he can regard and claim as peculiar to being a psychoanalyst and not distorted, repetitive, odd behavior, peculiar to himself as an individual?

One can imagine even the Spanish Inquisition beginning to glaze over at this juncture, so that the idea of calling in the authorities has lost a certain zest. Still the exchange suggests that what is going on in the hour is not insulated from the context in which the hour and the analysis both are set, though the unselfconsciousness of the two, and P, while the session is going on may keep them and ourselves from noticing this. For despite the cleavage temporally introduced by the threat to the *Pair* by the authorities, they, like the infant and mother before them, have formed a *Pair* with which to do their work on the relationship between themselves as a *Couple*.

15. Session: Tuesday

P : [Sigh.]

Ψ: [Raised eyebrows.]

P : [Silence.]

Ψ: [Silence.]

P : Shit, I forgot your check.

Ψ: Check. I forgot your shit.

P : Well, it's true, I am angry about yesterday's session. I felt I worked my ass off and you just sat there.

Ψ: And now . . .

P : Right. You're still just sitting there like some kind of stone wall. . . I don't know: is it that I envy you because you can just sit there and choose your time and place to say something? Or do I feel that this analysis is just too one-way? I can't *make* you talk, I know that. But that seems to me to give you a special obligation *to* talk. I mean, you hold all the cards, you're the dealer—so give. God, you're infuriating. Fucking Buddha, just sitting there. What I should do is get off this god-forsaken couch and walk out.

Ψ: You are thinking about what walking out would be like?

P : I love the idea of it. Me just striding out. You just sitting there with this "Huh?" expression on your face. "I've gone too far this time."

Ψ: Not giving a shit, not moving my bowels for you? "Why can't *I* be the Mother-Buddha-God for a change? What need keeps me from turning the tables? What has she got that I don't have?"

P : Well, of course, you're the analyst: you have the knowledge I need to get well.

Ψ: That is no longer an angry and envious baby talking; that is a pious believer appeasing his gods.

P : Well, at least today you are talking!

Ψ: Go with the flow, don't bite the breast that feeds you?

P : Say what you like; when you talk I have a chance of learning something.

Ψ: Flattery. You are more interested in my talk than in what I have to say. The talk is like nursing to you. You are not so much interested in the contents as in the experience of the sucking and the flow.

P : But you don't understand. It makes a difference when you talk. The whole session is different. It's like there is something there, not just a vacuum. Sometimes I feel I could—you know, like a spacecraft—get sucked out into the void. . . . You are not going to say anything? I feel you are settling back to listen. Did I say something wrong?

Ψ: I was settling back to listen. I had thought perhaps you were going to go into the question of why my simply listening is so frightening and hurtful to you. You were starting to say that my silence is like a hole—the hole session—that is empty for a little moment before you fill it with your wish to suck everything into your emptiness and feeling of void. When you have transferred your own wishes into the hole-silence your wishes come *at* you and frighten you very much. You went on to say that when this happens you feel it is something you have done. Perhaps it is not merely that you want me to talk but that when I do not you feel your sucking void coming at you ready to destroy you.

P : It's just that I never know when you are going to and when you are not.

Ψ: In those circumstances would one not want to huff and puff and blow the house down—suck and suck and swallow the breast right into the void?

P : . . . Are you going to stop talking again?

Ψ: Probably.

P : What you are saying is helpful.

Ψ : What you are saying is more flattery. You are hoping to find a way to keep me talking—to take some sort of charge of me. Earlier you wished I was shit, because one can control shit, keep it in, let it out, choose, as you said, one's "time and place." I am wondering if your envy of my being able to choose does not inspire a wish in you to make me into a nice shit that you can keep with you to fill the void, like the check that is kept with you.

P : When you remind me I have forgotten the check, *I* feel like shit. I don't like the idea of controlling you that way. I apologize. It slipped my mind.

Ψ : "I evacuated my bowels before I came here because you treat me like an asshole and make me talk and pay."

P : [Laughs.] I remember something like that with my mother—playing outside, having to go, but waiting until the last minute and then running like all get out hoping I hadn't left it to too late. Once or twice I did. I remember one day. My sister was home sick from school, but not so sick that she had to be in bed. She was kind of bored and she started teasing me or something and then we started wrassling and she being bigger got me down and was on top of me, on my stomach, bouncing like, and all of a sudden I really had to go bad but she wouldn't let me up ... ? Well that was something. ... What were we talking about? I got off the track, somehow.

Ψ : Jumped the track. The choo-choo got very excited and angry that it was pinned down, so it jumped the track.

P : Choo—makes me think of chew. Chew-chew. I remember that was how I was fed if my mother wanted me to finish up or maybe hurry up. "Here comes the choo-choo," she'd say, kind of bringing the fork to my mouth. "Into the tunnel. Open up. Here it comes." Kind of sing-song. "Here it co-om-es." Oh, my God! I just thought of something! That's what *I* say when I'm about to come: "Here it com-m-m-es!" Weird. [Silence.]

Ψ : [So the breast-feces-penis links gradually reappear. Shall he be able to maintain them, or is the silence to undo them? And what about this bouncing sister. Was she masturbating? Did he feel any genital excitement? Or was it already pushed back into the anal choo-choo. And where was mother in this?

He started with her and keeping her waiting for her "check" and then running to the inside, P feels bad for not going. Today, having withheld the check or let it "slip," he has taken Ψ's interpretations and used them. His idea seems to be that the asshole can control the breast as if the latter were a b.m. He will doubtless wonder what he did today to "make" me flow, and then wonder what the receipt is for shutting me down. This is dangerous for him because the shit and the sphincter quickly reverse. When I do not submit to feeling like shit, as I did yesterday, giving those associations, he does. One of us has to, it seems. Either and Or played a game to see which could make the other come and go. Where's number Three—that is the congestion.]

P : I surprised myself.

Ψ: That you went in your pants?

P : No. That . . . Now I am confused.

Soon P and Ψ are going to leave matters there for the day. They work the fifty-minute hour but both, I think, would have welcomed a slightly earlier cessation. Some analysts do not. They work when the patient is in a mood to and discontinue when the silences start or can be heard underneath the chatter. Or they discontinue when they feel that one or both simply have said what needed saying. But there is a fashion, not perhaps unlike the scheduling of programs on television, in which matters end on the hour or half-hour no matter how little or much there is to them. The container is given precedence over the contents. This twosome does not seem to consider this aspect of the matter, though it is noting something of the toilet container aspect of the session-as-session for both himself and P, who "slipped" up with the check. Despite this, however, both faithfully adhere to the idea of putting the right thing in the right place at the right time. The culture of the fifty-minute regular session cloaks the cloacal nature of this activity.

The analysts who do observe the fifty-minute session do so in the belief that though the patient may "resist" revealing much to the analyst or to himself, the reasons for such concealment are as worthy of detailed study as what would otherwise be revealed. But Ψ is having some trouble with this. Yesterday he correctly told P that he wanted to put P's impatience back into him. But he might have added that one of his reasons for wanting to do so was because he was having enough trouble with his own impatience. But P knew this anyway. He had become adept at noticing and evoking impatience in both his mother and sister, as he told Ψ in today's session, as long ago as preschool. Indeed, Ψ has begun to wonder if impatience hasn't a sexual quality for P as yet unnoticed by him, and not alone for P but for P's sister and mother. He seems quite likely to soon link impatience with anxiety and anxiety with sexual excitement, as aspects of a total experience, out of which P has a penchant for attending to the anxiety element. P's laugh suggests that the pleasure component is not so far off today as yesterday and that this pleasure component has to it a slightly sadistic quality. Certainly sadistic qualities were being reflected in Ψ's impulses in respect to P in earlier sessions—"putting the boot in" and that sort of thing. Ψ seemed to feel that P was at one and the same time stimulating him to impatience, excitement, and sadism while P was sanctimoniously denying such impulses in himself. "Speak for yourself, John Alden," Ψ wanted to say back to P. Therefore as soon as P did speak for himself, in today's session, Ψ was able to relax. P had stopped evacuating his impatience and excitement into Ψ, as if Ψ were a pair of pants that P wanted to dirty. Still, Ψ is left wondering about P's sister—and gushy-liking T also—and how P feels about their excitement. He suspects a degree of envy from P there, too.

But this has now become all about P; Ψ has a way of forgetting about his own role in this, no matter how much P tries to call it to his attention. Why did Ψ feel so put upon—so impatient and sadistic? It was possible to think that Ψ was already laboring with tensions of his own, perhaps even with envy of P for being able to get others going while he stayed still. In respect to these tensions, Ψ has three alternatives. One is to "cure" P of behaving in ways that Ψ finds difficult. A second is to cure himself of whatever is there to which P is merely adding. A third might be to change the rules of the game by declining to allow P to take his frustrations out on Ψ—or, more accurately, putting his frustrations into Ψ. Ψ attempted this by giving P the hickory limb of "key" words to which to associate ("Broken—Closed off," etc.), but P declined really to use them. This evoked in Ψ his rather mordant ruminations concerning sticks and bushes, lambs and slaughter. Ψ was feeling what it was like to feel teased and impotent and taken— like a lamb to a slaughter. But if he didn't like it, why did he not say so, except in his mutterings to himself?

Ψ might say that it was vital for him to experience what at that moment P could not, so that in time, when P could tolerate it, he could return the experience to P. And he might point out that no later than the next day he was, in fact, able to help pre-own the experience. Today he did not accept what he called P's flattery, which he regarded as a further effort on P's part once again to insinuate blame for any frustrations the *Couple* experienced into Ψ. As a result of this refusal, P started to attend to what he himself had experienced in the past and felt dumbfounded when he realized the extent to which the past was not limited to the past.

There is a story about Atlas who stood for years with the world literally upon his shoulders. One day Hercules chanced by, returning from one or another of his own labors. He paused to chat, and in the course of the chat Atlas asked Hercules to shoulder the burden for just a moment while he caught his breath and worked out a kink in his muscles. Hercules obliged—but with that, Atlas darted away, leaving Hercules holding the bag. "Well, well," cried out Hercules. "I can see what a chore this has been for you and why you so eagerly get shed of it when you can. I myself cannot hold it a minute longer unless I have my lion skin between it and my shoulder." At this, Atlas returned to take back the world while Hercules adjusted his lion skin, but now it was Hercules who strode away.

It is to be hoped that the worries of the world are not, like a hot potato, being passed from one part of the *Pair* to the other. And yet it seems that somehow they are. According to Ψ, P needs to project so that he can see in Ψ what he cannot endure seeing in himself. But according to P, if Ψ would talk more, that would be the factor which would make P's experience more endurable. And indeed Ψ did talk more. And P was more confiding. P does not ask for particular portions of information or insight—he does not tell Ψ what he wants Ψ to say. He specifies only that Ψ talk. And this Ψ regards as a desire for mother's breast—he feels that P wants not so much food for thought as soothing. Ψ suspects a quid pro quo in the re-making: check-shit for breast-talk. His guesses along these lines puts P in mind of the game he played when young. But why should Ψ play this game with P? Why should he not remain quiescent until P decides to abandon the quid pro quo and get down to work once more?

I think we should not be surprised to find this very question among P's thoughts. His "I am confused" is at once a fact and an accusation. Will Ψ accept the responsibility for P's confusion and "talk"? We must hope not, for both their sakes. It is no good for Ψ to be doing what makes him impatient and angry—to hope P will be "cured" before he, Ψ, is overburdened. And it is no good for P to feel guilty for what Ψ permits P to do, only then to have to find fault with Ψ to excuse himself. Wednesday's session should be of interest in this respect—how will the two work this predicament out?

16. Session: Wednesday

Unlike the analyst in the "Who listens?" joke, Ψ feels tired at the end of the day. Not only does he listen, he goes through experiences P brings to him. Perhaps too much so, but Ψ is only human and from time to time has preoccupations of his own; at such times his container runneth over. But then Ψ believes that there is a model of communication that requires P to communicate through projections with which Ψ then identifies himself. P hopes to distract both himself and Ψ from experiencing those experiences as if they were P's. He feels if he can get Ψ to musing about himself, Ψ will have less time and energy to call P's attention to what P has no immediate wish to feel or know.

Ψ also feels that he must lend himself to P for use as a transference object, so that P's experiences can come to dramatic life. Otherwise P would be restricted to the narrative form, telling stories and giving news reports. But when Ψ allows P to cast him as one of the figures in what otherwise would be the same old stories, this allows them both at once to participate in and observe the story as it unfolds. Ψ's silence, therefore, can serve, as his talk does, to symbolize anything from, as it were, milk to nuts. Moreover, as P fleshes out his playlet with attributions of intent, the characters take on the motivations that are the basis of any good drama.

Ψ, however, has to decide how far he will lend (or rent) himself for such casting. What he decides may not prevail, but it may at least sometimes have some influence. For example, instead of playing the analyst for whom flattery is either necessary or in order, he refused. He told P that P was himself trying to draw his own attention from the "greedy baby" aspect of his wishes by playing at being the eager, responsible student. In doing so, Ψ also rejected the role of the baby in whom P could find the greed he was trying to keep undiscovered in himself. This, he felt, it was time now to do—that P could stand the experience of his own greed and wishes to own and control others. P's laugh suggested that such a discovery frightened him. He could also begin to note the pleasurable truth in it. Yet in his story, he implicates Mother and Sister as the greedy, impatient ones. If Ψ won't accept the role, he will cast others for it. Ψ has noted this and when, after the silence, P attempts to regain his innocence (for he was troubled by the implications of the fusions he has effected between eating, going, and coming), Ψ brings him back to his letting out of the secret confession as being a current equivalent of going in his pants.

Were we to interview P on his way to today's (Wednesday) session, and asked him if he understood anything of what transpired yesterday, we shouldn't feel surprised were he to say no. Nor would Ψ say more than a qualified no. For Ψ has been at some pains not to explain matters to P. He does not want this analysis to turn into a tutorial. He feels that the knowing portion of an experience should not be purchased at the expense of the fullness of the experience itself. He is no ally to the way in which P has paid attention selectively. Indeed, as with the flattery issue, he has fairly forcefully interfered with P's customary way of selectively paying attention—in this case trying not to pay further attention to the greedy-baby wishes that are alive in himself by cultivating a taste for flattery on the part of Ψ. P's efforts to have Ψ explain fall into the same category. Ψ suspects P of wanting to diminish the potential of a full flowering of the experience by heading it off with intellectual "insights" into it. Ψ appears to have some idea that people assimilate information into an experience without necessarily taking note that they are doing so. If P were to say "Oh, I see what you are getting at: I have unconsciously set up a series of analogies between the nipple, the anus, and the penis, such that what issues from any of these is interchangeable one with the other, and I did so in order not to feel the loss that would come with the realization that analogies are just likenesses, selectively arrived at, so that when I lose any one of the possibilities I want, I cannot substitute for it," Ψ would probably give up doing analysis and take up farming. For this realization would have as much of a chance to help P experience who he is and what he is about as it does you and me.

Ψ, knowing this, knows that to point to any aspect of P's experience is to highlight it at the expense of others. Every interpretation from Ψ alters P's own patternings. Alas, this is even the case should Ψ move in his chair, sigh, or sneeze. Ψ's view, therefore, is least said, soonest mended. (But he does not try to suppress his sneezes.) The experience that unfolds must, as much as possible, be P's own.

P has been to some extent busy at trying to experience certain intentions as coming at him rather than from him. He wishes to reassign the authorship of these to Ψ. He has used accusation, flattery, and an air of being victimized—all to induce Ψ to spare him the further misery of feeling that these intentions are his own.

Ψ has had to move somewhat delicately back and forth from accepting these intentions and refuting them. He has been guided by his estimate of where the experience can best come to reflorescence. It can emerge wholesale, defended against only—yet entirely—by P's assurance that it is Ψ of whom he is talking when he speaks of these intentions. Or, bit by bit, it can emerge as an experience P can stand to associate with himself. For example, it is sometimes possible for P to disown an aspect of an experience by inserting the words "not" or "don't," as in, "I don't feel angry at her," or, "It's not that I wanted anything more, it's just. . . ." These words disown the part of the experience P would find it painful to feel, but they do not oblige Ψ to own them instead of P. Such demurrers bespeak the fact that P does accept part of the experience—the minus K part of it—and may soon enough become aware of the "minus-ing" he is so careful to do. The matter of degree guides Ψ. Were P to begin talking of an entire half of the world who, unknown to anyone but himself, has fearful designs on P's sister, Ψ might well feel that P was less "ready" to discover such designs closer to home. Were Ψ to ask P, for example, whether it ever crossed his mind to do such a fearful thing to his sister, he could expect P to not understand the question, possibly even not to hear it. Ψ designs his own activities accordingly; he is forever asking himself where the experience is now, how it got there and how and when to open it up to P's attention. As the Parisian couturier explained patiently to his nouveau riche client, "I charge, madame, not just for what I put on, but as much for what I know to leave out," so too might Ψ say. And so, not surprisingly, this is how Ψ designs his work this morning:

P : . . . Once again I seem to be tied in knots.

Ψ: You have had dreams of people tied in knots.

P : What do you mean? Dreams? Did you say dreams? I don't know what you mean. I don't remember any dreams of knots.

Ψ: Am I perhaps being tied in knots. Or himself?

P : You always refer everything to yourself. It's as if I cannot breathe, eat, . . . or live without it having something to do with you. You think you are the center of the universe. Does the sun also rise and set on you?

Ψ: [Silence. What P has said is rich with feeling and meaning. The envy is patent. So too is the statement, concealed in barest irony: "I cannot breathe, eat, . . . or live without it having something to do with you." The reference to *The Sun Also Rises* may or may not refer to one of the themes in P's life. The reference to the Omphalo (the umbilicus), Ψ feels, is unmistakable. Yet perhaps most impressive of all is the degree to which P's knots have loosened as he ties into Ψ. Earlier he bound himself and Ψ in a kind of stalemate, of which nothing could come. Ψ's noting for P that P was concentrating only on his own "(k)nottedness" to obscure what he was also, in fact, doing to Ψ, turns the cords that bind to another use. P lashes out at Ψ, experiencing his outrage and envy of him for occupying the place at the center and core that P would like to occupy.]

P : [Talking of T, a woman friend of his.] She—she's such an asshole. I said to her, "Look, let's—." She is *such* an *ass*hole, I can't believe it. I said to her, "Look let's—you know . . . mess around now, and then we can eat." So she says, "Dinner is almost ready, so why don't we eat now and, you know, later." She calls it "you know." She can't even say it. [Silence. P seems to be stewing T in his thoughts.]

Ψ: Perhaps T stands for me and us both for the breast that had to be received when it and not you were ready. Perhaps you had to know that I, who gives you dinner, is not the same person who can give you "you-know."

Ψ could have said what he did without doing what P would call "bringing himself into it." That is, he could have talked of T and, beyond T, to mother and sister. Or he could have again said nothing and waited. But Ψ appears to be harboring the suspicion that this talk about T is not merely talk about T, women, and mother, but talk that is also designed to take away the center of P's interest that P had not so long ago reluctantly accorded Ψ. P is feeling tied to something by T. Is he also tying to a post of unimportance?

Ψ's choice from the range of alternatives is in one sense technical and in another perhaps a matter of style. But as Ψ's habit is to keep wondering where the experience not being experienced has gotten to, it is probable that he consulted himself and found himself feeling a little envious of T. "Why should she be the one with the dinner and the you-know? What's the matter with me?"

Happily, Ψ can stand such petulant thoughts today. If he could not, he might have intervened exactly as he did, only without knowing that he did so because he had become gifted with P's earlier envy. Or, were the envy so strong as to be repellent to Ψ, he might not have been able to intervene, for fear that the intervention would make his envy public. In the event he believes that P has caused him to feel envious, and since P has already demonstrated a capacity for feeling his own envy today, Ψ returns the gifted envy by adverting to himself as well as T.

Whether, however, Ψ would appreciate that I am making his inner tensions and petulance so public is another question. In any case, P assuredly does not like Ψ's re-introduction to P of the envy P had been hoping to replace with disparagement.

> P : I am trying to get some insight into T. Well, myself and T. You seem to be saying that I regard T as a mother who I want to suck and fuck both. But I do not. You seem to be suggesting that I am overreacting to T. But you may like everything in lock-step order—probably in fact you do, considering the way this goddamn analysis is arranged. But why shouldn't I—look, she was cooking. I was having a glass of wine. She was

wearing a shortish T-shirt. I kind of slid my hand up from her waist and grabbed her boobs. It felt good. I felt horny. I thought, "Who wants to eat—"

Ψ: —these boobs anyway? These are not boobs, these are holes. These are assholes. The only thing that likes to eat assholes are pieces of shit. I am not a piece of shit, no matter what the boobs say. I am the asshole that controls the shit, and when I say now, I mean now, no shit: now means now. We'll soon find out who is in charge here—who controls whom. No boobs are going to make me hungry just because I feel starved.

P : Yeah . . . yeah. Okay. Because when we were doing it— she agreed to wait dinner—I kept feeling, "God, I got to get it up. I have to make it last." Perform. She was excited. I felt she wanted to climax. But I kind of lost my excitement. I felt I had to get *her* off. . . .

Ψ: She had become a hungry mouth to feed? An empty hole to fill?

P : Yeah. Sometimes I feel small—my penis.

Ψ: The breast cuts the penis back down to size. . . . It takes its revenge for being made into a hole.

P : I have often thought how much easier it is to be a woman than a man.

Ψ: Or an analyst than a patient.

P : Same fucking difference, you're right. [Bitterly:] As always.

Ψ: I haven't stayed tied in "nots." Sometimes I am right?

P : Well, I haven't left yet.

Ψ: "Yet!"

P : [Laughs.] You're an asshole, but I like you. It helps, this stuff we are doing. Even though some days all I want to do is tell you to stuff it.

Ψ: You feel more cheerful now that you have told me a fuller story? But now we have come to the end for today.

Whether or not "we have come to the end for today" may be easier said than done. Certainly neither party will stop, on the instant, thinking of the session. Indeed, it is likely that P at least will have more than one brief fantasy about the session—more than one brief dialogue with Ψ. After all, if his disposition is, as Ψ thinks it is, to own and possess without regard to the time schedule—perhaps indeed the very needs of the other—he will keep Ψ "tied up" in imagination and not let him go in sphincter-like docility just because Ψ says it is time to eat or go or come or leave or as Ψ wills. To do this—to keep Ψ in "nots"—is after all to gain some redress from Ψ's dominion. Just as Baby will have analogized his processes of mind to colonic possession in order to be able to forgive and forget Mother's actual self-possession, so now will his heir, P, imagine that in "of mind" is in "of body." P will have walked out of the consulting room tractably enough, but what he did afterward with Ψ is anybody's guess.

It is more or less a free country, so that what P does with Ψ, T, or anyone else in his imagination should concern no one. The difficulty is that P's forebear, Baby, did not distinguish between affairs of state and affairs of the mind. When Baby held Mother in siege, imagining that he and not she was the regent of all doings, he did not wish to view this as a mere, and to him, paltry act of imagination. To him sleights of mind were rather the equivalent of sleights of hand—or body; he did not care to notice the difference. Thus, just as P, in calling T an "asshole" rendered her the inverse of a freely held and attracting Breast—only to "pay" for it later when his acquisition of the breast-penis could not feed her hungry-baby mouth—so his use of Ψ will not seem to him a mere curl of his mind, but a deed as real and actual as steel. For the luxury of this maintained delusion, he will undergo a retributive amount of pain. Perhaps that is why at the end of the session Ψ calls P's attention to the value of words, as contrasted with deeds, in his remarks about "fuller" communication. It is not clear whether P is interested in this clarification at the moment. If he were, he would from then on just sit about having chats with Ψ about what he thought, felt, imagined, and wished. But he may not yet (or ever) wish to trade the heavy liabilities of deeds done for the lighter one of thoughts thought, for the former gives one illusions that the latter takes right away.

17. Session: Friday

People come about people, it is often thought—about relationships. This is what P said while reproving Ψ for his introduction
of himself into P's attempts to gain insight into his relationship
with T. From this point of view, Ψ was iatrogenically causing a
problem for P by Ψ's steadfastness or unwillingness (or inability)
to deal with P's relations with the actual world of events and
people. Ψ put this down in part to his own envy of P's other
relationships, but he discounted this feeling as one given him by P
that P wanted him to feel so that P could feel disparaging instead.
P is rather at Ψ's mercy in this. Ψ may only be claiming that P
"projected" his, P's, envy; in truth, it might be all a function of
Ψ's envy that from the theatre experience on, Ψ has rather stub-
bornly been dealing with what he would call P's relationship with
fantasy or internalized or introjected objects. Ψ could cite chapter
and verse on this from the psychoanalytic literature. Indeed, had
Ψ had the time (or inclination) to read the present text, he would
have said that P's attempts to conduct relations with actual people
in actual events was impoverished by P's preoccupation with inner
versions of people, something P accomplished in order to feel less
helpless about the actual turns of events while still a baby. He
would cite P's continual movement of attention, now paid to this,
now to that, each time to reduce the impact of anyone actual in
any event. He would argue that if indeed P was absorbed in T, he,
Ψ, would not have reintroduced himself into the proceedings; and
as things turned out, T, having complied with what seemed at first

223

blush like P's simple longing for spontaneous sex, was doomed to play a role in the sexual act that she had not—perhaps—bargained for. If, Ψ might maintain, P's relations with T *had* been actual, everything might have been (as the song has it) "satisfactual." But P had T confused with another play and another time.

That confusion, one might suppose, could be more easily cleared up were Ψ, or someone better trained, seeing P and T as a *Couple.* Moderating a discussion of the evening's events, the couples therapist might have asked each of the partners to state what he or she were feeling at each moment of the encounter. This might help each of them to see their distortions of one another and to begin to ponder the origin of those misperceptions. As it is, T gets no help with hers (if indeed she has them) and P is shown his by Ψ's implication that P has stigmatisms in respect to T of the same sort and from the same motivation as he does with Ψ. P feels a bit as if this were a matter of two against one and if T were willing, P might contemplate switching sides so that it is T and P riding off into the sunset with Ψ left gloomily (and, no doubt, repentantly) behind. Many a psychoanalysis has been stopped by a third party's decision to force an issue. There can be little question that there is a triangle of sorts in place: P with T, P with Ψ and Mrs. Ψ (whomever she might be), and T with Ψ (whomever he might be) and P.

This may be one of the reasons—apart from all the other reasons which drew Ψ to psychoanalysis and not family or couples therapy or (for that matter, psychotherapy)—for Ψ does not do couples work. Believing that the triangles replicate themselves like glass chips in a kaleidoscope, believing that it would make as much sense for himself and P to be seen as a *Couple* as it would T and P, he goes on with his work on the unseen triangle—the relations between himself and P and P's inner others, of whom T is an objective correlative in the same way as the people at the theatre who so spooked P. Poor T may ask after each session what Ψ might have had to say about this event or that, and P would be hard put to answer. He would not—for doubtless very good reasons—want to say, "Oh, he is only interested in you as a displacement of himself or my mother's penis or nipple." Many people would find that either uselessly humorous or dolorously worrisome; happily, most are spared such replies, whatever the truth to them.

For his own reasons P has not selected one of the other therapies. By now he is only too well aware of how Ψ works and he sees that Ψ's view of him as someone who sees the actual world only in glimpses is accurate. Somehow he has come to trust that when Ψ speaks of T, someone he does not know, has never in fact even met to look at, he speaks, as he does of himself, as if he knew the difference between P's experience of her and the actual T. Or of him. So when P tells Ψ that T is an "asshole" he does not expect Ψ to believe him. Nor does he expect Ψ to disbelieve him. He expects Ψ to gain an idea of P contemplating T, when T is as he experiences her to be. Knowing this, Ψ can interrupt P's description of T's boobs and imply P is sourly trying to trash what are good, sweet grapes. Ψ assumes, correctly or otherwise, that P might find some pleasure in T having good, sweet boobs, instead of shitty, controlling holes (which he has then guiltily to feed with his mother-penis). And in compensation for this switch of the way P attends to T (and Ψ), P might accept the pain of envy. Thus without speaking at all about the actual T, Ψ assumes that if P can tolerate his envy of T, T will appear far more desirable than she does when P, to protect himself from that envy, has to disparage her. P's relative acceptance of Ψ at the end of the last session is for Ψ a proof of this line of thought. Whether the envy can remain subdued by gratitude will depend on whether P can enjoy what he has with the help of Ψ and T. This, in turn, will depend on whether P can allow Ψ and T their pleasures. And that will in turn depend on whether P can be free enough of guilt to enjoy and allow enjoyment, for if his guilt over his wish to deprive and disparage is too great, he will be unable to enjoy himself—and so his envy of others can only increase. Where will P come in on this cycle? Ψ awaits Friday's session.

P : Hi.
Ψ: Hello.
P : [Rubs his eyes.] Tired. Hot today. Weather . . .
Ψ: Something you have seen has made you tired. You are

tired of something you have seen. The question seems to be whether.

P : Funny you should say that. You have some sort of growth. Outside, I mean. It was greyish. At first I thought it was some kind of animal, then brain—animal brain. I looked at it, horrible, greyish but like flesh. Split down the middle, sort of crumbling. Holes in it, one, two, I don't know. It had a brother, I noticed, but the brother was more like a regular mushroom. Thickish stem, rounded buttontop head. But the other was— and to make it worse, it had a snail on it. Slimy. You should have it removed. If they go over it with a . . . whadyacallum— cutter—*lawn* mower—lawnmower, it could burst open and its spores could explode out—everywhere. . . . What were we saying? Oh, the weather. Bright and sunny today. Blue sky. . . . Why is he talking about the weather, is what you're thinking, I bet. Looking down your nose. It doesn't make any sense, but it is the best sense I can make. . . . Some things don't. You just have to accept that. Make the best of it, as my mother likes to say. Don't look past it. Make the best of it. . . .

Ψ : We are in the presence of mother.

P : I guess so. . . . Who knows? All very puzzling. I mean I can see her, like from childhood, five, six, maybe smaller— three. Flour on her arms, dab on her forehead. Wisp of hair. Hair in a bun? Short now. Same grey eyes. I have grey eyes. Got them from her. "Look-alikes" comes to mind. Only her hair is getting greyish now. Me, I'm losing mine. Feel dizzy. What's the expression: "Chicken with its head cut off." I saw that once. Farmer's wife grabbed the damned chicken by the neck, put its head on an old tree stump, bango! Off with its head. And blood. . . . Ugh. Yech. Gushing. How they can eat them after that, *I* don't know. Matter of upbringing, I suppose. Got me stumped. "Stumped"! How far's the "Old Stump Inn." First dirty joke I heard. Kids in confirmation class. Way off the track now. Of course, there is no track—that's what you would say. "Track"? Did I say "track"? I thought I said "crack." Meant crack. "T" turned to "c." Lost my bearings. "Barings"—get it? I can't bare it any longer—bear it. Bear. My old nemesis. Old Fuzzy was- he. Had no hair. Gave his mother forty one. I'm cracking up.

Farmer's daughter joke that I don't remember. "Did you have an accident, dear?" "No, just a crack up." Supposed to be funny, but I don't . . . not . . . think so . . . or sure. Was thinking about the traveling salesman. Can't remember his role in this. Is any of this supposed to make any sense? I hope it does to you. You know, this is lonely work over here. No one to talk to, all by myself, no one to look at, I'm sitting on the shelf. Ain't misbehavin'!—that's it. . . . Is it dark in here, or am I imagining things? . . . Nothing important. . . . I was just thinking my lips are dry, have to get some Chapstick. Stick, stuck, stump. Plump. Plump pullet. Pull it. They never said, I know some parents do, don't. Just "not in public." Along with "Now don't make an exhibition of yourself." "Ladies and Gentlemen you are now about to see, direct from, the biggest, the boldest, the . . ." Maybe "baddest." . . . "Ladies and Gentlemen take my advice, pull out—" No, that's not how it goes. . . . I'm doing all the talking. Showtime!!! That theatre, you know the one. . . . Dizzy as Hell. Couldn't breathe. More of a fucking show in front of the curtain than behind it. . . . Am I making sense or am I just whistling Dixie? Wish I were in the land of gotten, where all good things are not forgotten, look away, look away, look away, Dixie land. . . . "Cotton." Why did I say "gotten"? "Gotten" means "had." Like one has been had. "Had," tricked? Or "had" in the biblical sense? Talk about "forgotten," I have forgotten almost everything. . . . Something about privacy . . . or alone. Kids feel alone, you know. That door gets shut, poohm! It takes the wind out of you. God, how I hated it. "Just going to take a little nap, son." Nap, my eye! . . . Is this session going to be over soon? I feel that this session is going to be over soon. You know, nobody would believe. . . . Soon takes a long time, and that's the long and short of it. "Mom-my, when are we going to get there?" "Soon, darling, soon." But it would take forever. Geez, I am hungry. I am *hung*-gry. Like to die. [Silence.]

Ψ: You were hungry and excited, anxious, eager. Now you are dead. Had and be had. Now you are dead.

P : Yes, something came over me. I felt suddenly scared. I couldn't talk, not for the life of me. . . .

Ψ: No more exhibitions, no more big, bold, and bad. It is

safer to be chicken than to be *a* chicken, in a stump-eat-stump world. . . . And now the time is up—though you may wonder if that is because of something you were doing to me.

P : No no. I am glad to be out of here.

Ψ: [Such a good boy, who would hurt a good boy like that? But still he has to get out of here while he still can.]

Mommy, Daddy? How does the world end? What makes people die?

Ya wanna know? C'm'ere!

This, anyway, is how Ψ apparently views P's predicament. It is not alone what P wants to *do*. Even to *know* the secrets puts P in danger. He is excited to know. His excitement ticks through the session. He has seen through people. He has looked behind the scenes. He has even espied Ψ's secret "growth" out front which looked to him suspiciously like the adult female genital once did. Though he tries to look up at the sunshine and blue skies, he feels triumphant. He has penetrated Ψ's secret. Ψ is quote a Man unquote. Ψ has quote a Brain unquote. This discovery now colors P's communications. Everything is in quotation marks. These are sly digs at quote-unquote. P is feeling positively Promethean. But his hubris scares him to death. He is wary of Ψ. And, at the end of the session, which he has felt approaching like the blade of the farmer's wife, he wishes to escape before Ψ can tell him even more. Ψ, supposing this, tells him the end of the session is not a retaliatory castration; he is not being sentenced to death. Ψ emphasizes, not the narrative portion of what P is saying, but the drama taking place in the room.

Not everyone would agree with the path Ψ once again is taking. Why not help P reexperience the origins of his experiences? The car trips, the "naps," the beheadings? If Ψ believes the description of the fungus is a disguised recollection of seeing P's mother's genital, why not help P toward the actual recollection? Where were they? What were the circumstances? What was P's state of mind then? Good newspaper questions (Kipling's "Little Servants"): who, what, when, where, and how. Or, why not draw attention to the possibility that as P feels now, so he felt then: triumphant and scared, curious to know and too filled with hubris to dare know, knowing by the mind being (fairly ambitiously) confused by P with knowing in the "biblical" sense?

Well, as Ψ might say, it is easy enough to carp. What is the anxiety attached to having P recollect his childhood experiences? When the experience in the present is identified, can the past be far away? Will not P say, "Oh, yes. I remember feeling that way before. We were at the beach and the changing rooms were made of weathered boards, grey weathered boards. My mother took me in to change with her. She turned her back, but something—I think it was the idea of someone looking from the men's changing room next door, yes that was it, made her turn back toward me. Her suit was half way up her thighs, She was a bit plump in those days, and the suit sort of dragged and curled as she pulled it up. She was a little twisted around, as it was, because she didn't want me to see her either. 'Pull on your own suit!' No she wouldn't have said pull on—*put* on; where did pull on come from anyway. Oh, I know. Masturbation of course. Where was I? Oh, yes, so I saw her. I don't know what I expected to see. Maybe something like my sister, who had a cute little thing, though she never thought so. . . ." Or something of the sort? Once the attention can be once again turned, does it make a difference whether it is the past or the present that comes into being first—except that the present is more intense, as befits the experience?

One would have to concede that Ψ has a point. ("Not at the moment," he would reply. "At the moment, like mother, I do not have a 'point,' and the questions are what happened that I don't and will this happen to P?") The important thing—sh-h—is whether both the present and the past converge. And converge they have most certainly started to do. P goes from the here-and-now to the there-and-then almost effortlessly. The transference is as if on ball bearings. Ψ feels this to be potentially quite helpful. Nevertheless, he cautions P about misunderstanding "The End" of the session with other endings. This normally would suggest that P was quite ill—unable to discriminate between what is actual and what imaginary. And indeed, Freud's own name for this condition of P's was the "transference *neurosis*." How then can a neurosis be something for Ψ (and Freud) to feel sanguine about?

Freud's point of view on this was that people repeat what they cannot remember: that the repetition is, in effect, a way of coming to remember. The patient does not notice this aspect of his behavior: he wishes to imagine that what is happening is a first time occurrence. If it is, then maybe [this time] it will turn out okay. The "this time" is what the patient hopes to remain oblivious of; he does not want to learn from repeated experience. It falls to the analyst, therefore, to show the patient the patterns that make seemingly unique and first-time experiences both historically and contemporaneously repetitive. This reminder from the analyst supplies the missing ingredient. If the patient accepts the element of recurrence, which previously he tried not to notice, he will look for another avenue by which to succeed toward his goals. This makes the analyst a welcome partner, where, just moments earlier, he had been a grim threat.

Yet the transference is as prime example of repetitiveness as one could hope to find. P is acting as if what was true of mother in, let's say, the changing room (Ψ is partial to this irony of place) is true of the consulting room. The idea of change embraces both transformation of gender and psychotherapeutic change. Hence Ψ's warning to P not to confuse his ending of the session with a far more drastic change in circumstance. But then what *is* going on — an analysis, or a transcendence of sexual function, anatomy, and role? Is P changing, if he is, psychologically or in some bizarre reenactment of . . . of whatever?

This question is a difficult one. I don't think Ψ can answer it. He hopes, of course, that as P remembers more and more about what he experienced, it, meaning the unremembered unnoticed aspects of P's experience, will remember P less. In this we share the same theory with Freud. But were someone to tell us that P is changing what he feels, thinks, or does as a result, say, of believing himself to be undergoing a sex-change operation, we could not refute this. For example, not even Ψ knows why P had the session he had. Ψ was expecting some sort of pivot on the feeling of envy. The discovery of the "growth" might qualify for this. But was it the source of P's evident excitement? If not, was it something in the previous session? Or was it because P was experiencing one side or the other of the sex-change procedure?

Strachey, in an oft-quoted paper, considered this question. What indeed *was* mutative in psychoanalysis as a therapy? His answer was that the transference of the patient to the analyst gives the latter the position that the superego occupied—and, before the superego, the parent, or more accurately, the parent as perceived by Baby. As the patient encounters the analyst, he experiences a person rather different from the judgmental, retaliatory, punitive figure previously ensconced—he experiences a patient, accepting soul who listens for the most part attentively and with a benign, undemanding sympathy. An installation of such a mentality in place of the previously designed superego, Strachey suggested, was what altered a person's view of himself and others. This makes sense, as far as it goes. Ψ's farewell message to P suggests that Ψ is in Strachey's camp on this one. But Ψ and I do not agree, even though he appears to be losing no sleep over this fact.

I am a little worried about the railway tracks that convey people or superegos in and out of the mind as if it were a mine. Though I admire Ψ's imaginative anticipation of something I agree P might well feel, surely Ψ does not think he is performing sexual surgery on P? Why should he therefore make a bid to have himself installed in P's hall of fame as a good guy? Hasn't P had enough trouble with his previously installed figures? Why should Ψ use the same antiquated railway to install himself? Already as Baby, P started to imagine himself as part of a *Group* with Mother. To give an aura of authenticity to this illusion, P imagined himself and Mother as a pair with one mind and one view. He actually went so far as to turn on his own wishes to (form a) *Couple* with Mother, in which position he could enjoy and appreciate their differences one from the other—including those of gender. Now, if Ψ is to be believed, P is expressing triumph, if guilt, over his "discovery" that he and Mother are not as if One, but different— and not only merely different, but with himself being her superior. True, so far as the guilt is concerned, P is not expecting his once-partner to treasure this moment of his sneering ascendancy; we saw what price he had to pay T when he fed her empty and assish hole. Ψ linked T with himself and Mother as superego figures. And indeed, there is a case to be made that this interpretation of the matters helped P feel less bound to the rock face that Prometheanos fear. Today he was plainly looser and freer. So why replace one superego with another? Why not be rid of them all— and the railway to boot?

Ψ, it is to be hoped, would hardly say that he wishes to gain immortality by cloning himself into P's superego. Analysis can be no more a gene-spliced transplant than it can be a genital-sliced surgery. I suspect Ψ would have something to say to me about my analogy, but I shall permit myself to continue nevertheless: Ψ is not in the disk-drive of my superego; I am careful of mountebanks who stay for dinner. If P is afraid of the latter, which we hope is without foundation, should he not be also afraid (as am I) of the former? Knowing Ψ, I think he will get around to interpreting P's dreams of psychosurgery by showing him the wishes involved in it, particularly those of being a woman to replace mother and sister so to make merry and babies with father. . . . But how would he explain P's fear of being impregnated by an analyst who wishes to leave his clone—or, as P spoke of it today, his outburst of spores —in the form of superego babies? This would indeed spell an end to P's autonomy, sanctimonious reassurances from guilty Ψ not-withstanding.

Since the Strachey paper has become a classic in the field, Ψ may feel himself free not to note that it conceals, while licensing, a triangularly shaped victory by Ψ over P's mother or father—or whoever was the original model for the superego. Ψ knew about this in thinking out the rivalry implicit in the threesome of T, P, and himself. But now, having become a regularized part of the doctrine, it may escape him. In fact, the idea of this superego modification through identification with the analyst as good breast or good self-object is but a part of a much larger idea. That more extensive concept of cure involves giving the patient an "emotionally corrective experience." It is sometimes less a part of the culture of psychoanalysis than of other psychotherapies, but it is part of the lore and tradition of the psychoanalytic culture as well. One of its earliest exponents was Sandor Ferenzci. Later in the United States it became identified with Franz Alexander. In Kleinian terms it is expressed as the gaining or re-gaining of good relations with the good (enough) mother. It is an idea with powerful appeal since it lets its adherents loose of the constraints that they would otherwise have to join the patient in mourning.

Psychoanalysis, as I am sure Ψ would join me in attesting, is hard work. The degree of self-abnegation it requires would fell many lesser men than those mentioned. It is hardly a wonder that analysts and others, together with their patients, would be tempted to find shortcuts. Nor do I think that search should be abandoned. To the contrary. But to have different experiences of one's experience is something quite different from having different experiences. The latter can be done outside the analysis. So far as is yet known the former cannot, whether the analysis in question is the sort we are considering or those deriving from studies and practice of Zen, Taoism, and other paths to self-enlightenment. Whether the two are mutually nullifying is a question not entirely confined to theory. It is possible that Ψ wasn't altogether helpful to P today. This is bound to happen. The hope is that Ψ will find his way to knowing if a countertransference of his was involved, however much it looked like "mutative" work within the tradition. But then there is P to count on. He is an equal partner, and if for the moment he will feel delight at Ψ's small error, he may take pity and bring Ψ's exuberance to Ψ's attention. If he does so, let us hope that P will not retaliate by trying to modify Ψ's superego. There has already been quite enough of that.

18. Session: Monday

"Hi there."

"Hi yourself."

"Want a beer?"

"No, I'm fine, thanks. No. Yeah, a beer would be good. . . . Thanks."

"How was your session today?"

"O.K. I talked a lot."

"Isn't that good? I mean, weren't you worried about not being able to talk—you know?"

"Yes."

"So?"

"Well, yes. . . . Well, it's difficult to explain. But I feel he has changed. That he is being different. Less critical. He listens more. For instance, today I was talking about—well, scenes from my childhood. Reminiscing, sort of. I told him about some scene from the beach. Nothing special, just one day when we all went swimming. Well, not S; she was at camp. But the three of us. Changing. Different sexes, different setups. The usual thing. Nothing important—see, that's what's such a pisser about this! That's what is so, I don't know, confusing. It's that I don't talk about anything—you know, in the ordinary sense—and he makes a lot out of it. So nothing feels like something. See, when I talk about it to you, it doesn't flow that well. I mean I don't feel exactly fluent. It's like you're kind of watching me and I'm supposed to come up with something big. Only I can't? . . . Like

234

now. See? I'm trying to present you with something, but it just isn't coming. So I feel like I'm just standing there—here. Or maybe, it's on the spot."

"Well, I don't want to put you on the spot. I was just, you know, like asking, like just to talk. But I don't want . . .'"

"No no, it's not you. I know that. You were just asking. See, it's me. I mean that's what happens with him, too. I feel he is waiting for me to do something or say something."

"Well, isn't he? Waiting? I mean, isn't he supposed to wait for you, like until you're ready?"

"Yes. Exactly. Only I can't ever feel that way. I always feel he is waiting—for me to come out with something, come up with something. . . . I don't know what."

"That must be hard. For you, I mean. Do you tell him this? Can you talk to him about it? What does he say?"

"Well, see, that's the thing. That's the point, exactly! He acts like it isn't him, see? He acts as if I am, you know, in a way, laying this on him. Like it is me that's impatient and demanding and all. See, they all do that is what I heard. Hard to get. So naturally, you get to feeling like it's a long wait. I told him that 'soon takes a long fucking time,' I told him."

"So, what'd he say? When you told him?"

"I mean, see, that's the thing. He doesn't say anything. He just waits."

"Well, how is that supposed to help you? Why didn't ya say, 'How's that supposed to help?' I would."

"You would, huh. Well, he waits because he is supposed to wait. What he is interested in is why I feel what I feel. What in the past is cropping up again, so that I feel he is all impatient and stuff, when I know, as an adult, I know, he is supposed to wait and listen, that *I'm* supposed to listen—to *my*self. . . . It's hard to explain."

"Well, I sort of get it. You've said this more or less before. I know that he has to listen and that you kind of feel like you used to and after a while you know or remember what you used to feel like. But what I don't get is why, if he doesn't ever say anything, you wouldn't naturally, like, feel pissed? I would. See, if you weren't brought up okay and were under all that pressure, like you say, to act right and do right and shape up, how does him putting you under the same pressure help? It seems to me that it would hurt, being more of the same thing. . . . Or is it supposed to toughen you? I don't get it. . . . I'm going to open some wine. I have a nice fumé blanc D's boyfriend recommended."

"Fuck D's boyfriend!"

"If you don't mean that, you shouldn't say it. I'm *not* what's's name, you know!"

"Yeah, I know. I'm sorry. I guess I wish you were."

"Well, thanks a bunch! Anyone else I can be while I'm at it?"

"See! that's it! *I* want to fuck D's boyfriend."

"Ex-cuse me? Did you say what I thought you said?"

"Yes, I see it now. This is good. I see it now. Tch! I remember now. I was taking a leak at the same time. Around the bowl. Him and me. I mean, I thought his was so-o big, but beautiful, perfect in its way—I'm not explaining this properly."

"Do you think I don't know how beautiful a penis is—*your* penis is? . . . Oh, don't cry! Why are you crying?"

P : So, I said to her—I could hardly speak, I was so touched —"Thank you. Thank you, at last." And she said, "But I thank *you.*" So I cried some more and I thought, "She forgives me." . . . And I took her in my arms and we made love—and it was a disaster. Just like the last time.

Ψ : She forgave you, but you hadn't forgiven her?

P : I HATE THIS I *HATE* THIS. I will not put up with this one instant longer. I cannot stand this. . . . I cannot . . . I . . .

Ψ : This . . .

P : No I simply will not put up with this. And *fuck* "this." I don't give a shit about any "this." As far as I'm concerned there is no "this." You can take your "this" and shove it. Just shove it. Choke on it. *Die* on it! [Cries.]

Ψ : This is the this that is everything that is beautiful.

P : [Bitterly.] Right! *Right!* Everything bright and beautiful. His cock, her fucking chardonnay, or whatever it was—

Ψ : —D's boyfriend's and your Daddy's urine, perhaps?

P : —Yes, all right. But her kindness, her forgiveness.

Ψ : You feel so bad for wanting to destroy all of the "this-es" out of your envy of them and your jealousy. How can you be loved, after that, how can you be forgiven? It is possible even to envy her love for you and her forgiveness.

P : Right, you got it. When we were screwing—no, I don't want to say that—when we were lovemaking—I felt obligated somehow. I was truly grateful—and touched. But I resented it. It came so easily to her—from her; I don't know what I mean. It was so *easy* for her—

Ψ: —That instead of being able to receive it with pleasure and joy, you fell to wanting that ease, that givingness for yourself.

P : Yes, you're fluent too, you know!

Ψ: What to do? Resent it—or appreciate it. Take from the Breast—or bite it into assholes? . . . Drink the wine or piss on it?

P : It's easy for you to say!

Ψ: Exactly.

P : Don't sound so smug. You could be wrong, you know!

Ψ: I haven't forgotten your ability to beat plowshares into swords.

P : Ha-ha—very funny. You like this, don't you? You're elated because you think this is progress. You know, you shouldn't be. But I forgive you!

Ψ: You are right. If I am elated, I shouldn't be—and I apologize.

P : No no. I was kidding. Don't apologize—

Ψ: —Nevertheless, if I want you to progress, I apologize.

P : What for? Of course you should want me to progress. This is weird. Stop apologizing!

Ψ: I think you are worried that I am setting a tone here in the way of apologizing. You may not be ready to apologize—or for that matter, think it necessary for you. But if I need you to progress and be "better," I must apologize. Who and what you are is no one's business but your own. But here we must end.

How very helpful of P to bail Ψ out from his egregiousness the previous session! Not too superego-ish at all. The help T and Ψ gave him about his envy allowed him to forgive, or almost forgive, Ψ's enthusiastic preemptions of P's well-being. Doubtless Ψ will hear, in replay, the excessiveness of his apology and it will alert him to the continuation of this countertransference of his. But P does rather have a way with him in bringing out these excesses. He seems to be adept in stimulating people to regret how they are. Ψ seems to have become heir to this. Still, one can see that P is embarked on that portion of an analysis that puts together what tricks of attention persuade one that they have nothing to do with one another.

And yet there is much to *be* put together. And the problem as always is when to conjoin what with what. For example, is there significance to the fact that P had a portion of his analysis with T? And told Ψ about it only by narrative? Ordinarily, the way he works, Ψ would be alert to this; but there is the possibility that a degree of suppressed jealousy on his part has moved him from being a contestant to being an (over)enthusiast. But Ψ might respond that everything cannot happen all at once, and he takes what P can do where he finds it. There will be time enough for P to notice that he and Ψ as Father are not peeing in the same bowl: "It's easy for you. . . . You're so fluent." At present it is the fluent breast that occupies P's attention, regret, and desire.

19. Session: Wednesday

Ψ: [To himself: His hands clench. He lies stiffly, arms close to his side. He is silent. He is dead. My god, he is dead! What from? What am I to do? Is it something I have done? What did I do? I take it back, I take it back. Really—back. Start again. All over. Fresh start, new leaf. I confess. I confess!] I confess.

P: [Laughs.] So *you* did it! Well, it's about time you admitted it! Is that what I want—for you to confess? Yes. *You* confess.

Ψ: You laughed at what I said.

P: Yes, it tickled me. Yes, I would like it to be your fault. I am sick of feeling so guilty, so wretched and afraid. Maybe you killed her. My mother was distraught. I didn't know what to do. What am—was I supposed to do?

Ψ: Confess.

P: Yes, and die instead, I suppose.

Ψ: And die instead. Someone must pay.

P: But why? I didn't want him to die. He was her mother, nothing to me. She did the right thing. I would do that for her, if she were sick and dying. Have her to my house. Nurse her, let her die at home. It would give me a great deal of pleasure. Reciprocation, of a sort, I suppose. My father is no good at that. He runs the other way. Bright and cheerful—cheer them up, make them laugh. Forget about the trouble. Look on the bright side. When he was sick—I was four; it was just before grandmother. Well, not sick, laid up from the accident. Leg in a cast. Couldn't bend it. Stuck out straight. Had to be careful not to bump into it. "For Christ's sake, W, don't be so cheerful all the time." "Bad enough being laid up. Don't have to feel sorry for myself on top of that." Bad English movie, stiff upper lip, and all that sort of pip, pip. I mean, I wanted to feel sorry for him. But, "You're the man of the house now, son." See, I told you this. He tripped over the drapes. He was hanging the drapes in our new place, and somehow his foot caught. And he went down —hard. Bruises all over his face. Busted rib. Leg broken in two places. My big daddy. But he wouldn't take any sympathy. Held his place—the Big Guy. Down but not out.

Ψ: Confess. . . .

P : Me? You mean me? Oh, I think you meant him. "Confess, big guy, confess you're out of it. Confess you don't fucking have it anymore, and I can feel a little sympathy for you."

Ψ: "I confess—"

P : No, not *you*, asshole, *him. Him.* Jesus, you infuriate me. . . . Can't you ever . . . I suppose you mean well. But you are so intrusive. Sticking yourself into *every*thing I say. Keep out of it for once. Just give me a break. Just once, give me a break.

Ψ: "Or I'll give you one?"

P : . . . And then my mother's mother came along, and mother nursed her until she died. And that was that. . . . This isn't going well. I can't fight with you and try to accomplish something at the same time. I can't. I need you, so don't make me too angry. I just lie here and feel terrible. Can't move . . . can't talk. [Silence.]

Ψ: Dead as father; dead as grandmother . . .

P : My father is not dead. Aren't you listening? My grandmother died, is what I was talking about. . . . The revenge of the living dead. Yes, I saw that movie, horrible. Could hardly stand it. . . . I wish you were more friendly. Why can't you be more sympathetic? You say good stuff, but you seem so distant, so remote. Why can't you be more likeable?

Ψ: Is that, I wonder, how you felt? Dad, why can't you be more likeable. I don't want to resent you. I don't want to wish you dead? Don't make me wish that.

P : Yes, exactly. Because then I'll hate you, and then you'll hate me, and then . . .

Ψ: And then and then and then.

P : And then and then and then. And you too. Let me ask you something. Are you this way with all your patients?

Ψ: You suspect me of being something with them that I am not with you.

P : Well, but you didn't answer my question. Nothing is fifty-fifty around here, I answer your questions, but do you answer mine? No! So it is not fifty-fifty.

Ψ: You have switched away from thinking how I am with others to how you and I are different. As if for a moment there were more than the two of us and now we are only two? Perhaps the two of us stand for mother and you without grandmother and father, and the three with them. And when there were three, you felt jealous.

P : I don't know why I just thought of this—yes I do. But that patient who precedes me? I find her unpleasant. Of course, as you well know my sister was my father's little darling. Nothing was too good for her. . . . I don't want to go on with this. It seems unconvincing somehow. . . . Perhaps I was trying to tell you a story. "Please like me and not her, because my father liked me and not her." Well, he didn't. It was the other way. I only wish!

Ψ: Perhaps it is that you wish there were favorites among the children, so that you wouldn't have to give up your hope of getting a better share of it. If I like you better than another sister-patient, there isn't any mommy here.

P : [Long silence.] I don't seem to have anything to say.

Ψ: So that is the way today ends.

The trouble with dead people, ruminates Ψ, watching P leaving the session, P walking the least bit stiffly from his ordeal in the box that is also the coffin, is that they don't always know when they are dead. They think they are merely on to a new part, the dead person part. Noises off, so to say. These are are no-things. The presences of what is absent. They exude hostility the way a rotting corpse exudes the stink of decay. The Yellow River people, Ψ remembers hearing from an anthropologist friend, do not go out at night, at least out away from the central commons, after some-one has just died. They expect that the dead person will not feel reconciled to that death for a while yet, so will enviously lurk on the edges of darkness to exact retribution from the merry-making living. But they expect that this is just a phase that the newly dead must go through. Terrible Twos: Ungrateful Dead. We do not have a tradition to help out, Ψ muses. Death, Purgatory, Hell, or Heaven is really so much the dead person's Odyssey that the living aren't quite part of it. No one has said to P, "Well, Grandmother is dead now and you will be in danger for a week or two, so don't enjoy yourself too blatantly. Wear black, cry either loudly or a lot, and she will presently become resigned to her fate." Indeed, nowadays, there are no instructions for the soon-to-be-dead. They also don't know how to comport themselves, how to feel. It is difficult for them to plan for the transition. If Grandma could have said to P, "Well dear, I shall be leaving soon, and for God knows where. But I am packed and ready, and I shall be just fine. And for Heaven's sake (or Hell's—it doesn't matter, sweetheart; you know Granny, she'll make do, get her way in the end) don't fret. Even if I wanted to, I can't do anything with you, just as I never really could, if you'll remember. (Anyways she'll have her hands full with them over there, if there are any, which I wish there aren't, at least now.) I'm tired and don't need a new fuss, so take care of *you*, my nice grandson, and I forgive you a thousand sins in advance, if I have such pull, which I will if there is a something there, but won't if there is just a nobody and a nothing—get Granny her pills, there's a good boy."

P would have transposed this backward to his father's "death," and felt the stiff, cast-plastered old boy, fallen, draped in his own disaster, but unforgivingly, coming back after him, making him afraid, so angry, so vengeful, so self-imposedly helpless, and so angry all over again and envious and scared. The VIP.

"R'you enjoying the theatre, old son, pip pip? (VIP-RIP?) Not looking behind the drapes, are you? No Mommy-Sister-persimmon stuff, y're old Dad hopes and trusts. Wouldn't take advantage of a dead man, would you son? Wouldn't want to disappoint y're old Dad, now. Helpless and such like Granny and next thing to dead too. Wouldn't be thinking of hurrying him along, would you dear boy? He's got a lot of life left in him for a dead man. No permission for the persimmon, har-har."

This, Ψ muses further, is the price P is paying for the privilege of thinking that death is not death, just in case it's P who's dead.

If P could stand his own mortality, he could believe that others could. But P can't or won't, so he knows how wretched death is and has thus something to wish on his worst enemies. How clever those cultures who say, "Kill me, and the sooner to our Maker in Paradise I'll be. Do me a favor. Make my day." Oh P, how unreconciled you are! You always felt you had to fight for it—that life wasn't for free, that people lived at one another's expense. There was nothing that said to you, "No, it has already been decided; you're one of the ones who will live and not to worry. It's a birthright, don't y'see? You're not taking the staff of life out of anyone's mouth, so bite down hard, m'boy: it's yours for the taking. Don't even have to pay protection money to a shrink, no propitiation of the gods needed. Stay, no pay."

"You knew, all too soon, before your illusions were still undried, that the interest of the Other in you was strictly functional. That as long and only so long as you did the Others some good in their own quests for ascendancy and competitive advantage were you worth a dime to them. Once you ceased to help in the *Pair* and *Group*, you became immediately redundant, and the only other purpose you could serve was to make yourself scarce. On the other hand you could give up the *Pair* that weds you to the *Group*."

But would P have been able to stand being so deprived, Ψ wonders? To live at no one's expense, isn't that a bit of a downer? Why sell himself so cheaply? P doubtless believes that since he didn't ask to be born, but arrived nonetheless, and without undue complaint, that if he wasn't C.O.D., at least they should pay in full later. Is he supposed to come for free? [Here Ψ checks his notations of receipts, and as he thought, P is late again in paying.] But on what basis can P in conscience submit a bill like that? Would he not be thought unconscionably egotistical—narcissistic—enti-*tle*d? Who exactly does he think he is, he would be asked, perhaps first by his sister. "You must think you are *some*thing!" she would say in a voice dripping acid and spite. And what would P say? "Yes, my girl: because I just happen to be born with a something instead of your no-thing. And that is why they went on and had me instead of quitting in contentment after you were hatched. So put that in your pipe and smoke it." Perhaps that is why it is difficult for P to pay until the last minute: he feels it is a tribute exacted for the sin of simply being endowed as himself.

"Me, P, no ands, ifs, and buts!"

Well, all right, cousin P, why not let peace break out—you know, live and let live? Let Mom have it to give. Let Dad have Mom, and Mom Dad. Wish Sis well. Forgive and forget. Let the dead be dead, bury them with honors. And so if someday you'll join them? Well, live while you can, eh? No ands, ifs, and buts, as someone once said. Oh, yes. You'll say, "You make everything sound so simple." As if that's a crime, huh? And I'm supposed to feel, "What kind of a shrink am I, making everything so simple for this nice man?" And you'll say, "Right. Life is complicated. People are complex. You know? One of these days you'll have to learn to give the devil his due, as *you*'re so fond of saying to me." But is that my due? How you don't notice my due, when your eye is so firmly on your own! I wanna/wanna/wanna/wanna/wanna/wanna/ wanna. Is that so hard to say? What's the federal case with every- thing? You wanna? All right, you wanna. Plain. Simple. Ah—here she is, there will be much in why is she late today. . . .

And so Ψ prepares for his next patient, having taken care to keep from closing his mind to her with speculation and theory.

"Hit 'em where they ain't," a leading batsman said by way of explaining his success. Ψ is adopting that policy. Ψ would not make a very good dance partner. He allows P to lead, but he doesn't follow. He seems to want to be where P was and not where P is going. He plainly thinks that when P implies someplace is empty of significance by moving elsewhere, that is just exactly where he should tarry.

Understandably P objects. He is trying to move along to hear a story. The story is that P didn't do it, that it is a bum rap (what Ψ might interpret as an undeserved rap on P's bum, though he might go on to wondering to P whether P thought that he needn't be diapered, spelling "rap" with a "W"). P feels that bad deeds should be punished, and this feeling has got him into being sauced. Why then should the gander keep wanting to sauce the goose? Ψ wants to open this question; P merely wants someone else to get the sauce. This puts them at cross purposes. P, liking to think in terms of will-nots, feels that blame is due the one who could but won't. Ψ introduces the notion of can-nots. This ruptures the *Pair*. P turns on Ψ with rage. Ψ interprets another of P's wishful thoughts— that there is no difference between mothers and sisters, and if there is none between them, there is none between other women and mothers and sisters: ergo, it is not as if mothers and sisters cannot; it is that they will not. Therefore someone must be punished. As much as P doesn't want it to be himself, he wants punishment meted out even more. For believing that he is confronted with a will-not, he is naturally very angry.

P also feels more directly betrayed because he has thought that psychoanalysts believe in "will" and "won't" and not in "can" and "can't." He thought that the whole purpose of a psychoanalysis is an enabling one: to turn what patients experience as cannots into neurotic blocks and baseless fears which, when analyzed, yield over to being able to do what previously one could not.

On this basis he felt that he and Ψ and formed a *Group*. The *Pair* of them believed in this, even though others in other *Group*s did not. But in today's session, Ψ is proving to be rather unreliable as an ally. P is trying to escape from the deadness he experiences and the anxiety, such as at the theatre, he feels from time to time when anticipating that feeling of deadness. Ψ understands that P would gratefully, if guiltily, fob that feeling off on himself, and then proceed to make a case in his defense for doing this fobbing off later. Perhaps it could be defended by Ψ's superior interest in another patient, for after all if your analyst can't love evenly, who can one trust? In this fashion P is hoping to free himself of the crippling anxiety and deadness that interfere with his life. He has counted on Ψ to be his partner and ally in this. Father never took the rap, except when he fell; but even then he didn't act contrite and confess. If Ψ would confess, that could be referred backward —in much the way Grandmother's death was referred backward to Father's breakages. And P could feel that this was the long-awaited confession at last. With the guilty party having finally confessed, P could receive his pardon and go forth a free man.

Ψ interprets this for P, but P is hard put to take Ψ's thoughts on the situation. He feels that if someone else is not guilty, it reverts to me. It is wrong of Ψ to do this to me. He is guilty of poor practice. I have tried to correct him, and he would not listen. Now there is nothing more to say. He has done the deed and become bad. I should leave him with that. But being merciful, I do not. I lie here wounded and helpless, not even taking myself off to another doctor, on the off chance that he will feel contrite and confess. I have died for his sins? Must I do more? "I cannot think of anything [more] to say."

Ψ's closing remark, "Me, P, no ands, ifs, and buts," is curious. It seems to convey a sense of helplessness, even of regret. One might wonder if Ψ was feeling prescient at the start of the session, anticipating the ending that eventuated—anticipating that no matter what Ψ did there was a very high chance that P would end up reproachfully dead. For by session's end, P failed to pass off the deadness to Ψ, so Ψ was left with a dead P on his couch: "Well, Ψ, do you like this better?"

Ψ responds with an internal soliloquy wishing the dead would either get reconciled to their fate or, if not, to stop taking their pain out on others. Like himself. For he worked hard, some would say too hard, not to have P hold so tightly to his cleft stick, on which either P was dead and Ψ did him in or Ψ was dead and his death was deserved. Ψ is feeling that there is no respite for him. Even while dead, he is being belabored and reproached. Couldn't P just confess and stop from feeling guilty? No. P does not want to have to feel guilty, he wants Ψ to vindicate what P has done to him and confess his own sins.

Couldn't you just want things without so much guilt? Ψ asks P in his musings. Just wanna, without also having to make a federal case. No, and neither can you, replies P. But I can—and do. Hear me! I am wanna-ing you to forgive and forget. I am wanna-ing you guiltlessly and shamelessly to live and let me live and I am wanna-ing this of you and wanna-ing this of you—and you can't make me stop by being dead. Deadness is not necessarily a contagious disease, and I don't have to be dead just because you are. O Grandmother, what long teeth you have! Ψ is trying to protect himself, but not, he hopes, at P's expense. Won't P defend *him*self, and stop doing the dead thing?

Look, Ψ says, just give up some of your hopes for a world of wills and won'ts. Don't feel so terrible for surviving that you have to blame and punish the dead. Just enjoy the life you have. But P says, No. I was selected to be born, because my sister didn't have it. And I was selected not to die, because my grandmother didn't have it. And I feel selected to have what I want because others don't have it—and that includes you—either as the someone I get to have or, if you insist, as another have-not. But what about

Mommy? Ψ says just before P kills him by laying his guilt and his dead body upon him.

So the analysis proceeds. No one seems to be saying anything much intelligible. If P came for reasons having to do with his dissatisfaction with his current life or the way he functions at the job of living, he doesn't speak of it—although doubtless initially Ψ asked P to "put into words as best words will serve, everything you experience while you are here with me," and P awkwardly and tentatively attempted to comply. It is as if now there is no choice. The river flows, and each session dips into it a bit while it keeps on flowing, day and night, on and on.

And the river flows for Ψ as well, this time into the interval between P and Ψ's next patient. What he had wanted to "return" to P was declined by P, who, for that matter, upped the dosage. So like Hercules in the story, Ψ is holding P's Atlas world upon his own shoulders. This is one meaning of what Winnicott called the "holding environment." Temporarily the analyst has to hold and contain what the patient is too frightened or miserable to endure for himself. And the analyst must contain himself about giving it back. Sometimes Ψ finds it a bit difficult to do this. One can feel him pressing to clear the way for P to understand and take back his burden. P, of course, knows this and is not unwilling to sidestep these efforts of Ψ's. When P is very angry, he uses these times to offload even more for Ψ to hold. In today's instance there was time enough between patients for Ψ to uncontain himself and so be empty enough to receive what his next patient had in store for him.

But, barely. And that fact implies that P is doing more than asking Ψ to take in his experience and make some manageable sense of it. P is giving Ψ a dose of Ψ's own medicine. Ψ, P feels, is very selective as regards what P is attempting to communicate. There is a continual need on P's part to fashion his experiences according to what Ψ can respond to. Tap him in the right place and Ψ is resonant; in the wrong, thump. This exercises a continual pressure on P to avoid Ψ's dead spots. If he does edit and select his "free" associations, they can have quite lively sessions. Ψ's milk flows. But P feels it more like being a trained rat rewarded with pellets. Does the rat control the scientist, or is the rat being selectively fashioned by the scientist?

This rather paranoid view of the psychoanalytic transaction is normally regarded as betraying on P's part an excess of narcissism. And doubtless P does suffer (or makes others, like Ψ, suffer) from the grandiosity and prickliness that betrays an entitlement of the narcissistic sort. Moreover P is not unaware of this. His fear of death by deselection is barely covered by his fear of castration, but plainly more difficult to even think about. It is almost as if he wishes castration was all there was to it. If it were, he could take it and be done with his anxieties in the *Pair*. But P senses that what is required of him in being a member of a *Pair* with Ψ as its other member is something else—a deindividualization process. This terrorizes him, because the last one he can complain to about that is Ψ.

So they are both dipping into the river and behaving for all the world as if this is a sensible and even meaningful way to spend time. The question of whether this is a *folie à deux* has inevitably risen before, as it now must again. What has happened to what in the jargon is sometimes called the "presenting problems"? Plainly they have been redefined; that is much of what Ψ considers his function. P says "This" and Ψ draws his attention away from This and over or back to That. By looking at matters in terms of That and not This, matters are redefined and experienced differently. They are also lost.

But many systems of thought have practitioners who do such work. Alcoholics Anonymous has as its effort and prayer the plea to know the difference between what can be helped and what cannot. Such redefinitions put things in a different light, beginning with the concept of whether alcoholism is a will-not weakness or a can-not illness. And many feel themselves indisputably helped by viewing the limits to their will and will power differently.

Ψ's system is no different. It sees vast and important confusions regarding which are the will- and which the can-nots, and puts these to P for re-view. But where P uses the power of the *Group* and of prayer to assert the differences, Ψ has no such power to employ. His power, such as it is, consists in his ability to *demonstrate* to P when, how, and why P goes about blurring or inverting the distinctions in ways P does not notice or wish to pay heed to. He does this with first one thing, then another, and then again and again. By observing to P that P's wish to compare himself with another patient is designed to overlook the differences between "sister-people" and "mother-people" and having done that, to go on to blur the differences between "stranger-people" and "family-people" in order then to go on further to become or remain oblivious to the differences between Ψ and P's father, and the "here and now" and the "then and there," is a demonstrable instance of P's rewriting possibility through a sleight of mind, just as he does and did in other instances in which he wanted his wishes or hopes to be served.

All very well and good: but is there a grain of truth to these allegations? Should P listen to him? *Why should* P listen to him, if he does? And if he does, why doesn't Ψ call this peculiarity to P's attention?

The answer to the last question could of course be Ψ's self-interest. If Ψ were conscious of the motivations that flow from his self-interest, would he still use P as a means to his ends? Ψ probably knows pretty clearly about the money. Bills come in for every month (sometimes, it feels to him, like more often than that). Ψ also is likely to know of his interest in being a professional in a Western capitalistic country, and the illusion of being self-employed his profession affords him—though of course it is his patients who employ him, and as an hourly laborer to boot.

Perhaps a little less clear to Ψ might be his need for proving again and again that how he sees things is correct. Such quantitatively repetitive proofs draw one's attention from the questions of quality that lurk nearby. Thus, "What's Ψ trying to prove—and to whom?" might make an apt question. Is he trying to prove something to P; and if so, who does P then stand for? Or is it to himself, against his own doubts, that he is trying to prove that what he doubts is really true (again and again)? But "again and again" doesn't necessarily make anything true, as Ψ might be the first to say regarding the continual assertions of astrologers. Is it perhaps, then, that in making a *Pair* with P, and observing P gradually come to the same conclusions about how things work and what they mean, Ψ's doubts will be assuaged? But how will P's conversion to the Analytic *Group* help? Ψ has his own *Group* (or Society, to give its more formal name) of converts. Are they not enough to keep the wolf of doubt from the door? Indeed, if Ψ has grown up outside the convent, he will be long acquainted with the number and substantiality of the doubters. He will have heard people doubt everything from the mercenary cast of his motives to his sanity in believing rot such as he and his fellow cultists parade before one another and their poor patients—too sick to distinguish gibberish and balderdash from sense. Indeed, he will have heard from people that the very transference of which he so learnedly speaks, *by his own definition and admissions*, makes P prey to the very exploitation that Ψ may, out of his own self interests, be visiting upon P. Isn't the transference making P sicker and more in need of the so-called treatment Ψ pretends to provide? And, for that matter, would Ψ be going around dipping sticks in the great rivers of the unconscious, or whatever, if P happened not to be able to afford it?

20.   Session: Thursday

". . . And so," Ψ is saying, unburdened with the weighty issues we have been considering, "And so?"

P is silent. He is debating whether to answer this as a question or as Ψ has instructed him to (just what comes to mind, please). He doesn't know what he is to do. What *is* it that Ψ wants, anyhow. [This is such a misery. This is so very bad. Of all the people in the entire world P would like to talk this situation over with. Something has gone badly wrong, and if he had to define it, he would say that he simply cannot *talk* to Ψ without Ψ listening to what P has to say "in the transference." Psychoanalysis, like any other true nightmare, appears to be one of those games in which there are *no time outs!* No making a "T" with your hands, right horizontally banging on the perpendicular left, and everyone waking up for a moment and talking like people. Real people: a man, himself, and another, an analyst, whom he is consulting. He remembers those times of old—he *thought* they were of old—when he was caught up in his sleep so hard and deep that he had lost himself to his dreams, and needed getting back, awakening, to someone who would anchor him against the calls from the deep. "Mo-mmy. Da-ddy," whispered into the night. "-y, y!" but -y doesn't answer in real person either. There is no real life, No Exit, as the Sartre play put it. I'd like to have a word with you. You see, I'm not feeling at all well these days, and it is rather frightening. You see, things are untrivially worse than when first I saw you, and as my analyst, I think I should tell you this. But you will say something like, "As my analyst?" and I will say I didn't mean that I was my analyst speaking to you, and you see the entire experience is a nightmare. I suppose you have been analyzed, and I suppose you have been through something like this before, and I suppose you have been through it with other patients of yours, and I suppose, what with the one thing and the other, you are inured to it and don't know that this is an emergency This Is an Emergency! And the dream has got to stop here—now—here—now. I have to talk to you. I have to tell you something. And that is not to say, "What comes to mind?" Or, "Have you perhaps experienced something like this before?" You see, what you think is "transference" is not. I am locked up with a monomaniac who can only think: "This is transference." But I happen not to be a "transference." I happen to be me and I happen to be caught in an insane asylum where the more I say, please, for God's sake be real, you say, "Ah, so now you see how sick you really are, eh?" And if I say, "The keeper, it's the keeper who is mad," you say, "Well, gentlemen, you have heard it with your own ears. The man is mad. We shall have to keep him for a while before we next consider his parole." And they murmur, "Yes, we see" and "Yes, we see," and I am doomed. EMERGENCY!! EMERGENCY!! Is there a living man to hear me? A person, not a figure in a dream? You see, I remember you. I remember my first phone call. You were brisk, businesslike. "I cannot talk with you now, but if you'd still like to talk to me, please call me back between. . . ." Yes, and I got the "if you'd still." Ah, I said to myself, yes, he knows how disappointing it is finally to get up the courage to call and find you can't speak. So maybe you know how even more disappointing it is that I still can't speak. Or, *won't*, as you would say: that I am waiting for conditions to improve. And that you said it on the first phone call, if I "*still* . . ." Well, as you see I *don't* "still" wanna anything. Me, I am out of here, gone, history. Or you are. Dead, finished, finito. "Goodbye—and good luck," "Bye By-ye." And, Goddamn you, you are not even asking me anything. Ask me to talk! Ask me, "So-o—what's happening?" What are you, fucking made of stone? You know, you are a madman! Yes. Yes. Yes, crazy. Yes, *you*'re the one who's crazy. And I am outta here. . . .]

Ψ: Nothing respectable?

P : [Oh, Jesus, weeps.]

Ψ: Nothing suitable for my ears.

P : [Right. He's nuts. I'm in the middle of a nightmare, and he's like on Waikiki. Excuse me, could we just, you know, talk a minute, you know, talk? T A L K? English word, meaning "speak." Meaning "speak" as human beings do? Without "interpretations"? See there is something I would like to ask you. "Why am I feeling worse, and acting crazier than when I first started?" Just that one little question. I mean, am I not supposed by this time to be better, clearer, more in control of my life? Could it be that you are no good as a shrink, in fact lousy? Isn't *that* a respectable question? I guess not, since you don't, I mean won't—wouldn't, *would*n't—answer it. And, Goddamn it, why not? What do you take me for? Answer that: What Do You Take Me For?]

Ψ: Nothing sufficiently respectable—

P : —What? What!

Ψ: I appear to have guessed correctly. That scared you, that I guessed?

P : No. . . . No. I was just thinking about T. We smoked a little, and some funny stuff happened. Nothing special, nothing serious. . . .

Ψ: Nothing "respectable," either, I expect?

P : Easy for you to say.

Ψ: Too easy.

P : I know you won't answer this, but is it possible for an analysis to make people worse?

Ψ: You must feel frightened of what I might say, if you ask the question in the confidence that I wouldn't answer it.

P : No, frightened? No. I was just wondering. I heard that analysts can't always tell beforehand whether someone is "analyzable" or not. Don't people sometimes have breakdowns or something during the analysis?

Ψ: Or something.

P : See. I can't talk to you. You are playing games with me. Word games. Apparently you can't take what I say seriously. So what's the use, really, of talking. [Silence.]

Ψ: [Silence. . . . What can I say to help? A'parent'-ly something has happened, and the fault of it is too much. I am to take
the bum rap. Anything I can say now will feel to him that I
don't want to take it, and that the fault lies with him. Nor does
he want to make it "easy" for me to say. As usual, when he is
pained, he wants to take me with him. Last time I was dead,
now I am trying to escape the noose. Whatever he has done, he
wants to put the blame on me. But there is more to it. He is
afraid that he is misusing the analysis, that somehow he is not
talking with me, but secretly acting in defiance of me. He doesn't
want me to think of this in transference terms, but as a consequence of an actual transgression of mine. But if it is actual,
why will he not come out and say so. Is it that he fears me—
that having transgressed in some actual way, he cannot trust
me to not transgress again. Or is it that he wishes to use my
transgression to justify actions of his own? His silence is not, at
the moment, designed to help me to understand his animus. It
is accusatory. He has trapped me into being a "word" game
player. The *Word Child*—the Murdoch book. "Dear Iris, I love
you very much. You are a wonderful writer. . . ." Writers understand the immense potency of speech, their stock in trade. Like
us. "Only" talk. "How does talking help?" How many times
have I heard that question. When I was younger, I used to take
it seriously and try to answer it, never realizing that I never
could—all I could do is help prove that talking doesn't work.
Finally I learned to be silent. "Why don't you answer my question?" "If talking doesn't help, why talk?" Word games, in a
way. But serious. When the child learns to talk. . . . It is immense, isn't it. Promethean, in its way, if In the Beginning was
the Word. What differs the adult from the baby—the baby can't
talk. But, Oh, when he can! He is different from the beasts of
the field and the birds of the air. Tower of Babel. The Lord God,
lad, this one here. Rather be a bad lad than a sad lad, is what it
is. Hope in badness. Hope, most of all, in hopelessness and
despair. Lose heart all you who are buried here. And gain pain.
The pain in Spain—oh! I see: he put his penis into her bottom.
That's what's troubling him so.]

P : I feel I am doing worse.

Ψ: [Shall we come to *the* choice? Or shall I first take him to his choice of choice? Better to let him tell it. Shit, you are already talking!] You are fascinated with the good and the bad, the better and the worse. These are choice choices?

P : You have said this many times before, and I still don't understand where you are coming from. I *feel* bad, horrible, in fact, and all you can say is "I'm sorry.". . . I didn't mean to say that, about "sorry."

Ψ: Um, like yesterday's "I confess." [Be quiet! What's gotten into you?]

P : Well, *you* may say that better and worse don't exist, but I will tell you frankly that that is psychopathic. How am I to feel being in analysis, if that is still what this is, with someone who doesn't know good from bad. I mean, don't you ever think, I did well this session, I was really helpful, and Oh, dear, last session I bombed, I really fucked up good. . . . And don't say, Oh *Dear*. For chrissakes. I mean, Don't say it. OK? And don't say I'm frightened. I am. I am frightened about being with someone like you, who doesn't know an ear from an asshole. . . . Well, you might as well know that I—well, why not say it? I fucked T up her asshole.

Ψ: "Ear from an asshole."

P : That's exactly right, I don't. I don't even know what that is supposed to mean. It certainly doesn't help. What you should do is ask me why I thought I had to do that, what was going on between me and T that this gross, sick perversity happened. [Silence.]

Ψ: [Are there any non-ear fucking questions, at this point? How can I say that he is wanting to do *as* it seems to him *I do* —that he hates me for reminding him of any wish he might have for me to insinuate *some*thingness into him. For he was hoping to ease such an experience of having a "hole" for me to fill. By discovering it elsewhere (into me, in a need to ask questions, and in T) he was trying to move the holes out. If T and I have the question-holes, he has the answer things to fill them with. But he does so want the VIP(enis) in him to have and to hold, to give him strength and audacity—backbone, really, as he imagines his father did to and for his mother, put an armature in her anus or "analysis" and set her up for life. And he doesn't want to know he wants that from me, if only through his ear, but that as a last resort, although he is making do, by not knowing his ear from his asshole. . . . "Oh dear," he says to his father. "Oh my dear."]

P : This is stupid. I don't talk to you and you don't talk to me. What are we saving it for? Now don't tell me the time is up. It is, I can tell, and I can leave by myself, thank you all the same.

Ψ: [Yet another end to it, that un-sad, sad lad; ends being the same in the dark, as the bottom observed to the pussy.] Goodbye.

21. Session: Friday

And sad he is, but not quite yet. There are hopes and options. Mourning has not become electric, as Ψ might say in his tongue-tied way. And it is impressive, thinking of the child P was, to see unfolding the sense of option and opportunity he was able to contrive for himself. He is frightened, of course, of exactly that. He feels incorrigible. He feels he will never "grow up," a feeling he has felt always, a feeling that probably so scared him into "outgrowing" himself that he never had time to *grow* up. This is another prong of death's ubiquity; he feels he is stalling and that Death will "get" him for that hubris. "Stay, Moment: thou art so fair!" But this time around he does not wish to hurry. He wants the power and the glory he feels he missed out on. He wants, as Ψ might term it, an earful that is an assful that would fill him with the pure substantiality that he feels somehow he missed out on. Words he can do without; they simply occupy the space where the infusion might otherwise take place. They might also, if well taken, induce P further to believe that words—as in a talking therapy—are enough. Having temporarily given up on the mouthful of the maternal breast, P is now looking for the assful-earful that is more filling than mere words. But he hates his want, and, envying Ψ for being in the position either to provide or not to provide for P's wants, hates him too—and usurps Ψ's role of provider by himself "providing" T. And all of this is going on in a way incomprehensible to P, the adult on the couch.

Thus Ψ the social director! "Excuse me, P, have you met P-at-three? P-at-three, this is you heir. This is the fellow who is going to get it done for you—you know, all the things they said you would have to wait for until you were bigger or grown up? Well, this is the person you deferred to! He is doing the doings.

"P, meet P-at-four; you've seen him in yellowed photographs. Well, here he is in the flesh, so to say. Yes, he is one sad little fellow. And, no, I agree, he feels you are not anxious to meet him. Yes, embarrassing for both of you. Grown apart, I should judge, as people do. But he loves bottoms too! No, I won't tell him. But why don't you? Something in common. That's the way he thinks about bottoms, as a matter of fact: fronts divide, backs unite. From the back, you can't tell the players without a scorecard. Saves jealousy, saves envy, all around a good leveler. Yes, substitutability, that's his motto. Modular. Disappointed in you? Well, I suppose. But what can you expect of kids? He shelved a lot, never gave it up quite, put it in mothballs. A holding pattern. Sure, waiting. Waiting for you to come along. Big guy, well-educated, a lot of class, big dick. *Act*-tion Country!!! as he might say. No, I don't know why he is shy. Perhaps he feels it is prudent to keep a low profile. No stickee no choppee. Waiting for you, stronger, wiser, to take it on. But why ask me, here he is, ask him yourself.

"No, he *is* you. More like Superman? I see, you would be Clark Kent, go into your telephone booth, as if a caterpillar into a chrysalis, and Bang-o-o! Exit Su-per-man! Yes he knows it. Feels rather the same way, as a matter of fact. What went wrong? You also feel something went wrong. Well, what do you think? More candy, huh? You're not quite sure about the candy. More food? The more the food, the bigger the b.m., I see, Make a splash. That's a good play on words. It's not a play on words? Okay. Sorry. Peed with Daddy. Yes, impressive. Big thing, big yellow stream. Enema? Oh, yes, a big stream from you too. Yes, it is a bit. So he goes into you and you go a big stream into the toilet. Oh, into Mommy? I see. And then it's as good as Daddy. Uh-huh, done some thinking about this, it seems. Firemen. Right, the hose connection. Oh, up Mommy's bottom. And fix her thing-ey. Make it come out. Oh, like yours would come out more. Water pressure, like the firemen's hoses. On TV. Swell right up and leap about, eh? Then woo-oosh. Yes. Pause that refreshes, some people have called it. Never mind. From my own childhood. Well, why not ask him, he's right here.

No, that one's you at twelve. Well, I expect he is sad about grandma. Oh, right, you don't know about grandma, except that she smelled from a lot of stinkstuff. Well, you've some catching up to do. . . . No, I am what's called a psychoanalyst. P, that is now-P, talks to me and I listen. How is talking supposed to help? Now, look here young man. . . . Yes, more in common than you might think."

An interpreter is by way of being a translator. Insofar as P-now and P-then talk different languages, Ψ has to translate. A good and faithful translator does simply that; he does not add anything of his own. But first it is prerequisite for each P to talk clearly to. Only after that occurs can Ψ try and find the language to put P-now to P-then and P-then to P-now. P-now has so ardently tried to outgrow P-then, as Ψ sees it, that P-now doesn't want anything to do with P-then. P-at-four is quite unembarrassed at his wishes. He has, at their prompting, given the science of life a good deal of research and much thought. He has figured out a thing or two, on which P-now is, indeed, currently acting. But P-now is mortified. Both he and P-then have imagined that by the present P-now would be a much finer fellow than they think he is. It is understandable that P-at-four should be too young to understand. He doesn't even know anything about Grandmother's dying and death, only perhaps that she hid the decay in her with too much scent. P-at-twelve knows about this, but there is the danger that he has outgrown P-at-four and would regard him as a little wimp. P-at-four seems a proud lad and would not, I think, like to be so regarded especially by someone whose age and manner remind him of his sister. If he has given way, he has yielded the future to someone rather like Dad or, better, Superman, not to a twelve-year-old who only knows about baseball cards and spin the bottle. P-at-twelve would probably retort that the only problem with him is that P-at-four keeps hanging around, weighing him down with all his kid's stuff. P-now, as we have seen, feels the reemergence of those two to be a re-emerge-ancy. He yearns to talk to Ψ as adult to adult, but the kids are in the way. They have captured or captivated him and he feels hogtied. As each did *his* predecessor, P-now feels the best course of action is to get off speaking terms with both of them and outgrow them as quickly as possible. He feels Ψ's refusal to talk to him, man to man, as an adult, to take away the only recourse he (and they) have found to get and keep out of touch. Ψ's idea of a family reunion is not a popular one. But people often feel that the other is getting far too much attention, and why should the Ps be an exception to this? Still, there is always the possibility that as they get to know one another better, their respect and sympathy for each other and what each of them was trying to do to contribute to the success of the Ps will grow. But at the moment P-at-four was doing something with T that P-now doesn't much want to know about. P-at-three is yelling for P-now to get them both the heck out of here. He doesn't know about it either, but he can feel it evolving and doesn't think he wants any part of it. "Run," he counsels P-now. "Dummy up, the way I did in nursery school once. Bite him, like P-at-two and I do. Call him a good name. Call him a do-do. 'Psychopath?' um-n, that's a good one."

Ψ would like to be heard from here. "You see," he wants to say to me, "this is the way the presenting problem—the problem of the present—so quickly becomes irrelevant. It is only the present version of the old problem, history in modern dress. I can say to P, 'Look here, grow up, you're acting like a child.' But if he is a child, my remark is childish, for only children in their inexperience misestimate how difficult or easy things are. Many 'children' come to therapy or analysis or somewhere and whom they meet is also a child. The person they meet may also underestimate things as children do. 'Here take this medicine. Take two a day for ten days. Take it even after you start to feel better.' But the patient of this physician does not. Nor does the one who is told to stop smoking or to lose weight or to lower his cholesterol. 'Hit the pillow, that's it, hit it hard. Hard. Don't hold back. That's more like it. Now I want you to do a visualization. I want you to remember an incident in which someone made you really angry, only you couldn't express it. Right? Take your time. . . . All right, what have you got? Mother? Okay, she called you Friday afternoon at work and suggested dinner. Not a lot of notice. Takes you for granted. Never imagines you have anything else to do. All right, the pillow is mother. "Hello, Mrs. Snarl." Okay, hit it and tell her, Tell her, what you would like to tell her, what you wanted to tell her Friday, but couldn't, what you have wanted to tell her all your life. No, you're tapping it! Hit it! It's okay to hit it. You know, you are looking irritated with me. Am I pushing you too hard? Yes?

Good. Make the pillow me. Hit it and tell it what you would like to tell me. Excellent, excellent, we are making progress. Aren't you feeling better already. You know, when you walked in here you looked pale and morose. Your posture was slumped. Now you have color and a sparkle to your eye. Yes, we are making very good progress indeed.'

"So two children play at house, pretending that to express one's self and assert one's self is beneficial. One plays the grown-up, the other the child. 'I love you better than your mother does and ever did; I love you enough to allow you to hit and be angry. Now hit and be angry or mother won't love you so much. And I want your cheeks pink and your eyes to sparkle—aren't I nice? Now do what I tell you.' I can't speak for the mother, it appears she can speak for herself, but the real mother may have changed and washed her daughter's diapers while her new mother, for a fee, will give her 'support' and a pillow to hit. Only a child could offer and accept that kind of deal.

"You have questioned the self-interest that leads me to use the transference. What you say is true, though some of the doubt-and-reassurance part I have not thought about so deeply as you think I might. But let me say this. First, I have no choice in regard to the transference. If God knows what patients think is going to go on, if they come to consult me, He or She doesn't tell me. *I* don't know what I am letting myself in for. All I know is that someone like P seems remotely, how shall I say, discernable to me. I think it is possible for me to come to know and feel and sense what he is about as a person in this world—that I won't need something I don't have, like an infrared scanner, to receive him. So this is enough to start.

"If we also finish what we start, he will know everything I know about his transference. If he is changing the way he feels or acts because he thinks that I'm dressed in leather and beating him with whips, he will find that out. And find out that I am not going to start. After he finds that out, he may not want to change. (As I said to him about calling back, '*If* you still want to. . . .') Or after he finds out I don't intend to marry him or hit pillows with him. So maybe he has become assertive and has pink in his cheeks, and this is all for me in the transference. Do you think he will not know this as we are going along? I am not a Pavlov or a Skinner, like my good friend with the pillows. He may start with very little choice; he ends, I hope, with very much more: he becomes his own man. And now I am through with you. I have work to do, and pleasant as this has been, I cannot stand about gossiping, especially with people who uninvited look over my shoulder."

That remark about me looking over his shoulder would refer to his analyst of course, and before her, his mother, who probably also looked over his shoulder to see how things were doing in the hindmost parts.

One can only feel how difficult it is for Ψ that he must work so coolly. He must be a little intimidating to his patients. I wonder if he knows that? Freud, of course, made a point of it: "Above all one must stick coolly to the rules." But for Ψ it seems to involve a real effort of self-denial. He is a chap with *bonhomie*. I think he misses being friendlier with his patients: He would have liked, I suspect, to have answered the question about whether P is analyzable or is having a breakdown. There is a feeling too of his analyst working through him, like the dead people who refuse to get dead he was talking about. If you don't "work through" the loss of your analyst, *he* "works through" you.

It is not just a matter of being under observation by the "participant-observer," as Sullivan named that dignitary. It is truer, perhaps, to say with Bion,

> that in actuality a stream of elements exists, some of which are *seen* to unite at a moment that, like the elements themselves, is selected *by the predisposition of the observer* and are seen to issue in a process of change and its attendant effect—events that are the peculiarity of the observer's outlook. I suggest then that the stream of elements remains constant in actuality, but the union of those elements and the choice of the elements that are supposed to unite, together with the choice of the moment at which the union is supposed to be effected, depends upon the observer and in particular on what we should call the observer's disposition (if we are analysts) or scientific discipline. (1992: 6–7)

How else can we account for Ψ's turbulence upon discovering P's turpitude? If the psychoanalyst cannot make the new baby via P's internalization of him, as in the Strachey modus operandum, what then can he do to justify his *Group's* tolerance of him? The *Group's* sense of at one-ness requires adherents who in turn will inspire identificants. This is the messianic ideal. It is the *Pair*'s alternative to heterosexual reproduction. The threat to this method arises in the *Couple*'s idea of reproduction as a consequence of a heterosexual activity. The geneity of the *Pair* and *Group*, out of which samenesses are valued, can be satisfied by onanism and homoerotic activity. In effecting sodomy between himself and T, P becomes a convert to Ψ's modality, but without Ψ himself, either as subject or object. This is a horse of a color different from finding rivals for Ψ in the *Coupling* department: this is an insurrection against the acts of mutual identification necessary to form and preserve a *Pair*. In Ψ's stout defense against allegations by P concerning his exploitation of the transference, what is obscured is Ψ's interest in effecting a *Pair* with P. Ψ has underrated the strength of his passion as social director. He is a better member of his *Group* than perhaps he credits himself with.

The difficulty, of course, is how these intimations of one's mandate from the *Group* make themselves known. It would be feckless to suggest that they are taught because it is in the nature of the *Group* to work anonymously. Members of the *Pair* and *Group*, indeed, express their identity by surmising the values and rules precisely without having to be told. Mum's the word. The very same mumness asked of any member is returned when he, any other member, wished anonymity. It is not just the Mafia in which no one knows anything. Rather more, or perhaps especially more, respectable *Group*s offer Ψ the same sort of anonymity, if "unconsciously." For example, could Ψ say that in P he would like to inculcate the following disposition? Of course not! So how can he know why P's defection upset him so?

> We that had loved him so, followed him, honored him,
> Lived in his mild and magnificent eye,
> Learned his great language, caught his clear accents,
> Made him our pattern to live and to die! (Robert Browning 1895, on
> Wordsworth as Judas)

Ψ is interested in encountering the stream, and his work shows every indication of taking another leaf from the Bionic book— to wit:

To the analytic observer, the material must appear as a number of discrete particles, unrelated and incoherent. The coherence that these facts have in the patient's mind is not relevant to the analyst's problem. His problem—I describe it in stages—is to ignore that coherence so that he is confronted by the incoherence and experiences incomprehension of what is presented to him. . . . This state must endure until a new comprehension emerges. (Bion 1970: 15)

P and Ψ seem able to do this in respect to the associative stream that bodies forth upon their encounters. But what if they were asked to do this in respect to the "coherence" of the Analytic Encounter?

P breaks in with a lip-smacking "amen!"

"That is what I have been trying to tell him. But he refuses to talk with me about that, treating everything I say as a further ring on the changes of the transference. I don't deny that some of the feelings I have are crazy: I mean, I know that psychoanalysis is not a suppository but a supposition. All the same, when he refuses to talk with me outside of the transference, I feel he is even more demented than I and quite literally dangerous. It is like being in a dream from which you cannot awaken—or you think you are awake, but the characters in the dream refuse to dissolve. See, I wanna say, 'Okay I am awake now, let's talk about the dream,' and he acts as if the dream is not over and I am just dreaming it is. So I feel I'm in *his* dream—stuck there because the bastard won't wake the fuck up.

"It's a fucking one-way street with him. He's always right, and I'm the one who's crazy. But what good is it to tell you that? You are some sort of analyst too, aren't you? So you probably believe that whatever else someone can say about the situation, it works. Right. But is it working for me? I'd like to have your opinion on that! I'm not exactly worse, but am I better? Or am I just slowly but surely sinking into getting used to being sick? Maybe *that* is what patients are supposed to do in psychoanalysis."

In his final remark P attempts to make the idea that he might be narcissistically invested in himself seem quite ludicrous. This is probably another example of what Ψ means when he wishes P could just "wanna" in his own behalf and not lie about sifting and scanning everything for what it reveals as to what Ψ wants of P. Ψ, of course, hopes to foment desires, the stuff of *Coupling*, sufficiently in kind and intensity to bring them to the threshold of P's notice. These promptings from within would help distract P's fascination with Ψ's innards.

Meanwhile, however, P's "*Pair* crisis" reasserts itself. He is asking rather basic questions. How do I know which are events taking place in something called sleep, which in wakefulness? When I am asleep, I do not know that I am asleep—which is how I know that I am asleep. When awake, I know I am awake so long as I know when I am awake. My wakeful mind can scrutinize my sleeping mind: does my sleeping mind do the same for my waking mind? "Wake up," he wants Ψ to tell him, "it's only a transference." A patient of my own once said, "I feel like I am having shock treatment, only inside-out shock treatment." This patient also was beginning to tolerate the disorientation people feel when nothing is wanted for them or from them by the analyst. In other people this freedom from *Pair* requirements brings on vast rages commonly expressed as suicidal intentions. "I quit!" They feel as if when someone has nothing in mind for them they are no longer here for some purpose. This no-thing in turn engenders vast feelings of being put upon, as if the freedom to one's own devices is a very-bad-thing not only in and of itself, but something cruelly set in motion without one's permission and informed consent. On the other hand any implication that time and tide are indifferent to the affairs of human beings excites in P feelings of profound anxiety. P wants to climb out of the session to a mountain top, so to gaze beyond the previously farthest horizons in quest of *purposes*, the fulfillment of which might yield him meaning, direction, and fulfillment. For in contemplating Ψ, even in the augmented images of the transference, P sees a visage too like his own. (See also Boris, "The Self Too Seen," forthcoming c.)

P awaits the voices, the signals, the scents carried in breezes that are pregnant with the scents of flowers and musk. And while awaiting he spasmodically busies himself in small vagrant journeys ten yards to the east and two feet to the west. He dares not go far or become occupied with what he finds for fear he will miss the signal. When Ψ talks to P, P is polite enough; but withal there is a tendency for P to look past the Ψ of the *Couple* transference toward Ψ of the *Pair*.

Ψ now wants what must be a final word. "Work with patients

has always put me on edge. I have other patients in addition to P, you know. They are in no real sense a *Group* beyond being 'my' patients. Occasionally one patient bumps into another coming or going, but they do not constitute a face-to-face *Group* in any other sense. *Nevertheless* if two patients cancel or even come late, just two, not to speak of three or more, I can experience that as an entire *Group* protesting the way I do analysis. Doubtless this reflects some insecurity on my part, but insecurity is a requirement for properly doing analysis, for what *is* there to be secure about? Analysis is by way of being a basic research project: one is bound to learn something, if negatives are also counted. So it is not quite that kind of insecurity. It is more like coming under a spell. The envy I bear myself for having the right to be, and feel myself to be, a 'good enough' analyst, is always lonely for company. Any indication that my envious nature is not alone cheers it up immensely and makes it quite fractious. My envious nature derives these indications from lateness and absence, by forgetfulness or cancellation, on the part of my (I am almost saying 'other') patients. In turn, I begin to experience self-doubt of the 'Look upon me and die' sort that Banquo wished to instill in Macbeth. And there precisely is where the analytic *Group* is so helpful. A few minutes' chat with a colleague ('Since they have no borders, borderlines never can tell when enough is enough') can restore my sanguinity. It's now no longer them against me: but my *Group* against theirs, and mine is better. You are an admirer of Bion's (1992) thought (if, that is, you are not the devil quoting scripture), so hearken to this:

> The individual analyst has two main contacts: his patients and society. In the first certainly, and in the second probably, he will have it brought home to him how little he knows and how poor his work is. In this respect his position is not unlike that of the soldier in war who is aware of his own troubles but not of his enemy's. It must therefore be borne in mind that the fundamental importance of our work demands that kind of fortitude and high morale which places the welfare of the analytic group and its work before the welfare of the individual analyst and sometimes before the welfare even of a particular patient. This, taken in conjunction with the isolation in which analyst and patient work, means that the analyst must, in addition to the commonly recognized equipment, possess a social consciousness of a very high degree. . . . Or, to put it another way, the analyst must never cease, even

in the midst of his analytic work, to be a member of one or more social groups.

To this I would but add that as analysts, we need a refuge not only from the patient's insanity, but from his sanity as well."

Part Three

Conclusion

22. Conclusion

In the pages now recumbent under the reader's left thumb, I have put forth some paradigms and paradoxes as ways of further explaining the conflicts of motive to which people are subject. The gist of these conflicts is that we behave as if we had been genetically lumbered by our forebears to take a hand in our own genetic destiny. So far as biologists are concerned, such a genetic imposition is commonplace, for it has long been evident that behavior patterns are as heritable as morphological traits are. I do not argue as to whether such a heritage is good or bad for us as human beings; whether or not it is adaptive in the competition of the species, only time or wisdom will tell. The genetic endowments that have proved adaptive in a previous generation may be rather like the Maginot line. I do argue that without altogether noticing it, we are all concerned to live and breed in ways that we imagine may help the species of which we and ours are charter members.

My own understanding is that a powerful, even proactive, receptivity to influences on the subject of fitness exists, which then turns us to sources deemed "like-us" for information with which to be filled out. This conceptualization borrows from Kant's notion of "empty categories."

The *Pair* is one of these basic categories. In a *Pair* disposition, we look to the culture, as made manifest in the identity of the *Pair*, for our symbols: Roberts (in Green 1986: 48) has described the symbol as "an object cut in two, constituting a sign of recognition when its bearers can put together its two separate pieces." Since

271

it is the nature of cultures to be discriminate, our sensitivity imbibes values and tastes as well as techniques and meanings. These fulfill the mandate of our nature to be selective as to fitness. Nature tells us at once to be selective and to offer what is necessary for our *Pair* to select selectively. In this sense what may *look* like narcissistic preoccupation is very likely to be the individual's attempt to be better than and different from others; better, but not so much better as to seem unapproachable; different, but not so different as to be mutant. Individuals must be, in short, one of a kind without being absolutely unique.*

Indeed such a proactive "readiness" subjects the newborn (perhaps even earlier, the fetus) to influences that threaten its feelings of narcissistic aloofness and grandeur. The nice feeling, "we-R-me," is shocked again and again by the requirements in the *Pair* to get along by going along (this is possibly what the patient mentioned in chapter 21 meant when he or she talked of "inside-out shock treatment"). An ongoing amount of confusion exists as to the source of the influence: is it the Other, the Tauskian Machine, Society. . . . What? When susceptibility and responsiveness become confused, a primary paranoia comes into being. That paranoia is based on a confusion created by mental realizations. When a preconception and its realization meet, it is by no means always clear to the experiencer which created which. It is also based on the opposite experience, in which preconception and realization do not meet. In this circumstance, there is no such thing as nothing, only sourceless, roving no-things that never find rest. The ability of folklore and legend to give realizations for these dark surmises is a comfort; movies like "The Night of the Living Dead" take up where Hamlet left off.

As one would expect, there are bodies upon bodies of information about what constitutes fitness. Cultures and subcultures have this information. To my knowledge there is as yet no found culture which is without (1) a deity; (2) a kinship system; (3) an aesthetic. This fact suggests that the genetic program Human Being needs

---

*The latter position is left for the godhead or the transfiguring one. This is because the unique tends to form its own species and, by definition, cannot therefore reproduce except through parthenogenesis, analogous perhaps to Zeus's birthing of Pallas Athena.

these categories. Deity is the twin realization for the Beginning or Origin and for the End or Return. The kinship system marks who may be used for purposes of *Pairing* and who, beyond the incest barrier, for *Coupling*. *Coupling* is the state of mind or affairs which needs differences of kind in order for it to function for everything from seed/egg exchange to the exchange of other commodities; *Coupling* creates an urge for fission in regard to the object world. The more discrete objects, the wider the possibilities for exchange. The aesthetic is based on selective superiority: in selection, one has to be choosy and there have to be choices: there is no point to the one without the other. This is why it is incumbent upon the individual to offer Others a choice.

At his birth, if not before, the infant needs to be selected into the *Pair* by a member of the *Group,* or else he is at risk of becoming a lifelong failure to thrive. I believe there is a syndrome of physiological features of this failure, beginning, but not ending with diminished immunity, even auto-immunity. I also believe that there are mental representations of this lack of selection, and these are the no-things. Thus unselected babies, if they grow up at all, grow up feeling that they haven't a leg to stand on. I quoted Vaclav Havel (1990) as to the feelings that persist:

> One of them is a profound, banal, and therefore utterly vague sensation of culpability, as though my very existence were a kind of sin. Then there is a powerful feeling of general alienation, both my own and relating to everything around me, that helps to create such feelings; an experience of unbearable oppressiveness, a need constantly to explain myself to someone, to defend myself, a longing for an unattainable order of things, a longing that increases as the terrain I walk through becomes more muddled and confusing.

From the psychoanalytic viewpoint, Havel, in the words that follow "a longing for," is speaking about the greed that persists despite the unselected's every effort to cultivate appetite.

Greed, as I use the word, refers to wants that cannot be fulfilled because they have neither beginning, middle, nor end. Appetite, in contrast, represents the whittling down of Greed into satisfiable proportions. The Hope that impregnates Greed has been abandoned in favor of Desire, moving the orientation of the individual from that of the *Pair* to that of the *Couple*.

The ideal, of course, is when the realizations of both states of mind dovetail: when the person we select in the *Pair* to select us in turn is one and the same as the person we choose in the *Couple* and who chooses us in turn. Repletion and completion synchronously synergize, lending to the experience a different order of magnitude. In our culture this feeling is often synonymous with falling in love, that mild mania of delight in which gratitude and admiration beggar envy, security stills jealousy, and want abounds with joy. (There are several opposites to this happy condition, not least of which is the *petit mort* of desire fulfilled while hope lies languishing.)

From nature's point of view, not only does "best adore best," but their adoration leads to a consummation that will produce progeny. Can we imagine that this part of the procedure in our own and other species has helped improve adaptability? Other strategies for reproduction would include "If you're not near the girl you love/you love the girl you're near." This, in the desert island condition, would help propagate the race, even in the absence of the brightest and the best. On the other hand it would be a poor reproductive strategy were choices to abound and the choosers not be choosy.

Of course, in these scenarios, nature is dealing the cards and playing the hands: we are but her minions. And in these scenarios it feels very much as if there is a "we" involved and the "we" is us. But the cells of which we are made up also have DNA to spend: they have lives no less gripped by the tropism of survival than our own. From this perspective, we as a species may be also the means by which other species find viability and reproductive immortality. These other species and we may live in symbiosis or in the condition following a hostile takeover. The virus not only shapes our immunity cells, but is shaped by them; it propagates itself by insinuating its DNA into our cells and replacing what it finds with its own. In this sense, one that Wilson and other sociobiologists have used, what we call us is not unlike a colony of ants or bees. The division into queen and worker is akin to our *Group*, in which differences are employed for making divisions of labor and specializations in function. Since all differences are jealously employed as variations of homo-differences, this use of differences ultimately goes toward cloning as a form of reproduction.

I have been proposing that in the mental domain the four absolutes—species, gender, death, and reproduction—likewise form the core of human preoccupation. Every life is about them; therefore every analysis is as well. Most analytic observers agree that at the heart and soul of each analysis is a series of minute acts of mourning and grief that must take place if there is to *be* an analysis. I would suggest that, closely examined, the mourning and grief will be seen to attach to the four constants, about which so very little can be done.

It is in the nature of the *Pair* to view things, selectively, in a competitive-comparative hierarchy, from first to last, least to most, worst to best, and in so far as we are members of the psychoanalytic *Group*, we arrange data from oral to genital, from pre-oedipal to post-oedipal, from narcissistic to interpersonal or from disintegrated to integrated. So natural do these seem that it is a struggle to fit in other categories of thoughts, like nonhierarchical (non-erier) thoughts. The most difficult part of developing the ideas I am presenting here has been the strain against this current of *Pair* thought. The most difficult part of presenting these ideas is the entirely natural disposition on the part of readers and listeners to listen for the "er-iest" or better-best schema that they feel must be contained in here somewhere. As I am with myself, so the reader is perhaps with him- or herself: we wonder and then, so what? He must have something in mind or he wouldn't have written all of this.

And indeed I do have something in mind. I am reporting on relationships that emerge from slight turnings of the psychoanalytical kaleidoscope. I have gleaned these ideas from working with a category of patient I have (to myself) called the "Unselected." Gradually it occurred to me that this sense of being unselected is so much a part of the human condition that I had to attend to it in many, if not most, of my patients as well as the people whom I have seen in groups. This enabled me to merge group and individual dynamics. It became possible, for example, to understand that people in *Group*s can engage in affiliative behavior, based on mutual and vicarious identifications, only in so far as there are opportunities for *Coupling* outside the perimeters of the *Group* and these are either faring well or drawing near—a dialectic that also, of course, governs the relations between the *Pair* and the *Couple*. This idea made it easier to understand why the early analysts urged sexual abstinence on their patients. It also made it easier to understand why the extraordinary events on the political landscape of Eastern Europe and the former Soviet Union occurred (we had been thinking of power as imposed by the state and not as power invested, as always, temporarily, in the reification called the state).

So my purpose in writing this book has been to draw attention to such relationships, which occur both as states of affairs and states of mind. The dialectic concerning which of these relationships occur, and where at any given time, may be made more explicable by considering projective and introjective identifications, and other sorts of relations with the object, as occurring in a Lewinian "field," whose dynamics can become comprehensible. The "Un-selecteds," those psychological "failures-to-thrive," for example, may appear to be devaluing, entitled narcissistic folk with little or no sense of time (i.e., how long things take and when a session begins or ends) and put one in mind of Freud's "Special Types." But if we understand that these patients feel themselves to be living on borrowed time and in soul-deep fear of the Bergmanian Reaper, who sooner or later *will* play them chess, we can see the degree to which they can but feel that they have prepaid for what they now barely feel eligible to do. (Regarding time, see Boris, "About Time," forthcoming d.)

If, as I think, facts do not exist outside of the relationships we make among them, the differences between the states of mind that follow from the egoistic pleasure principle and those that follow from the identifications that form the webbing of the *Pair-Group-Species* are immense and determinative. The propositions advanced in this work, as I said earlier, are drawn from interpretations I found myself making of the "it is as if" sort. Such interpretations approximate realizations to inchoate experience and experience neglected by *Group* consensus. One such "experience" has to do with the patient's feeling, "I have no right to have an analysis. I ought come but once a week. I mustn't spend such money on myself. The whole premise of psychoanalysis is antisocial. How can you live with yourself?"

What the patient says may very well be true: nevertheless the patient is with the analyst and not in once-a-week therapy. This fact therefore invites an interpretation. Since the experience is by no means limited to the occasional patient with the occasional analyst, many analysts will have tried to approximate it with many interpretations—as I myself have. The ambiguous nature of the reproof, for example, will not fail to catch one's ear. But some interpretations "work" and others do not. An interpretation of the patient's relation to the breast will be just right for some; others will be left cold by this and will need, perhaps, to reinterpret it into an Oedipus reference implying sexual abuse. Listening to the worry on one day, one may hear guilt; on another, dread. The same interpretation will not "work" on both days. One day the plaint will, if taken far enough, lead to the problem of pleasure and frustration in the *Couple* and give rise to the hypothesis of a pleasure principle. On another (or, of course, a scant moment later) the plaint will lead to surmises of the sort I have been setting out here.

If, as I also think, nature works through her creatures in the form of tropisms, one of these must surely be a tropism toward reproduction for purposes of generational survival of species. We are, as one reading has it, "to be fruitful and multiply." Tropism, as I use the word, registers as influence. The influence is felt in the form of suggestibility or susceptibility: as a leaning toward. When this influence registers very strongly, it takes on a certain stridency, such as that so beautifully described and analyzed by Beach (1991) and Tausk (1919). But even at lower amplitudes, it asserts itself in our preoccupations with truth and beauty and with the design the Deity(s) has for us not only now, but in the hereafter. We are not merely to live, but to live well; not merely to breed but breed well. When Mr. or Ms. Right Now is also Mr. or Ms. Right, hope and desire fuse, the *Pair* and *Couple* integrate, selection needs and needs to choose and be chosen are all met, and the baby and the future converge.

It is as if nature—her demands reposed in the *Pair*—so requires this deference to "right" as to make the *Couple* and *Pair*, up to this point of suffusion and convergence, deadly adversaries in ongoing conflict and negotiation. In forming a *Pair* the infant or individual may think that he is being assimilated into the *Group*, which, as represented in Mother, has a very nice breast for him, and is in every other way full of welcome. But he discovers that the Species-

Group, as reposed in the *Pair,* is interested in him only insofar as he contributes to its future—either by becoming selectable and himself selecting well, or, by having the decency to make himself scarce.

Such considerations may be at work in the plaint of the patient who cannot afford to ask for much. When guilt is on the day's menu, interpretations concerning the *Couple* will be needed; when dread comes into being, an alternative set of interpretations will be required. These will concern the relations within the *Pair.* Those relations and their predicaments are very much a part of the fabric of psychoanalytic training itself. The preparation of candidates relies heavily on the scope and depth of their own personal analyses. Scope and depth in turn depend on the extent to which the training analysis includes a study of the candidate in his capacities as member of the analytic *Pair* and *Group.* Analytic societies and institutes, as most members readily attest, are hardly models of the Socratic Academy. Power struggles abound; factionalism is commonplace. To these variations of the oedipal interpretation are offered. This is as needs be, *for who has been analyzed in also the Pair/Group respect that he or she may in turn analyze the young?* What many regard as a dearth of creative thinking and research in psychoanalysis may reflect less the quality of the candidate and his or her mentors than the neglect by the psychoanalytic group of the study of the psychoanalytic *Group.*

If very sketchily, there now follows some of the markers that when followed out, lead me to my conclusions. I begin with the divagations in selective attention that one hears especially well in free-association. I end with the categories *Couple* and *Pair* as these in turn "exply" the presence of a third principle of mental functioning.

Table of [Kaleidoscopic] Elements

Orientation of attention

CONTRAST: Sharpening of distinctions

COMPARISON: Leveling of differences

Sensory attunement

CLOSE: Smell, touch, taste, tactile
SIGN: Small gesture, part body

DISTAL: Hearing, vision
SIGNAL: Auditory, visual

Tropism

OBJECT CREATION: Fission, distinction

OBJECT COALESCENCE: Fusion, agglomeration; indistinguishability

REPLETION: Release, satiety

COMPLETION: Suffusion, restoration

Quality of object relations

DESIROUS: Appetitive, rivalrous, given to guilt and terror, subject to jealousy, capable of ecstasy, gratitude, love; fascinated by the novel; linear in perception of time

HOPEFUL: Greedy, possessive, loyal, given to dread over issues of integration, wholeness, boundaries; subject to shame, covetous of acceptance; absorbed with acquisition, status, attainment; circular in perception of time

ENVIOUS: Grateful; admiring; traducing

Quality of internal object relations

OBJECT REPRESENTATIONS: Kept individualized, not lumped, e.g., as superego. Objects experienced as in contact with one another; erotic activities and libidinous dispositions are maintained.

These are doomed to frustration, except through masturbation and masturbatory activities, forcing either a shift over to *Pair* orientation or to the resumption of actual relations with others.

OBJECT REPRESENTATIONS: Grouped into agencies and attitudes. Self continues to hope to find identity with these, i.e., with the ego ideal; feelings of bliss follow from fantasies of at-one-ment.

Great store is put in internalized object relations, since the emotional palette involves affiliative and vicarious feelings for which the actual object is of little consequence.

Nature of object relations

POLYMORPHOUS: Malleable, adaptable, transferential

PROJECTIVE AND IDENTIFICATORY: Rigid

Motivational valency

EGOISTIC: Libidinal; copulatory

SPECIES: Progenerative; affiliative; vicarious

State-of-mind

Couple

Pair

References

Adams, R. 1989. "Juggler." Review of *Foucault's Pendulum*. *New York Review of Books*. 9 November.

Anders, T. F. 1989. "Clinical Syndromes, Relationship Disturbances, and Their Assessment." In *Relationship Disturbances in Early Childhood*, edited by A. J. Sameroff and R. N. Emde. New York: Basic Books.

Angier, N. 1991. "In Fish, Social Status Goes Right to the Brain." *The New York Times*. 12 November.

Balint, M. 1968. *The Basic Fault: A Contribution to the Theory of Regression*. Madison, Conn.: International Universities Press.

Beach, D. M. 1991. *Windows of Insanity*. Unpublished manuscript.

Beebe, B., and F. Lachman. 1988. "The Contribution of the Mother-Infant Mutual Influence to the Origins of Self and Object Representations." *Psychoanalytic Psychology* 5 (4): 305–37.

Berger, P., and T. Luckman. 1967. *The Social Construction of Reality*. New York: Anchor Books.

Bion, W. R. 1961. *Experiences in Groups*. New York: Basic Books.

———. 1962. *Learning from Experience*. New York: Basic Books.

———. 1963. *Elements of Psychoanalysis*. New York: Basic Books.

———. 1966. Review of *Medical Orthodoxy and the Future of Psychoanalysis*. International Journal of Psycho-Analysis 47: 575–79.

———. 1970. *Attention and Interpretation*. New York: Basic Books.

———. 1979. *The Dawn of Oblivion*. Perthshire: Clunie Press. Reprinted as *A Memoir of the Future*. 1991. London: Karnac Books.

———. 1985. *All My Sins Remembered*. Abingdon: Fleetwood Press.

———. 1992. *Cogitations*. London: Karnac Books.

Birdwhistell, R. L. 1970. *Kinesics and Context*. Philadelphia: University of Pennsylvania Press.

Bloom, H. 1973. *The Anxiety of Influence*. New York: Oxford University Press.

Bollas, C. 1979. "The Transformational Object." *International Journal of Psycho-Analysis* 60 (1): 97–107.

———. 1987. *The Shadow of the Object: Psychoanalysis of the Unthought Known.* New York: Columbia University Press.

Borges, J. L. 1964. *Labyrinths.* New York: New Directions Press.

Boris, H. N. 1971. "The Seelesorger in Rural Vermont." *International Journal of Group Psychotherapy* 21 (2): 159–73. Reprinted in Boris (forthcoming a).

———. 1976. "On Hope: Its Nature and Psychotherapy." *International Review of Psycho-Analysis* 3: 139–50. Reprinted in Boris (forthcoming b).

———. 1984a. "The Problem of Anorexia Nervosa." *International Journal of Psycho-Analysis* 65: 315–22. Reprinted in Boris (forthcoming a).

———. 1984b. "On the Treatment of Anorexia Nervosa." *International Journal of Psycho-Analysis* 65: 435–42. Reprinted in Boris (forthcoming a).

———. 1986. "The 'Other' Breast: Greed, Envy, Spite and Revenge." *Contemporary Psychoanalysis* 22 (1): 45–59. Reprinted in Boris (forthcoming a).

———. 1988. "Torment of the Object: A Contribution to the Study of Bulimia." In *Bulimia: Psychoanalytic Treatment and Theory*, edited by H. Schwartz. Madison, Conn.: International Universities Press. Reprinted in Boris (forthcoming a).

———. 1989. "Interpretation of Dreams, Interpretation of Facts." *Contemporary Psychoanalysis* 25 (2): 212–25. Reprinted in Boris (forthcoming a).

———. 1990a. "Identification with a Vengeance." *International Journal of Psycho-Analysis* 71: 127–40. Reprinted in Boris (forthcoming b).

———. 1990b. "Beyond the Reality Principle." In Boris (forthcoming a).

———. 1992a. "Fears of Difference: Early Envy, Part II." *Contemporary Psychoanalysis* 28 (2): 228–50. Reprinted in Boris (forthcoming b).

———. 1992b. "The Equalizing Eye: Early Envy, Part III." *Contemporary Psychoanalysis.* 28 (4): 572–93. Reprinted in Boris (forthcoming b).

———. Forthcoming a. *Sleights of Mind: Selected Papers. Vol 1.* New York: Contemporary Psychoanalysis Books.

———. Forthcoming b. *Envy.* Northvale, N.J.: Jason Aronson Inc.

———. Forthcoming c. "The Self Too Seen: Early Envy, Part IV." *Contemporary Psychoanalysis.* Reprinted in Boris (forthcoming b).

———. Forthcoming d. "About Time: Early Envy, Part V." *Contemporary Psychoanalysis.* Reprinted in Boris (forthcoming b).

Bowlby, J. 1969. *Attachment and Loss.* New York: Basic Books.

Brazelton, T. B., and B. G. Cramer. 1989. *The Earliest Relationship.* Reading, Mass.: Addison Wesley.

Browning, R. 1895. "The Lost Leader." In *The Poetical Works of Robert Browning*, edited by G. R. Stange. Boston: Houghton Mifflin, 1974.

Chomsky, N. 1972. *Language and Mind.* New York: Harcourt Brace Jovan-ovich.

Darwin, C. 1859. *On the Origin of Species by Means of Natural Selection or the Preservation of Favoured Races in the Struggle for Life.* London: Murray.

———. 1872. *The Expression of Emotion in Man and Animals.* London: Murray.

Durkheim, E. 1933. *The Division of Labor in Society.* Translated by George Simpson. New York: Free Press. London: Collier Macmillan, 1964.

Edelman, G. 1987. *Neural Darwinism.* New York: Basic Books.

Eigen, M. 1986. *The Psychotic Core.* New York: Aronson.

———. 1991a. *Coming Though the Whirlwind.* Wilmette, Ill.: Chiron Pub-lications.

———. 1991b. "On Bion's No-thing." In *New Ideas in Psychology* 9 (forth-coming).

———. 1992. *The Electrified Tight Rope.* Northvale, N.J.: Jason Aronson.

Emery, E. Forthcoming. "The Envious Eye: Concerning Some Aspects of Envy from Wilfred Bion to Harold Boris." In *Melanie Klein and Object Relations.*

Erikson, E. 1950. *Childhood and Society.* New York: W. W. Norton.

Feiner, A. H. 1982. "The Relation of Monologue and Dialogue to Narcissis-tic States." In *Narcissism and the Interpersonal Self,* edited by J. Fiscal-ini and A. Grey. New York: Columbia University Press.

———. 1988. "Countertransference and Misreading: The Influence of the Anxiety of Influence." *Contemporary Psychoanalysis* 24 (4): 612–49.

———. 1992. "Misappropriation, Misattribution and Change." *Contempo-rary Psychoanalysis* 28 (1): 152–71.

Freud, A. 1965. *Normality and Pathology in Childhood.* Madison, Conn.: International Universities Press.

Freud, E., ed. 1961. *Letters of Sigmund Freud, 1873–1939.* London: Ho-garth Press.

Freud, S. 1900. *The Interpretation of Dreams. Standard Edition. Vols. 4–5.* London: Hogarth Press, 1964.

———. 1911. *Formulations on the Two Principles of Mental Functioning. Standard Edition. Vol. 12.* London: Hogarth Press, 1968.

———. 1915a. *The Unconscious. Standard Edition. Vol. 14.* London: Ho-garth Press, 1968.

———. 1915b. *Thoughts for the Times on War and Death. Standard Edition. Vol. 14.* London: Hogarth Press, 1968.

———. 1916. *Some Character-Types Met within Psychoanalytic Work. Stan-dard Edition. Vol. 14.* London: Hogarth Press, 1968.

———. 1917. *Mourning and Melancholia. Standard Edition. Vol. 14.* Lon-don: Hogarth Press, 1968.

———. 1918. *From the History of an Infantile Neurosis. Standard Edition. Vol. 17.* London: Hogarth Press, 1964.

Freud, S. 1919. *A Child Is Being Beaten. Standard Edition. Vol. 17.* London: Hogarth Press, 1964.

———. 1920. *Beyond the Pleasure Principle. Standard Edition. Vol. 18.* London, Hogarth Press, 1964.

———. 1921. *Group Psychology and the Analysis of the Ego. Standard Edition. Vol. 18.* London: Hogarth Press, 1964.

———. 1923. *The Ego and the Id. Standard Edition. Vol. 19.* London: Hogarth Press, 1964.

———. 1925. *Negation. Standard Edition. Vol. 19.* London, Hogarth Press, 1964.

Freud, S., and J. Breuer. 1893–1895. *Studies on Hysteria. Standard Edition. Vol. 2.* London, Hogarth Press.

Fromm, E. 1964. "Causes for the Patient's Change in Analytic Treatment." *Contemporary Psychoanalysis* 27 (4): 581–602.

Ghent, E. 1990. "Masochism, Submission and Surrender." *Contemporary Psychoanalysis* 26 (1): 108–36.

Glover, E. 1931. "The Therapeutic Effect of Inexact Interpretation." *International Journal of Psycho-Analysis* 12: 397–411.

Goodman, N. 1978. *Ways of Worldmaking.* Cambridge: Hackett Publishing Company.

Gould, S. J. 1987. *Time's Arrow, Time's Cycle.* Cambridge: Harvard University Press.

Green, A. 1986. *On Private Madness.* Madison, Conn.: International Universities Press.

Greenberg, J., and S. Mitchell. 1983. *Object Relations in Psychoanalytic Theory.* Cambridge: Harvard University Press.

Grotstein, J. 1983. *Do I Dare Disturb the Universe? A Memorial to Wilfred A. Bion.* London: Maresfield Reprints.

———. 1990–1991. "Nothingness, Meaninglessness, Chaos and 'The Black Hole.'" *Contemporary Psychoanalysis* 26 (2): 257–90, 26 (3): 377–401, 27 (1): 1–33.

Hartmann, H. 1959. "Psychoanalysis as a Scientific Theory." In *Psychoanalysis, Scientific Method and Philosophy: A Symposium,* edited by S. Hook. New York: New York University Press.

Hartmann, H., E. Kris, and R. M. Lowenstein. 1946. "Comments on the Formation of Psychic Structure." *The Psychoanalytic Study of the Child.* Vol. 25 (2): 11–38. New York: International Universities Press.

Havel, V. 1990. "On Kafka." *New York Review of Books.* 27 August.

Heimann, P. 1950. "On Countertransference." *International Journal of Psycho-Analysis* 31: 81–84.

Hoffer, W. 1950. "Development of the Body Ego." *The Psychoanalytic Study of the Child.* Vol. 5: 18–23. New York: International Universities Press.

Kafka, F. 1935. *Parables and Paradoxes.* New York: Schocken Books, 1958.

Kant, I. 1781. *The Critique of Pure Reason.* Chicago: Encyclopaedia Britannica Press, 1952.

Kellman, P. J., E. S. Spelke, and K. Short. 1986. "Infant Perception of Object Unity from Translatory Motion in Depth and Vertical Translation." *Child Development* 57: 72–86.

Kempton, A. 1991. Review of *Native Sons*, by Jewell Taylor Gibbs. *New York Review of Books*. 11 April.

Klein, G. S. 1967. "Peremptory Ideation: Structure and Force in Motivated Ideas." In *Motive and Thoughts: Psychoanalytic Essays in Honor of David Rapaport*, edited by R. R. Holt. New York: International Universities Press.

———. 1975. *Psychoanalytic Theory: An Exploration of Essentials*. New York: International Universities Press.

Klein, M. 1928. "Early Stages of the Oedipus Conflict." *International Journal of Psycho-Analysis*.

———. 1930. "The Importance of Symbol-Formation in the Development of the Ego." In *Contributions to Psycho-Analysis, 1921–45*. London: Hogarth Press, 1948.

———. 1945. "The Oedipus Complex in the Light of Early Anxieties." *International Journal of Psychoanalysis* 33: 433–38.

———. 1952. "Some Theoretical Conclusions Regarding the Emotional Life of the Infant." In *Developments in Psycho-Analysis*. London: Hogarth Press.

———. 1957. *Envy and Gratitude*. New York: Basic Books

———. 1961. *Narrative of a Child Analysis*. London: Hogarth Press.

Kohut, H. 1977. *The Restoration of the Self*. New York: International Universities Press.

Kolata, G. 1990. "Living and Dying in the Wild." *The New York Times*. 26 July.

Kuhn, T. 1962. *The Structure of Scientific Revolutions*. Chicago: University of Chicago Press.

Lacan, J. 1949. "The Mirror Stage as Formative of the I." In *Ecrits*. 1977. London: Tavistock Publications.

Laing, R. D. 1971. *Self and Others*. Baltimore, Md.: Penguin Books.

Levi, P. 1990. "Psychophant." *The New Yorker*. 12 February.

Lévi-Strauss, C. 1973. *From Honey to Ashes*. New York: Harper & Row.

Lewin, K. 1951. *Field Theory in Social Science: Selected Theoretical Papers*, edited by Dorwin Cartwright. New York: Harper.

Lorenz, K. 1966. *On Aggression*. Translated by Marjorie Kerr Wilson. New York: Harcourt, Brace & World.

Mahler, M. 1968. *On Human Symbiosis and the Vissictudes of Individuation*. New York: International Universities Press.

Mayr, E. 1982. *The Growth of Biological Thought: Diversity, Evolution and Inheritance*. Cambridge: Harvard University Press.

Meltzer, D. 1978. *The Kleinian Development, Part III*. Perthshire: Clunie Press.

Milgram, S. 1974. *Obedience to Authority: An Experimental View*. New York: Harper & Row.

Minuchin, S., B. L. Rosman, and L. Gailer. 1978. *Psychosomatic Families: Anorexia Nervosa in Context.* Cambridge: Harvard University Press.

Mitchell, S. 1991. "Contemporary Perspectives on Self: Toward an Integration." *Psychoanalytic Dialogues* 1 (2).

Modell, A. 1990. *Other Times, Other Realities: Towards a Theory of Psychoanalytic Treatment.* Cambridge: Harvard University Press.

———. 1991. "The Therapeutic Relationship as a Paradoxical Experience." *Psychoanalytic Dialogues* 1 (1).

Morrison, A. P. 1989. *Shame: The Underside of Narcissism.* Hillsdale, N.J.: Analytic Press.

Murdoch, I. 1956. *The Flight from the Enchanter.* New York: Viking Press.

Ornstein, R. 1986. *Multimind.* Boston: Houghton Mifflin.

Phillips, A. 1986. "On Being Bored." *Nouvelle Revue de Psychanalyse* (Automne).

———. 1992. "Playing Mothers." *Nouvelle Revue de Psychanalyse* (Printemps).

Posner, M. I. 1988. "Structure and Functions of Selective Attention." In *Master Lectures in Neuropsychology,* edited by T. Boll and B. Bryant. Washington, D.C.: American Psychological Association.

Posner, M. I., and D. E. Presti. 1987. "Selective Attention and Cognitive Control." *Trends in Neuroscience* 10: 13–17.

Riesman, D., R. Denney, and N. Glazer. 1950. *The Lonely Crowd.* New Haven: Yale University Press.

Rosenfield, I. 1988. *The Invention of Memory.* New York: Basic Books.

Sacks, O. 1990. "Neurology and the Soul." *New York Review of Books.* 11 November.

Saussure, F. de. 1959. *Course in General Linguistics.* 3d ed. Edited by C. Bally et. al. Translated by W. Baskin. New York: Philosophical Library.

Shapiro, D. 1965. *Neurotic Styles.* New York: Basic Books.

Segal, H. 1957. "Notes on Symbol Formation." *International Journal of Psycho-Analysis* 38: 391–97.

Spark, M. 1957. *The Comforters.* New York: Avon Books, 1965.

Spelke, E. S. 1990. "Physical Knowledge in Infancy: Reflections on Piaget's Theory." In *The Epigenesis of Mind: Essays on Biology and Cognition,* edited by S. Carey and R. Gelman. Hillsdale, N.J.: Lawrence Erlbaum.

Stern, D. 1985. *The Interpersonal World of the Infant.* New York: Basic Books.

Strachey, J. 1934. "The Nature of the Therapeutic Action of Psycho-Analysis." *International Journal of Psycho-Analysis* 15:127–59.

Sullivan, H. S. 1953. *The Interpersonal Theory of Psychiatry.* New York: W. W. Norton.

Tausk, V. 1919. "On the Origin of the 'Influencing Machine' in Schizophrenia." In *The Psycho-Analytic Reader,* edited by R. Fleiss. New York: International Universities Press, 1948.

Trilling, L. 1972. *Sincerity and Authenticity.* Cambridge: Harvard University Press.

Winnicott, D. W. 1986. *Home is Where We Start From.* London: Penguin Books. New York: W. W. Norton.

——. 1988. *Human Nature.* London: Free Association Books.

Zukav, G. 1979. *The Dancing Wu Li Masters.* New York: Bantam Books.

Index

289